simple & delicious
COOKBOOK
BRAND NEW EDITION

RDA ENTHUSIAST BRANDS, LLC
MILWAUKEE, WI

Taste of Home Reader's digest

A TASTE OF HOME/READER'S DIGEST BOOK
©2013 RDA Enthusiast Brands, LLC
1610 N. 2nd St., Suite 102, Milwaukee, WI 53212-3906. All rights reserved.
Taste of Home and Reader's Digest are registered trademarks of The Reader's Digest Association, Inc.

EDITORIAL
Editor-in-Chief: Catherine Cassidy

Executive Editor, Print and Digital Books: Stephen C. George
Creative Director: Howard Greenberg
Editorial Services Manager: Kerri Balliet

Editor: Christine Rukavena
Associate Creative Director: Edwin Robles Jr.
Content Production Manager: Julie Wagner
Layout Designer: Catherine Fletcher
Contributing Layout Designers: Matt Fukuda, Holly Patch
Copy Chief: Deb Warlaumont Mulvey
Copy Editor: Mary C. Hanson
Recipe Editor: Mary King
Content Operations Manager: Colleen King
Recipe Testing: Taste of Home Test Kitchen
Food Photography: Taste of Home Photo Studio
Executive Assistant: Marie Brannon
Editorial Assistant: Marilyn Iczkowski

BUSINESS
Vice President, Publisher: Jan Studin, jan_studin@rd.com

General Manager, Taste of Home Cooking Schools: Erin Puariea

General Manager, tasteofhome.com: Jennifer Smith

Vice President, Magazine Marketing: Dave Fiegel

READER'S DIGEST NORTH AMERICA
Vice President, Business Development: Jonathan Bigham
President, Books and Home Entertaining: Harold Clarke
Chief Financial Officer: Howard Halligan
VP, General Manager, Reader's Digest Media: Marilynn Jacobs
Chief Marketing Officer: Renee Jordan
Vice President, Chief Sales Officer: Mark Josephson
General Manager, Milwaukee: Frank Quigley
Vice President, Chief Content Officer: Liz Vaccariello

THE READER'S DIGEST ASSOCIATION, INC.
President and Chief Executive Officer: Robert E. Guth

For other Taste of Home books and products, visit us at **tasteofhome.com.**

For more Reader's Digest products and information,
visit **rd.com** (in the United States) or see **rd.ca** (in Canada).

International Standard Book Number: 978-1-61765-356-8
Library of Congress Control Number: 2012922760

Pictured on front cover: Pasta & Broccoli Sausage Simmer, page 42; Oreo Cheesecake Pie, page 195; Sweet and Spicy Grilled Chicken, page 216; Cheesy Chicken Vegetable Soup, page 209.

Pictured on back cover: Marshmallow Pops, page 192; Spaghetti Casserole, page 240; Tomato Cucumber Salad, page 117; Provolone Chicken Pizza, page 217.

Pictured on spine: Tater Tot Casseroles, page 239.

Printed in China
1 3 5 7 9 10 8 6 4 2

contents

quick, easy & fun!

Savor the fast and fabulous recipes shared by busy cooks like you! You'll find many new favorites and speedy takes on all-time classics in Taste of Home Simple & Delicious Cookbook.

Weekday Meals: 100+ fresh ideas, on the table in 30 minutes or less.

Smart Cooks' Solutions: Using the slow cooker, bread machine and microwave.

Planned Overs: Delicious ways with leftover poultry, ham, beef and pork.

Stock the Freezer: Awesome meals you just heat and eat!

Gatherings: Celebrate with ease.

Handy icons throughout point you to recipes ready in minutes!

10 *quick hot sandwiches, instant pies, soups & more.*

20 *stir-fries, tacos, warm rolls and tasty sides.*

30 *scrumptious pork chops and chicken, homemade mac 'n' cheese, irresistible burgers, even homemade fish sticks.*

187 Kim's grasshopper pie

❝This quick pie is such an ego booster! My family compliments me the entire time they're eating it. A big hit at work potlucks, too, it's good to the last crumb.❞

—KIM MURPHY ALBIA, IOWA

50

16

69

Weekday Meals

"Some people call it dinner hour, but many of us call it rush hour. Slow down with this super-easy meal and have time to share with your family."

BRIGITTE SCHALLER FLEMINGTON, MISSOURI
about her recipe, Jiffy Pork & Penne, on page 16

30 Gnocchi with White Beans

Warm their hearts on chilly nights with this yummy skillet dish full of veggies, beans, gnocchi, melty cheese and Italian flavors. It makes a fast and easy complete meal.

—JULIANNE MEYERS
HINESVILLE, GEORGIA

PREP/TOTAL TIME: 30 MINUTES
MAKES: 6 SERVINGS

- 1 medium onion, chopped
- 1 tablespoon olive oil
- 2 garlic cloves, minced
- 1 package (16 ounces) potato gnocchi
- 1 package (6 ounces) fresh baby spinach
- 1 can (15 ounces) white kidney or cannellini beans, rinsed and drained
- 1 can (14½ ounces) Italian diced tomatoes, undrained
- ¼ teaspoon pepper
- ½ cup shredded part-skim mozzarella cheese
- 3 tablespoons grated Parmesan cheese

1. In a large skillet, saute onion in oil until tender. Add garlic; cook 1 minute longer. Add gnocchi; cook and stir for 5-6 minutes or until golden brown. Stir in spinach; cook until spinach is wilted.

2. Add the beans, tomatoes and pepper; heat through. Sprinkle with cheeses; cover and remove from the heat. Let stand for 3-4 minutes or until cheese is melted.

Editor's Note: *Look for potato gnocchi in the pasta or frozen foods section.*

20 Beef Tostadas

Chipotle sauce gives these meaty open-faced tacos just the right amount of heat to fire up a fiesta at the dinner table.

—TASTE OF HOME TEST KITCHEN

PREP/TOTAL TIME: 15 MINUTES **MAKES:** 6 SERVINGS

- 1 pound lean ground beef (90% lean)
- 1 cup chopped sweet red pepper
- ½ cup chili sauce
- 1 teaspoon taco seasoning
- ¼ teaspoon salt
- ¼ teaspoon pepper
- ½ cup sour cream
- 3 teaspoons chipotle sauce
- 6 tostada shells
- 3 cups shredded lettuce
- 1½ cups guacamole
- 1½ cups shredded Mexican cheese blend

1. In a large skillet, cook beef and red pepper over medium heat until meat is no longer pink; drain. Stir in the chili sauce, taco seasoning, salt and pepper; heat through.

2. In a small bowl, combine sour cream and chipotle sauce. Layer each tostada with lettuce, meat mixture, guacamole, cheese and chipotle cream.

Between busy work schedules and having three kids in sports, our family is constantly on the go. We often attend two soccer practices a night, with tournaments three weekends a month. Many nights, it's tempting to hit the drive-through, but that gets costly. So I plan quick meals we can eat in shifts if necessary.

We especially like this Italian menu, plus it's special enough for company. **Creamy Ham Fettuccine** is my most-requested main dish. I really like the thick, creamy texture of the sauce. It's great with any hearty pasta, like whole wheat penne.

The **salad was inspired by** one my husband, Bob, and I first enjoyed at a restaurant. It's fast, fresh and goes with almost any pasta dish. Bagged salad greens are convenient and worth the extra cost to me. When **I bake Italian Cheese Bread** to serve alongside, the aroma in our home is just wonderful! If there's room for dessert, we top this meal with spumoni ice cream.

10 Artichoke-Pepperoni Tossed Salad

PREP/TOTAL TIME: 10 MINUTES
MAKES: 6 SERVINGS

- 1 package (10 ounces) ready-to-serve salad greens
- 1 can (14 ounces) water-packed artichoke hearts, rinsed, drained and chopped
- 1 cup (4 ounces) shredded Italian cheese blend, optional
- 1 package (3½ ounces) sliced pepperoni
- ¼ cup chopped red onion
- 1 jar (2 ounces) sliced pimientos, drained
- ⅓ to ½ cup Italian salad dressing

1. In a salad bowl, combine the greens, artichokes, cheese if desired, pepperoni, onion and pimientos. Drizzle with dressing and toss to coat. Serve immediately.

30 Creamy Ham Fettuccine

PREP/TOTAL TIME: 25 MINUTES **MAKES:** 6 SERVINGS

- 1 package (12 ounces) fettuccine
- 3 tablespoons finely chopped onion
- 3 tablespoons butter
- 2 tablespoons plus 1 teaspoon all-purpose flour
- 3 cups heavy whipping cream
- 2 cups fresh broccoli florets
- 2 cups cubed fully cooked ham
- 1 cup shredded Parmesan cheese, divided
- ½ to ¾ teaspoon garlic salt
- ¼ teaspoon pepper
- ¼ teaspoon dried oregano
- ¼ teaspoon ground nutmeg

1. Cook fettuccine according to package directions. Meanwhile, in a large saucepan, saute onion in butter until tender. Stir in flour until blended. Gradually stir in the cream. Bring to a boil over medium heat, stirring constantly.

2. Add broccoli. Reduce heat; simmer, uncovered, for 7-10 minutes or until broccoli is crisp-tender, stirring occasionally. Stir in the ham, ½ cup cheese, garlic salt, pepper, oregano and nutmeg. Drain fettuccine; serve with sauce. Sprinkle with remaining cheese.

20 Italian Cheese Bread

PREP/TOTAL TIME: 20 MINUTES **MAKES:** 6 SERVINGS

- ¼ cup butter, softened
- 1 loaf (1 pound) French bread, halved lengthwise
- 1 cup (4 ounces) shredded Italian cheese blend
- 1 teaspoon dried oregano
- ¼ to ½ teaspoon garlic salt

1. Spread butter over cut sides of bread. Place on an ungreased baking sheet. Combine the cheese, oregano and garlic salt; sprinkle over bread. Bake at 350° for 12-15 minutes or until cheese is melted. Slice and serve warm.

10 Quick Salmon Chowder

I made up this quick creamy chowder one winter afternoon. I like to use a can of sockeye salmon for the best flavor. The soup can also be seasoned with tarragon instead of dill.

—**TOM BAILEY** GOLDEN VALLEY, MINNESOTA

PREP/TOTAL TIME: 10 MINUTES **MAKES:** 7 SERVINGS

- 3 cans (10¾ ounces each) condensed cream of potato soup, undiluted
- 2⅔ cups half-and-half cream
- 1 can (14¾ ounces) salmon, drained, bones and skin removed
- 1 teaspoon dill weed
- ½ teaspoon salt
- ¼ teaspoon white pepper
- ¼ teaspoon crushed red pepper flakes

1. In a large saucepan, combine all ingredients. Cook and stir over medium heat until the chowder is heated through.

20 Pizza Grilled Cheese

When I was 15, I created this easy sandwich because it combined two of my favorite foods and was so good. Dipping sauce makes it extra-fun!

—**ROBIN KETTERING** NEWVILLE, PENNSYLVANIA

PREP/TOTAL TIME: 15 MINUTES **MAKES:** 1 SERVING

- 1 tablespoon butter, softened
- 2 slices bread
- 1 slice provolone cheese
- 6 slices pepperoni
- 3 tablespoons pizza sauce
  Additional pizza sauce, optional

1. Butter one side of each slice of bread. Place one slice in a skillet over medium heat, butter side down. Top with the cheese, pepperoni, pizza sauce and second bread slice, butter side up.

2. Cook until golden brown, turning once. Serve with additional pizza sauce if desired.

top tip

When I make chowder, I like to add leftover scalloped potatoes or other cooked potato dishes to it. The soup that results is flavorful and filling.

—**JEAN J.** CHULA VISTA, CALIFORNIA

30 Tater Tot Taco Salad

Since I love potatoes and my husband and I both enjoy the flavor of tacos, this meal-in-one dish is a tasty supper for the two of us. It's not as messy as eating tacos...and the recipe can easily be doubled for friends.

—**ELEANOR MIELKE** MITCHELL, SOUTH DAKOTA

PREP/TOTAL TIME: 30 MINUTES **MAKES:** 2 SERVINGS

- 2 cups frozen miniature Tater Tots
- ½ pound ground beef
- 2 tablespoons taco seasoning
- ½ cup shredded cheddar cheese
- ¼ cup sliced ripe olives
- 1 cup shredded lettuce
- 2 tablespoons taco sauce
- ¼ cup sour cream

1. Bake Tater Tots according to package directions.

2. Meanwhile, in a large skillet, cook beef over medium heat until no longer pink; drain. Stir in the taco seasoning.

3. Divide Tater Tots between two serving plates or bowls. Top with taco mixture, cheese, olives, lettuce, taco sauce and sour cream.

30 ▸ Homemade Fish Sticks

I'm a nutritionist and wanted a healthy fish fix. Moist inside and crunchy outside, these sticks are great with oven fries or roasted veggies and low-fat homemade tartar sauce.
—**JENNIFER ROWLAND** ELIZABETHTOWN, KENTUCKY

PREP/TOTAL TIME: 25 MINUTES **MAKES:** 2 SERVINGS

- ½ **cup all-purpose flour**
- 1 **egg, beaten**
- ½ **cup dry bread crumbs**
- ½ **teaspoon salt**
- ½ **teaspoon paprika**
- ½ **teaspoon lemon-pepper seasoning**
- ¾ **pound cod fillets, cut into 1-inch strips**
  Butter-flavored cooking spray

1. Place flour and egg in separate shallow bowls. In another shallow bowl, combine bread crumbs and seasonings. Dip fish in the flour, then egg, then roll in the crumb mixture.

2. Place on a baking sheet coated with cooking spray. Spritz fish sticks with butter-flavored spray. Bake at 400° for 10-12 minutes or until fish flakes easily with a fork, turning once.

20 ▸ Cherry-Topped Chicken

Looking for an entree that's simple enough for busy weeknights, but special enough to serve company? This scrumptious chicken fits the bill. It goes together in just minutes and uses only four ingredients.
—**TABETHA MOORE** NEW BRAUNFELS, TEXAS

PREP/TOTAL TIME: 15 MINUTES **MAKES:** 4 SERVINGS

- 4 **boneless skinless chicken breast halves (4 ounces each)**
- 1 **tablespoon canola oil**
- ½ **cup cherry preserves**
- ¼ **teaspoon ground allspice**

1. Flatten chicken to ¼-in. thickness. In a large skillet, cook chicken in oil over medium heat for 5 minutes on each side or until no longer pink.

2. Meanwhile, in a small microwave-safe bowl, combine preserves and allspice. Heat in the microwave until warmed. Serve with chicken.

My husband preaches at different churches, and I do a lot of cooking for church functions and potlucks. We like easy, affordable meals that I can easily scale to feed a crowd.

I love to fill the 12-quart stockpot I got from my mother-in-law with homemade chili and invite folks over to enjoy it. Then I make **Chili Mac** with the leftovers, using 1 quart of chili per batch. (For quick preparation, canned chili is called for here.) **The salad I'm sharing** is colorful and has a variety of textures. It's a great way for kids to get their vegetables.

Shortcuts like a graham cracker crust and whipped topping mean you can enjoy this **delicious fluffy pie** any time. My youngest son wanted pies around his wedding cake, and this was one of his requests!

20 Pepperoni Salad

PREP/TOTAL TIME: 15 MINUTES
MAKES: 6 SERVINGS

- 24 slices pepperoni
- 4 green onions, chopped
- 2 cups fresh broccoli florets
- 1 cup fresh cauliflowerets
- ½ cup chopped celery
- ½ cup golden raisins

DRESSING
- ⅔ cup mayonnaise
- ⅓ cup sugar
- 4 teaspoons cider vinegar

1. In a large serving bowl, combine the first six ingredients. For dressing, in a small bowl, whisk together the mayonnaise, sugar and vinegar. Pour over salad; toss to coat.

20 Chili Mac

PREP/TOTAL TIME: 20 MINUTES **MAKES:** 6 SERVINGS

- 1 **cup uncooked elbow macaroni**
- 1 **pound ground beef**
- 1 **small green pepper, chopped**
- 1 **small onion, chopped**
- 2 **cans (15 ounces each) chili with beans**
- 1 **can (11 ounces) whole kernel corn, drained**
- 1 **cup (4 ounces) shredded cheddar cheese**

1. Cook macaroni according to package directions.

2. Meanwhile, in a large skillet, cook the beef, green pepper and onion over medium heat until meat is no longer pink; drain. Stir in chili and corn. Drain macaroni; add to the skillet and heat through. Sprinkle with cheese.

10 Peanut Butter Pie

PREP/TOTAL TIME: 10 MINUTES **MAKES:** 8 SERVINGS

- ¾ **cup peanut butter**
- 4 **ounces cream cheese, softened**
- 1 **cup confectioners' sugar**
- 1 **carton (8 ounces) frozen whipped topping, thawed**
- 1 **graham cracker crust (9 inches)**
  Salted chopped peanuts

1. In a large bowl, beat the peanut butter, cream cheese and confectioners' sugar until smooth. Fold in whipped topping; pour into prepared crust. Sprinkle with nuts. Chill until serving.

top tip

Make Chili Mac Go Further

Lee's yummy skillet dinner turns her favorite chili into a satisfying main dish. To stretch it even further, she sometimes mixes in canned black beans and boosts the flavor with taco seasoning..

30 ▶ Garden Turkey Burgers

These juicy burgers get plenty of color and flavor from onion, zucchini and red pepper. I often make the mixture ahead of time and put it in the refrigerator. Later, I can put the burgers on the grill and then whip up a salad or side dish.

—SANDY KITZMILLER
UNITYVILLE, PENNSYLVANIA

PREP/TOTAL TIME: 25 MINUTES
MAKES: 6 SERVINGS

> 1   **cup old-fashioned oats**
> ¾   **cup chopped onion**
> ¾   **cup finely chopped sweet red or green pepper**
> ½   **cup shredded zucchini**
> ¼   **cup ketchup**
> 2   **garlic cloves, minced**
> ¼   **teaspoon salt, optional**
> 1   **pound ground turkey**
> 6   **whole wheat hamburger buns, split and toasted**

1. In a large bowl, combine the first seven ingredients. Crumble turkey over mixture and mix well. Shape into six ½-in.-thick patties.

2. Moisten a paper towel with cooking oil; using long-handled tongs, lightly coat the grill rack.

3. Grill burgers, covered, over medium heat or broil 4 in. from the heat for 4-6 minutes on each side or until a thermometer reads 165° and juices run clear. Serve on buns.

30 ▶ Jiffy Pork & Penne

Some people call it dinner hour, but many of us call it rush hour. Slow down with this super-easy meal and have time to share with your family.

—BRIGITTE SCHALLER FLEMINGTON, MISSOURI

PREP/TOTAL TIME: 30 MINUTES **MAKES:** 5 SERVINGS

> 1½   **cups uncooked penne pasta**
> 1   **pound ground pork**
> ½   **cup chopped onion**
> 1   **can (14½ ounces) stewed tomatoes**
> 1   **can (8 ounces) tomato sauce**
> 1   **teaspoon Italian seasoning**
> 1   **medium zucchini, cut into ¼-inch slices**

1. Cook pasta according to package directions. Meanwhile, in a large skillet, cook pork and onion over medium heat until meat is no longer pink; drain. Add the tomatoes, tomato sauce and Italian seasoning. Bring to a boil. Reduce heat; cover and cook for 5 minutes to allow flavors to blend.

2. Drain pasta; add to skillet. Stir in zucchini. Cover and cook for 3-5 minutes or until zucchini is crisp-tender.

30 Tilapia with Jasmine Rice

This zesty tilapia is to die for. Fragrant jasmine rice brings a special touch to the meal. And it gets even better—each serving has only 5 grams of fat!

—**SHIRL PARSONS** CAPE CARTERET, NORTH CAROLINA

PREP/TOTAL TIME: 30 MINUTES **MAKES:** 2 SERVINGS

- ¾ **cup water**
- ½ **cup uncooked jasmine rice**
- 1½ **teaspoons butter**
- ¼ **teaspoon ground cumin**
- ¼ **teaspoon seafood seasoning**
- ¼ **teaspoon pepper**
- ⅛ **teaspoon salt**
- 2 **tilapia fillets (6 ounces each)**
- ¼ **cup fat-free Italian salad dressing**

1. In a large saucepan, bring the water, rice and butter to a boil. Reduce heat; cover and simmer for 15-20 minutes or until liquid is absorbed and rice is tender.

2. Combine the seasonings; sprinkle over fillets. Place salad dressing in a large skillet; cook over medium heat until heated through. Add fish; cook for 3-4 minutes on each side or until fish flakes easily with a fork. Serve with rice.

20 Speedy Shepherd's Pie

Turn your leftovers and a few pantry staples into warm comfort food in no time! You'll enjoy this deliciously different dish.

—**SHARON TIPTON** WINTER GARDEN, FLORIDA

PREP/TOTAL TIME: 20 MINUTES **MAKES:** 4 SERVINGS

- 1½ **pounds ground beef**
- 1 **medium onion, chopped**
- 2 **garlic cloves, minced**
- ½ **cup water**
- 1 **envelope taco seasoning**
- 2 **cups (8 ounces) shredded cheddar cheese, divided**
- 3 **cups leftover or refrigerated mashed potatoes, warmed**

1. In a large ovenproof skillet, cook the beef, onion and garlic over medium heat until meat is no longer pink. Stir in water and taco seasoning; heat through. Stir in 1 cup cheese.

2. Combine potatoes and remaining cheese; spread over beef. Broil 4-6 in. from the heat for 5-6 minutes or until golden brown.

20 Kielbasa Tortellini Alfredo

We combined just six ingredients to create a hearty and satisfying main dish. It's easy to put together and sure to please the whole family.
—TASTE OF HOME TEST KITCHEN

PREP/TOTAL TIME: 20 MINUTES **MAKES:** 4 SERVINGS

- 1 package (9 ounces) refrigerated cheese or spinach tortellini
- ½ pound smoked kielbasa or Polish sausage, sliced
- 1 medium sweet red pepper, julienned
- 2 teaspoons canola oil
- 1 jar (16 ounces) Alfredo sauce
- 1 cup chopped tomato

1. Cook tortellini according to package directions. Meanwhile, in a large skillet, saute kielbasa and red pepper in oil for 3 minutes or until pepper is crisp-tender.

2. Drain tortellini. Stir tortellini and Alfredo sauce into skillet; heat through. Garnish with tomato.

30 Peachy Chicken

Here's a sweet and refreshing chicken recipe that's great for weeknights, but special enough to serve to guests. It's wonderful over rice.
—BILL BROWN HADDONFIELD, NEW JERSEY

PREP/TOTAL TIME: 25 MINUTES **MAKES:** 4 SERVINGS

- 4 boneless skinless chicken breast halves (4 ounces each)
- 1 tablespoon canola oil
- 1 tablespoon butter
- 1 can (15¼ ounces) sliced peaches, undrained
- ½ cup packed brown sugar
- ½ cup orange juice
- 1 envelope onion soup mix
  Hot cooked rice, optional

1. In a large skillet over medium heat, brown chicken in oil and butter; remove and keep warm. Stir in the peaches with juice, brown sugar, orange juice and soup mix to the skillet. Bring to a boil; cook and stir for 2 minutes. Reduce heat; return chicken to the pan.

2. Simmer, uncovered, for 15-20 minutes or until a thermometer reads 170°. Serve with rice if desired.

10 Chicken Melts

PREP/TOTAL TIME: 10 MINUTES
MAKES: 2 SERVINGS

- 4 slices cinnamon-raisin bread
- 2 tablespoons jalapeno pepper jelly
- 1 package (6 ounces) thinly sliced deli smoked chicken breast
- 3 ounces Havarti cheese, sliced
- 1 tablespoon butter, softened

1. Spread two bread slices with jelly. Layer with chicken and cheese; top with remaining bread. Butter outsides of sandwiches.

2. In a large skillet over medium heat, toast sandwiches for 2-3 minutes on each side or until cheese is melted.

20 Apricot-Glazed Ham Steak

Want to prepare a small and easy meal? Try my savory-sweet ham steak. The apricot glaze gives it an attractive look and delicious flavor.
—**GALELAH DOWELL**
FAIRLAND, OKLAHOMA

PREP/TOTAL TIME: 20 MINUTES
MAKES: 2 SERVINGS

- 1 fully cooked boneless ham steak (8 ounces)
- 1 tablespoon brown sugar
- 1 tablespoon apricot preserves
- ¾ teaspoon ground mustard
  Dash ground cloves

1. Place ham steak in a baking dish coated with cooking spray. Combine the remaining ingredients; spoon over ham.

2. Bake, uncovered, at 350° for 12-16 minutes or until heated through. Cut in half to serve.

The secret to these toasty, tasty sandwiches is the touch of sweetness from the raisins and the zip from the jalapeno jelly. You could also sub in brick cheese for the creamy Havarti.
—**DIANE HALFERTY** CORPUS CHRISTI, TEXAS

30 Chicken a la King

Comforting Chicken a la King has a thick and creamy sauce that's perfect over biscuits. I've been making this recipe for 30 years. It's a wonderful way to create a quick lunch or dinner with leftover chicken.
—**RUTH LEE** TROY, ONTARIO

PREP/TOTAL TIME: 25 MINUTES **MAKES:** 4 SERVINGS

- 4 **individually frozen biscuits**
- 1¾ **cups sliced fresh mushrooms**
- ¼ **cup chopped onion**
- ¼ **cup chopped celery**
- ⅓ **cup butter**
- ¼ **cup all-purpose flour**
- ⅛ **to ¼ teaspoon salt**
- 1 **cup chicken broth**
- 1 **cup milk**
- 2 **cups cubed cooked chicken**
- 2 **tablespoons diced pimientos**

1. Bake biscuits according to package directions. Meanwhile, in a large skillet, saute the mushrooms, onion and celery in butter until crisp-tender. Stir in flour and salt until blended. Gradually stir in broth and milk. Bring to a boil; cook and stir for 2 minutes or until thickened.

2. Add chicken and pimientos; heat through. Serve with biscuits.

20 Fiesta Ravioli

I adapted this recipe to suit our taste for spicy food. The ravioli taste like mini enchiladas. I serve them with a Mexican-inspired salad and pineapple sherbet for dessert.
—**DEBBIE PURDUE** WESTLAND, MICHIGAN

PREP/TOTAL TIME: 20 MINUTES **MAKES:** 4-6 SERVINGS

- 1 **package (25 ounces) frozen beef ravioli**
- 1 **can (10 ounces) enchilada sauce**
- 1 **cup salsa**
- 2 **cups (8 ounces) shredded Monterey Jack cheese**
- 1 **can (2¼ ounces) sliced ripe olives, drained**

1. Cook ravioli according to package directions. Meanwhile, in a large skillet, combine enchilada sauce and salsa. Cook and stir over medium heat until heated through.

2. Drain ravioli; add to sauce and gently stir to coat. Top with cheese and olives. Cover and cook over low heat for 3-4 minutes or until cheese is melted.

FISH FRIES BRING OUR FAMILY TOGETHER

BY BARBARA KEITH
FAUCETT, MISSOURI

With four children, 10 grandchildren and two great-grandchildren, plus our own siblings, my husband and I are richly blessed with a large extended family. I often cook when we all get together, and we often have fish fries for our friends, neighbors and relatives.

Everyone likes my Mustard Fried Catfish. **Coating the fish with mustard and seasoned cornmeal** seals the fillets so they don't absorb the cooking oil, while giving them a very good flavor. My youngest daughter frequently makes this fish for her husband, as it is one of his favorite dishes.

No fish fry would be complete without **cool and creamy coleslaw**, and I prepare my mother's recipe. It uses just five ingredients and it is so delicious, I'm always asked to share the recipe. **Garlic New Potatoes** are easy to make, and they complement just about any entree. They're also delicious with a squeeze of fresh lemon juice over them.

20 Mustard Fried Catfish

PREP/TOTAL TIME: 20 MINUTES **MAKES:** 4 SERVINGS

- ⅔ **cup yellow cornmeal**
- ⅓ **cup all-purpose flour**
- ½ **teaspoon salt**
- ¼ **teaspoon paprika**
- ¼ **teaspoon pepper**
- ⅛ **teaspoon cayenne pepper**
- ½ **cup prepared mustard**
- 4 **catfish fillets (6 ounces each)**
  Oil for frying

1. In a shallow bowl, combine the first six ingredients. Spread mustard over both sides of fillets; coat with cornmeal mixture.

2. In an electric skillet or deep-fat fryer, heat oil to 375°. Fry the fillets, a few at a time, for 2-3 minutes on each side or until fish flakes easily with a fork. Drain on paper towels.

10 Sweet 'n' Sour Coleslaw

PREP/TOTAL TIME: 5 MINUTES **MAKES:** 4 SERVINGS

- 5½ **cups coleslaw mix**
- ½ **cup heavy whipping cream**
- ⅓ **cup sugar**
- 3 **tablespoons white vinegar**
- ½ **teaspoon salt**

1. Place coleslaw mix in a serving bowl. Combine the remaining ingredients; pour over coleslaw mix and toss to coat. Chill until serving.

30 Garlic New Potatoes

PREP/TOTAL TIME: 25 MINUTES **MAKES:** 4 SERVINGS

- 16 **small red potatoes**
- 3 **tablespoons butter, melted**
- 1½ **teaspoons minced garlic**
- 1½ **teaspoons dried parsley flakes**
  Salt and pepper to taste

1. Place potatoes in a steamer basket; place in a large saucepan over 1 in. of water. Bring to a boil; cover and steam for 15-20 minutes or until tender. Transfer to a serving bowl.

2. Combine the butter, garlic, parsley, salt and pepper; pour over potatoes and toss to coat.

20 Tomato Walnut Tilapia

Tomato, bread crumbs and crunchy walnuts dress up tilapia fillets in this delightful main dish. I often serve it with cooked green beans and julienned carrots.

—PHYL BROICH-WESSLING
GARNER, IOWA

PREP/TOTAL TIME: 20 MINUTES
MAKES: 4 SERVINGS

        4 **tilapia fillets (4 ounces each)**
        ¼ **teaspoon salt**
        ¼ **teaspoon pepper**
        1 **tablespoon butter**
        1 **medium tomato, thinly sliced**
    TOPPING
        ½ **cup soft bread crumbs**
        ¼ **cup chopped walnuts**
        2 **tablespoons lemon juice**
     1½ **teaspoons butter, melted**

1. Sprinkle fillets with salt and pepper. In a large skillet coated with cooking spray, cook fillets in butter over medium-high heat for 2-3 minutes on each side or until lightly browned.

2. Transfer fish to a broiler pan or baking sheet; top with tomato.

3. Combine the topping ingredients; spoon over the tops.

4. Broil 3-4 in. from the heat for 2-3 minutes or until topping is lightly browned and fish flakes easily with a fork.

20 Caesar Strip Steaks

I season New York strip steaks with a Caesar dressing mixture, then grill them for a tasty entree that's ready in minutes. As a side dish, I serve baked potatoes topped with chunky salsa and sour cream.

—MELISSA MORTON PHILADELPHIA, PENNSYLVANIA

PREP/TOTAL TIME: 20 MINUTES **MAKES:** 4 SERVINGS

        4 **tablespoons creamy Caesar salad dressing, divided**
        2 **teaspoons garlic powder**
        1 **teaspoon salt**
        1 **teaspoon coarsely ground pepper**
        2 **boneless beef top loin steaks (12 ounces each)**

1. In a small bowl, combine 2 tablespoons salad dressing, garlic powder, salt and pepper. Spoon over both sides of steaks.

2. Grill, covered, over medium heat or broil 4 in. from the heat for 7-9 minutes on each side or until meat reaches desired doneness (for medium-rare, a thermometer should read 145°; medium, 160°; well-done, 170°), basting occasionally with remaining salad dressing. Cut steaks in half to serve.

Editor's Note: *Top loin steak may be labeled as strip steak, Kansas City steak, New York strip steak, ambassador steak or boneless club steak in your region.*

20 Cajun Shrimp and Rice

I have a friend with celiac disease and I serve this when she comes over for lunch. A nice option to the same old meat and potatoes, it's now become an often-requested recipe!

—**RUTH MILLER** BOYERTOWN, PENNSYLVANIA

PREP/TOTAL TIME: 15 MINUTES **MAKES:** 4 SERVINGS

- 1 **package (8.8 ounces) ready-to-serve long grain rice**
- 1 **pound uncooked medium shrimp, peeled and deveined**
- 2 **teaspoons Cajun seasoning**
- 1 **tablespoon olive oil**
- 1 **tablespoon butter**
- 1½ **teaspoons minced garlic**
- 1 **package (6 ounces) frozen snow peas**

1. Cook rice according to package directions. Meanwhile, in a large skillet, saute shrimp and Cajun seasoning in oil and butter until shrimp turn pink. Add garlic; cook 1 minute later. Add peas and rice. Cook for 2-3 minutes or until heated through.

20 Beef Taco Skillet

Busy day? Save time and money with a stovetop supper the whole family will love. This one calls for handy convenience products, so it's on the table in minutes.

—**KELLY RODER** FAIRFAX, VIRGINIA

PREP/TOTAL TIME: 20 MINUTES **MAKES:** 6 SERVINGS

- 1 **pound ground beef**
- 1 **small red onion, chopped**
- 1 **can (15¼ ounces) whole kernel corn, drained**
- 10 **corn tortillas (6 inches), cut into 1-inch pieces**
- 1 **bottle (8 ounces) taco sauce**
- 1¼ **cups shredded cheddar cheese, divided**
  Hot pepper sauce, optional

1. In a large skillet, cook beef and onion over medium heat until meat is no longer pink; drain. Add the corn, tortillas, taco sauce and 1 cup cheese; heat through. Sprinkle with remaining cheese. Serve with pepper sauce if desired.

30 Cheesy Cauliflower and Potato Soup

PREP/TOTAL TIME: 25 MINUTES **MAKES:** 5 SERVINGS

- 1 **package (16 ounces) frozen cauliflower**
- 1 **cup frozen sliced carrots**
- 3 **tablespoons dried minced onion**
- 1 **tablespoon chicken bouillon granules**
- 2¼ **cups water, divided**
- 2 **cups 2% milk**
- 1 **can (10¾ ounces) condensed cream of potato soup, undiluted**
- ½ **teaspoon garlic powder**
- ⅛ **teaspoon ground nutmeg**
- 4 **teaspoons cornstarch**
- 1 **cup (4 ounces) shredded cheddar cheese**

1. In a large saucepan, combine the vegetables, dried onion, bouillon and 2 cups water. Bring to a boil. Reduce heat; cover and simmer for 4-6 minutes or until vegetables are tender.

2. Stir in the milk, soup, garlic powder and nutmeg. Combine cornstarch and remaining water until smooth; gradually stir into soup. Bring to a boil; cook and stir for 2 minutes or until slightly thickened. Stir in cheese until melted.

20 Ham and Swiss Biscuits

PREP/TOTAL TIME: 20 MINUTES **MAKES:** 10 BISCUITS

- 2 **cups biscuit/baking mix**
- ¼ **pound fully cooked ham, finely chopped**
- ½ **cup shredded Swiss cheese**
- ⅔ **cup 2% milk**
- 1 **egg, beaten**
- 1 **tablespoon honey mustard**
- 2 **teaspoons dried minced onion**

1. In a small bowl, combine the biscuit mix, ham and cheese. Combine the milk, egg, mustard and onion. Stir into biscuit mixture just until moistened. Drop by ¼ cupfuls 2 in. apart onto a greased baking sheet.

2. Bake at 425° for 10-12 minutes or until golden brown. Serve warm. Refrigerate leftovers.

30 ▸ Shrimp 'n' Noodle Bowls

PREP/TOTAL TIME: 25 MINUTES
MAKES: 6 SERVINGS

- 8 ounces uncooked angel hair pasta
- 1 pound cooked small shrimp
- 2 cups broccoli coleslaw mix
- 6 green onions, thinly sliced
- ½ cup minced fresh cilantro
- ⅔ cup reduced-fat sesame ginger salad dressing

1. Cook pasta according to package directions; drain and rinse in cold water. Transfer to a large bowl. Add the shrimp, coleslaw mix, onions and cilantro. Drizzle with dressing; toss to coat. Cover and refrigerate until serving.

30 ▸ Swiss Tuna Casserole

My husband tossed together this comforting casserole, and it was the best-tasting tuna dish ever!

—JOANNE CALLAHAN
FAR HILLS, NEW JERSEY

PREP/TOTAL TIME: 30 MINUTES
MAKES: 4 SERVINGS

- 4 cups cooked egg noodles
- 1½ cups (6 ounces) shredded Swiss cheese
- 1 cup mayonnaise
- 1 can (6 ounces) tuna, drained and flaked
- 1 cup seasoned bread crumbs, divided

1. In a bowl, combine the noodles, cheese, mayonnaise and tuna. Sprinkle ½ cup bread crumbs into a greased 9-in. square baking dish. Spread noodle mixture over crumbs. Sprinkle with the remaining crumbs. Bake, uncovered, at 350° for 18-22 minutes or until heated through.

Here's a great quick meal that feels like it came from a restaurant. Cooked shrimp, bagged slaw and bottled dressing reduce the time needed to get it on the table. **—MARY BERGFELD** EUGENE, OREGON

30 Turkey Piccata

Quick, flavorful and special, my lightened-up take on a classic recipe has the same buttery lemon-caper sauce that people love.

—LESLIE RODRIGUEZ EL CAJON, CALIFORNIA

PREP/TOTAL TIME: 25 MINUTES **MAKES:** 4 SERVINGS

- ¼ **cup all-purpose flour**
- ½ **teaspoon salt**
- ¼ **teaspoon pepper**
- 1 **package (17.6 ounces) turkey breast cutlets**
- 2 **tablespoons olive oil**
- ½ **cup chicken broth**
- 3 **tablespoons butter**
- 1 **tablespoon lemon juice**
- 1 **tablespoon minced fresh parsley**
- 1 **tablespoon capers, drained**

1. In a shallow bowl, combine the flour, salt and pepper. Add turkey slices, one at a time, and turn to coat.

2. In a large skillet, cook turkey in oil in batches for 2-3 minutes on each side or until juices run clear. Remove to a serving platter and keep warm.

3. Add broth to the pan, scraping to remove browned bits. Bring to a boil; cook until liquid is reduced by half. Stir in the remaining ingredients until butter is melted. Pour sauce over turkey.

20 Applesauce Barbecue Chicken

You only need a few ingredients to create this sweet and peppery chicken. The subtle flavor of apple sets this dish apart from the rest.

—DARLA ANDREWS LEWISVILLE, TEXAS

PREP/TOTAL TIME: 20 MINUTES **MAKES:** 4 SERVINGS

- 4 **boneless skinless chicken breast halves (6 ounces each)**
- ½ **teaspoon pepper**
- 1 **tablespoon olive oil**
- ⅔ **cup chunky applesauce**
- ⅔ **cup spicy barbecue sauce**
- 2 **tablespoons brown sugar**
- 1 **teaspoon chili powder**

1. Sprinkle chicken with pepper. In a large skillet, brown chicken in oil on both sides. In a small bowl, combine the remaining ingredients; pour over chicken. Cover and cook 7-10 minutes longer or until a thermometer reads 170°.

10 Chicken Enchilada Soup

Canned soups, enchilada sauce and a few other convenience items make this yummy soup one of my favorites. Use mild green chilies if they suit your taste, or try a spicier kind to give the soup more kick.
—**CRISTIN FISCHER** BELLEVUE, NEBRASKA

PREP/TOTAL TIME: 10 MINUTES **MAKES:** 7 SERVINGS

- 1 **can (10¾ ounces) condensed nacho cheese soup, undiluted**
- 1 **can (10¾ ounces) condensed cream of chicken soup, undiluted**
- 2⅔ **cups milk**
- 1 **can (10 ounces) chunk white chicken, drained**
- 1 **can (10 ounces) enchilada sauce**
- 1 **can (4 ounces) chopped green chilies**
  Sour cream

1. In a large saucepan, combine the soups, milk, chicken, enchilada sauce and green chilies. Cook until heated through. Serve with sour cream.

top tip

I dilute condensed tomato or vegetable soup with V-8 juice instead of water. Then I top the simmering soup with homemade dumplings for a main dish that tastes like it's from scratch!
—**ESTHER T.** PORTALES, NEW MEXICO

30 Burritos Made Easy

These easy burritos are packed with a beef-and-bean filling for a taste of the Southwest. And since the recipe makes eight big burritos, you can feed a crowd!
—**JENNIFER MCKINNEY** WASHINGTON, ILLINOIS

PREP/TOTAL TIME: 30 MINUTES **MAKES:** 8 BURRITOS

- 1 **pound ground beef**
- ¼ **cup chopped onion**
- 1 **can (15 ounces) chili with beans**
- 1¼ **cups chunky salsa**
- ¼ **cup canned chopped green chilies**
- 8 **flour tortillas (8 inches), warmed**
- 8 **slices process American cheese**
  Taco sauce and shredded lettuce, optional

1. In a large skillet, cook beef and onion over medium heat until meat is no longer pink; drain. Stir in the chili, salsa and green chilies. Bring to a boil. Reduce heat; simmer, uncovered, for 5 minutes.

2. Spoon about ½ cupful beef mixture off center on each tortilla. Top each with a slice of cheese; roll up. Serve with taco sauce and lettuce if desired.

30 Bacon & Tomato Spaghetti

Our summer-perfect pasta features baby spinach, cherry tomatoes and crisp bacon tossed with a tangy balsamic vinaigrette. It's ready in a flash.
—**TASTE OF HOME TEST KITCHEN**

PREP/TOTAL TIME: 25 MINUTES **MAKES:** 4 SERVINGS

- 8 ounces uncooked spaghetti
- ½ pound thick-sliced bacon strips, chopped
- 2 cups cherry tomatoes, halved
- 3 cups fresh baby spinach
- ¼ cup balsamic vinaigrette
- ½ teaspoon salt
- ¼ teaspoon pepper
  Grated Parmesan cheese

1. Cook spaghetti according to package directions.

2. Meanwhile, in a large skillet, cook bacon over medium heat until crisp. Remove to paper towels with a slotted spoon; drain, reserving 2 tablespoons drippings. Saute tomatoes in drippings until tender. Drain spaghetti; stir into skillet. Add the spinach, bacon, vinaigrette, salt and pepper; heat through. Sprinkle with cheese.

20 Blackened Chicken and Beans

My husband loves any spicy food, and this is one quick-fix and low-fat recipe we can both agree on. As the chicken cooks, whip up a salad of lettuce, tomato, avocado and shredded cheddar cheese. Dinner's done!
—**CHRISTINE ZONGKER** SPRING HILL, KANSAS

PREP/TOTAL TIME: 15 MINUTES **MAKES:** 4 SERVINGS

- 2 teaspoons chili powder
- ¼ teaspoon salt
- ¼ teaspoon pepper
- 4 boneless skinless chicken breast halves (4 ounces each)
- 1 tablespoon canola oil
- 1 can (15 ounces) black beans, rinsed and drained
- 1 cup frozen corn
- 1 cup chunky salsa

1. Combine the chili powder, salt and pepper; rub over both sides of chicken. In a large nonstick skillet, cook chicken in oil over medium heat for 4-5 minutes on each side or until a thermometer reads 170°. Remove and keep warm.

2. Add the beans, corn and salsa to the pan; heat through. Serve with chicken.

GREAT ITALIAN DINNER AT HOME

BY TALENA KEELER
SILOAM SPRINGS, ARKANSAS

My husband, son and I really enjoy Italian food. Once, following an especially good dinner we had at a local restaurant, I created my own version of the meal at home. My family now prefers this pasta over the restaurant's!

And my **chicken fettuccine is so easy** to serve when unexpected company drops by. I like to make it with California-blend vegetables (broccoli, cauliflower and carrots), though you could use any one vegetable or combination you prefer. Quick **homemade garlic bread** is a natural accompaniment.

As a finish, I use ready-made pound cake from my local bakery in the **Berries & Cream Desserts**. If you have more time, you could make your own pound cake—just be sure to allow enough time for it to cool completely before you cut it.

20 Berries & Cream Desserts

PREP/TOTAL TIME: 15 MINUTES
MAKES: 4 SERVINGS

- 1 loaf (10¾ ounces) frozen pound cake, thawed
- 1 package (3 ounces) cream cheese, softened
- 1 cup marshmallow creme
- 1 cup sliced fresh strawberries
- 1 cup fresh blueberries

1. Cut pound cake in half. Cut one half into ½-in. cubes (save remaining cake for another use). In a small bowl, beat the cream cheese and marshmallow creme until smooth.

2. In four small serving dishes, layer the cake cubes and fruit. Top with cream cheese mixture. Chill until serving.

20 Chicken Fettuccine Alfredo with Veggies

PREP/TOTAL TIME: 15 MINUTES **MAKES:** 4 SERVINGS

- 1 package (9 ounces) refrigerated fettuccine
- 3 cups frozen mixed vegetables
- 1 package (9 ounces) ready-to-serve roasted chicken breast strips
- 1½ cups Alfredo sauce
- ½ cup shredded Parmesan cheese

1. Fill a Dutch oven two-thirds full with water; bring to a boil. Add fettuccine and vegetables; return to a boil. Cook on high for 2-3 minutes or until tender; drain. Stir in chicken and Alfredo sauce; heat through. Sprinkle with cheese.

20 Buttery Parmesan Garlic Bread

PREP/TOTAL TIME: 15 MINUTES **MAKES:** 4 SERVINGS

- ¼ cup butter, softened
- 2 tablespoons shredded Parmesan cheese
- 1 teaspoon garlic powder
- 1 loaf (8 ounces) French bread, halved lengthwise

1. In a small bowl, combine the butter, cheese and garlic powder. Spread mixture over cut sides of bread. Place on an ungreased baking sheet.

2. Bake at 400° for 10-12 minutes or until golden brown. Serve warm.

30 Spinach Pizza

My vegetarian pizza is so easy to prepare. What a delicious way to serve a veggie-filled meal!

—DAWN BARTHOLOMEW
RALEIGH, NORTH CAROLINA

PREP/TOTAL TIME: 25 MINUTES
MAKES: 4-6 SERVINGS

- 1 **package (6½ ounces) pizza crust mix**
- ½ **cup Alfredo sauce**
- 2 **medium tomatoes**
- 4 **cups chopped fresh spinach**
- 2 **cups (8 ounces) shredded Italian cheese blend**

1. Prepare pizza dough according to package directions. With floured hands, press dough onto a greased 12-in. pizza pan.

2. Spread Alfredo sauce over dough to within 1 in. of edges. Thinly slice or chop tomatoes; top pizza with spinach, tomatoes and cheese. Bake at 450° for 10-15 minutes or until cheese is melted and crust is golden brown.

10 Tuna Delight

A handful of ingredients is all it takes to put a hot meal on the table. This makes one fast dinner on busy weeknights.

—MARIE GREEN
BELLE FOURCHE, SOUTH DAKOTA

PREP/TOTAL TIME: 10 MINUTES
MAKES: 3 SERVINGS

- 1¾ **cups frozen mixed vegetables**
- 1 **can (12 ounces) tuna, drained and flaked**
- 1 **can (10¾ ounces) condensed cream of chicken or celery soup, undiluted**
  Hot cooked rice or noodles

1. In a saucepan, combine the vegetables, tuna and soup. Cook and stir until heated through. Serve over rice or noodles.

30 Quick Creamy Chicken Enchiladas

These marvelous enchiladas taste amazing, freeze well and reheat easily in the microwave. If you prefer more zip, substitute pepper jack cheese for Monterey Jack.

—RACHEL SMITH KATY, TEXAS

PREP/TOTAL TIME: 30 MINUTES **MAKES:** 2 SERVINGS

- ⅔ **cup condensed cream of chicken soup, undiluted**
- ⅔ **cup sour cream**
- 2 **cups shredded cooked chicken breast**
- ½ **cup shredded Monterey Jack cheese, divided**
- 4 **flour tortillas (6 inches), warmed**

1. In a small bowl, combine soup and sour cream. Spread half over the bottom of an 8-in. square baking dish coated with cooking spray.

2. Place ½ cup chicken and 1 tablespoon cheese down the center of each tortilla; roll up and place in the baking dish. Top with remaining soup mixture; sprinkle with remaining cheese.

3. Bake, uncovered, at 350° for 18-22 minutes or until heated through.

EASY OVEN-FRESH COMFORT FOOD

BY JENNIFER HOEFT
THORNDALE, TEXAS

I'm very busy with the two businesses I run from my home. My husband, Daniel, works an hour away in Austin, and he calls before he leaves work so I can have a hot dinner ready for us when he gets home. Because we live in the country, a good 20 minutes from a small grocery store and an hour from the supermarket, I plan our menus for two weeks at a time.

This classic comfort food meal is surprisingly fast to make. The recipes are short and use mostly staples that are readily kept on hand. The baked **chicken with its crispy, flavorful crust** is always moist and tender. **Sour Cream Pan Biscuits** are light and fluffy on the inside with just a hint of sweetness. They bake at the same temperature and for about as long as the chicken, which makes them an easy accompaniment.

I created Spicy Garlic Green Beans to reproduce the same great flavor of the beans served at my favorite Chinese restaurant. These come very close and use just a few ingredients.

Tasty Onion Chicken

PREP/TOTAL TIME: 30 MINUTES **MAKES:** 4 SERVINGS

- ½ **cup butter, melted**
- 1 **tablespoon Worcestershire sauce**
- 1 **teaspoon ground mustard**
- 1 **can (2.8 ounces) French-fried onions, crushed**
- 4 **boneless skinless chicken breast halves (4 ounces each)**

1. In a shallow bowl, combine the butter, Worcestershire sauce and mustard. Place the onions in another shallow bowl. Dip the chicken in butter mixture, then coat with onions.

2. Place in a greased 11-in. x 7-in. baking dish; drizzle with remaining butter mixture. Bake, uncovered, at 400° for 20-25 minutes or until a thermometer reads 170°.

Sour Cream Pan Biscuits

PREP/TOTAL TIME: 25 MINUTES **MAKES:** 6 SERVINGS

- 2 **cups biscuit/baking mix**
- 1 **teaspoon sugar**
- ½ **cup club soda**
- 3 **tablespoons sour cream**

1. In a small bowl, combine all ingredients; stir just until moistened. Drop into six mounds in a 9-in. round baking pan coated with cooking spray.

2. Bake at 400° for 20 minutes or until golden brown. Serve warm.

20 Spicy Garlic Green Beans

PREP/TOTAL TIME: 15 MINUTES **MAKES:** 4 SERVINGS

- 1 **pound fresh green beans, cut into 1-inch pieces**
- 1 **teaspoon minced garlic**
- ¼ **to ½ teaspoon crushed red pepper flakes**
- ¼ **teaspoon salt**
- 1 **tablespoon canola oil**

1. In a large skillet, saute the beans, garlic, red pepper flakes and salt in oil for 10-12 minutes or until beans are crisp-tender.

top tip Dessert in a Dash

Want an easy idea for topping off Jennifer's delicious dinner? Try any of the following simple dessert options:

- Cube a purchased pound cake, then layer it with chocolate pudding and whipped cream in a large bowl for a fast trifle.
- Heat apple pie filling, spice it with cinnamon and serve over vanilla ice cream.
- Sandwich whipped cream and raspberries into store-bought croissants and dust them with confectioners' sugar.

30 Pork Chops with Dijon Sauce

Here's a main course that tastes rich but isn't high in saturated fat. It's easy for weeknights but the creamy sauce makes it special enough for weekends.

—BONNIE BROWN-WATSON HOUSTON, TEXAS

PREP/TOTAL TIME: 25 MINUTES **MAKES:** 4 SERVINGS

- 4 boneless pork loin chops (6 ounces each)
- ¼ teaspoon salt
- ¼ teaspoon pepper
- 2 teaspoons canola oil
- ⅓ cup reduced-sodium chicken broth
- 2 tablespoons Dijon mustard
- ⅓ cup fat-free half-and-half

1. Sprinkle pork chops with salt and pepper. In a large nonstick skillet coated with cooking spray, cook chops in oil for 4-5 minutes on each side or until a thermometer reads 145°. Remove pork chops and keep warm.

2. Stir broth into skillet, scraping up any browned bits. Stir in mustard and half-and-half. Bring to a boil. Reduce heat; simmer, uncovered, for 5-6 minutes or until thickened, stirring occasionally. Serve with pork chops.

20 Asian Beef and Noodles

This yummy, economical dish takes only five ingredients—all of which you're likely to have on hand. Serve with a dash of soy sauce and a side of pineapple slices. Or try it with ground turkey instead of beef!

—LAURA STENBERG WYOMING, MINNESOTA

PREP/TOTAL TIME: 20 MINUTES **MAKES:** 4 SERVINGS

- 1 pound lean ground beef (90% lean)
- 2 packages (3 ounces each) Oriental ramen noodles, crumbled
- 2½ cups water
- 2 cups frozen broccoli stir-fry vegetable blend
- ¼ teaspoon ground ginger
- 2 tablespoons thinly sliced green onion

1. In a large skillet, cook beef over medium heat until no longer pink; drain. Add the contents of one ramen noodle flavoring packet; stir until dissolved. Remove beef and set aside.

2. In the same skillet, combine the water, vegetables, ginger, noodles and contents of remaining flavoring packet. Bring to a boil. Reduce heat; cover and simmer for 3-4 minutes or until noodles are tender, stirring occasionally. Return beef to the pan and heat through. Stir in onion.

30 Chicken Cordon Bleu Pizza

Here's a combination of my two favorite foods—pizza and chicken cordon bleu. I have made this pizza for my family and also the teachers at my school. Now my teachers ask me to make it for them for lunch!

—JUSTIN RIPPEL COLGATE, WISCONSIN

PREP/TOTAL TIME: 30 MINUTES **MAKES:** 6 PIECES

- 1 tube (13.8 ounces) refrigerated pizza crust
- ½ cup Alfredo sauce
- ¼ teaspoon garlic salt
- 1 cup (4 ounces) shredded Swiss cheese
- 1½ cups cubed fully cooked ham
- 10 breaded chicken nuggets, thawed and cut into ½-inch pieces
- 1 cup (4 ounces) shredded part-skim mozzarella cheese

1. Unroll dough into a greased 15-in. x 10-in. x 1-in. baking pan; flatten dough and build up edges slightly. Bake at 425° for 8-10 minutes or until edges are lightly browned.

2. Spread with Alfredo sauce; sprinkle with garlic salt and Swiss cheese. Top with ham, chicken nuggets and mozzarella cheese. Bake for 8-10 minutes or until crust is golden brown and cheese is melted.

30 Broccoli Cheese Tortellini

When we lived in Seattle, my favorite restaurant served a wonderful dish I ordered every time I ate there. When we moved away, I came up with this to satisfy my craving.

—DARLENE BRENDEN SALEM, OREGON

PREP/TOTAL TIME: 25 MINUTES **MAKES:** 6 SERVINGS

- 2 cups heavy whipping cream
- 1 cup fresh broccoli florets
- 2 packages (9 ounces each) refrigerated cheese tortellini
- 2½ cups shredded Parmesan cheese, divided
- ¼ teaspoon coarsely ground pepper
- 2 teaspoons minced fresh parsley

1. In a large saucepan, cook cream and broccoli, uncovered, over medium-low heat for 5-6 minutes or until broccoli is crisp-tender. Meanwhile, cook tortellini according to package directions.

2. Stir 2 cups cheese and pepper into broccoli mixture. Bring to a boil. Reduce heat; simmer, uncovered, for 8-10 minutes or until mixture is thickened, stirring occasionally.

3. Drain tortellini; add to sauce and toss to coat. Sprinkle with parsley and remaining cheese.

20 Ham with Mixed Fruit

Apple pie filling and fruit cocktail are combined to create a sweet chunky sauce that nicely complements ham. I make this often for family birthdays—and it's so simple.
—**MRS. RAYMOND HOLTMANN** GERMANTOWN, ILLINOIS

PREP/TOTAL TIME: 15 MINUTES **MAKES:** 8 SERVINGS

- 2 **pounds fully cooked bone-in ham steak, cut into serving-size portions**
- 1 **tablespoon canola oil**
- 1 **can (21 ounces) apple pie filling**
- 1 **can (15¼ ounces) fruit cocktail, drained**
- ¼ **cup packed brown sugar**
- ¼ **cup butter, melted**

1. In a large skillet, cook the ham in oil over medium-heat for 3-4 minutes on each side or until lightly browned.

2. Meanwhile, in a large microwave-safe bowl, combine the pie filling, fruit cocktail, brown sugar and butter. Cook until heated through, stirring twice. Serve with ham.

30 Pasta & Broccoli Sausage Simmer

I created this hearty dish to use up a large head of broccoli. Now, my family requests it at least once a week, which is nice because we always have the ingredients handy.
—**LISA MONTGOMERY** ELMIRA, ONTARIO

PREP/TOTAL TIME: 30 MINUTES **MAKES:** 8 SERVINGS

- 3 **cups uncooked spiral pasta**
- 2 **pounds smoked kielbasa or Polish sausage, sliced**
- 2 **medium bunches broccoli, cut into florets**
- 1 **cup sliced red onion**
- 2 **cans (14½ ounces each) diced tomatoes, undrained**
- 2 **tablespoons minced fresh basil or 2 teaspoons dried basil**
- 2 **tablespoons minced fresh parsley or 2 teaspoons dried parsley flakes**
- 2 **teaspoons sugar**

1. Cook pasta according to directions. Meanwhile, in a Dutch oven, saute the sausage, broccoli and onion until broccoli is crisp-tender.

2. Add the tomatoes, basil, parsley and sugar. Cover and simmer for 10 minutes. Drain pasta; stir into the sausage mixture.

20 Zucchini Frittata

Here's a long-standing family favorite. When we plan a trip by car, I make this frittata the night before, stuff each half in a pita pocket in the morning and microwave them. After I bundle them up, we can enjoy a still-hot breakfast even when we're an hour down the road!
—**CAROL BLUMENBERG** LEHIGH ACRES, FLORIDA

PREP/TOTAL TIME: 20 MINUTES **MAKES:** 2 SERVINGS

- ½ **cup chopped onion**
- 1 **cup shredded zucchini**
- 1 **teaspoon canola oil**
- 3 **eggs**
- ¼ **teaspoon salt**
- 1 **cup (4 ounces) shredded Swiss cheese**

1. In an 8-in. ovenproof skillet over medium heat, cook onion and zucchini in oil until crisp-tender.

2. Beat the eggs and salt; pour into the pan. Cook until eggs are almost set, 6-7 minutes. Sprinkle with cheese. Bake at 350° for 4-5 minutes or until cheese is melted.

With leftover roast beef or deli beef, it takes almost no time at all to make hot, satisfying French dips. They're perfect for those hectic days. —HOLLY SZWEJ BRIDGEPORT, NEW YORK

20 Cheddar French Dip Sandwiches

PREP/TOTAL TIME: 20 MINUTES
MAKES: 4 SERVINGS

- ¼ cup butter, cubed
- 2 garlic cloves, minced
- 4 ciabatta rolls, split
- 1 cup (4 ounces) shredded cheddar cheese
- 1 pound thinly sliced roast beef
- 1 can (14½ ounces) beef broth

1. In a small skillet, melt butter. Add garlic; saute for 1 minute. Place rolls on a baking sheet; brush cut sides with garlic butter. Sprinkle with cheese. Broil 3-4 in. from the heat for 2-3 minutes or until cheese is melted.

2. In a large saucepan, combine beef and broth; heat through. Using tongs or a slotted spoon, place beef on rolls. Serve sandwiches with remaining broth for dipping.

10 Club Salad

I first made this tossed chicken salad for my cousin's baby shower, and everyone simply loved it!

—**BETH MARTIN SINE**
FAULKNER, MARYLAND

PREP/TOTAL TIME: 10 MINUTES
MAKES: 4 SERVINGS

- 1 package (10 ounces) ready-to-serve salad greens
- 1 package (6 ounces) ready-to-use grilled chicken breast strips, cubed
- 10 to 15 cherry tomatoes, halved
- 8 bacon strips, cooked and crumbled
- ¾ cup Italian salad dressing

1. In a salad bowl, combine the greens, chicken, tomatoes and bacon. Drizzle with dressing and toss to coat. Serve immediately.

Between working as the assistant manager and chef in a cafeteria and running my own catering business, I spend much of my day planning and preparing meals. When I get home, I rely on quick, nutritious recipes so my husband, our two daughters and I can gather around the table. Sharing our daily events over a hot supper is soothing to the mind and soul.

This menu is one of my favorites. It starts with an **easy chicken recipe** that I got from another family member, but I put my own spin on it one night with some additional ingredients I had on hand. Everyone enjoyed the results.

I'm always trying to get more fruit into our diets, and the **slightly sweet and tangy Fruited Rice Pilaf** delivers. It's great with the chicken. As an occasional treat, my family loves it when I make **Pistachio Cream Pie**. And I'm happy because they're eating a little more fruit without even realizing it!

20 Asian Chicken

PREP/TOTAL TIME: 20 MINUTES **MAKES:** 4 SERVINGS

- **4 boneless skinless chicken breast halves (4 ounces each)**
- **2 tablespoons butter**
- **1 cup teriyaki sauce**
- **½ cup water**
- **½ cup orange marmalade**
- **½ to 1 teaspoon minced garlic**

1. In a large skillet, brown chicken on both sides in butter.

2. Combine the teriyaki sauce, water, marmalade and garlic; pour over chicken. Bring to a boil. Reduce heat; cover and simmer for 10-15 minutes or until a thermometer reads 170°.

20 Fruited Rice Pilaf

PREP/TOTAL TIME: 15 MINUTES **MAKES:** 4 SERVINGS

- **1 package (6 ounces) rice pilaf**
- **2 tablespoons butter, softened**
- **½ cup pineapple chunks**
- **½ cup raisins**
- **¼ cup prepared Italian salad dressing**
  Toasted coconut, optional

1. Cook rice pilaf according to package directions. Stir in the butter until melted. Add the pineapple, raisins and salad dressing. Top with toasted coconut if desired.

20 Pistachio Cream Pie

PREP/TOTAL TIME: 15 MINUTES
MAKES: 6-8 SERVINGS

- **1 package (8 ounces) cream cheese, softened**
- **1 cup milk**
- **1 package (3.4 ounces) instant pistachio pudding mix**
- **1 can (8 ounces) crushed pineapple, drained**
- **1 graham cracker crust (9 inches)**
- **2 cups whipped topping**
  Toasted coconut

1. In a small bowl, beat the cream cheese, milk and pudding mix until smooth. Fold in pineapple. Spoon into crust.

2. Spread with whipped topping; sprinkle with coconut. Refrigerate until serving.

Fresh, Fast Side Dishes

Try one of these simple ideas to round out Lucille's healthy menu.

- Saute broccoli florets or snap peas until crisp-tender; toss in some sesame seeds near the end of cooking.
- Heat your favorite frozen vegetable stir-fry blend according to package directions.
- Toss baby spinach or broccoli coleslaw mix with bottled sesame-ginger vinaigrette .
- Serve a side of fresh fruit: pineapple, oranges, green grapes and/or mango.

20 Fish Taco Wraps

Here's a yummy recipe that takes just minutes. If they're less expensive, I'll sometimes thaw frozen tilapia fillets in the fridge overnight instead of using fresh fillets.
—**MICHELLE WILLIAMS** FORT WORTH, TEXAS

PREP/TOTAL TIME: 15 MINUTES **MAKES:** 6 SERVINGS

- ¾ cup salsa
- 1 can (4 ounces) chopped green chilies
- 6 tilapia fillets (6 ounces each)
- 2 tablespoons olive oil
- 2 tablespoons steak seasoning
- 12 flour tortillas (6 inches), warmed
- ¾ cup shredded cheddar cheese

1. Combine salsa and chilies; set aside. Drizzle fillets with oil; sprinkle both sides with steak seasoning.

2. Cook fillets, uncovered, in a large skillet over medium heat for 3-5 minutes on each side or until fish flakes easily with a fork. Gently stir in salsa mixture.

3. Spoon a heaping ⅓ cupful onto each tortilla; top with cheese and roll up.

Editor's Note: *This recipe was tested with McCormick's Montreal Steak Seasoning. Look for it in the spice aisle.*

30 Mexican Pizza

I love the ease and versatility of crowd-pleasing pizza with Southwestern flavors. You can add shredded chicken and taco seasoning for meat lovers or leave the meat off for a quick vegetarian meal.
—**KATHLEEN HALL** IRMO, SOUTH CAROLINA

PREP/TOTAL TIME: 30 MINUTES **MAKES:** 8 SLICES

- 1 large onion
- 1 prebaked 12-inch pizza crust
- 1 can (16 ounces) refried beans
- 2 cups (8 ounces) shredded cheddar cheese
- 3 cups shredded lettuce
- 1 cup (4 ounces) shredded Mexican cheese blend
- ⅓ cup chopped seeded tomato
- 2 tablespoons sliced ripe olives
- ½ cup coarsely crushed ranch-flavored tortilla chips

1. Slice half of the onion and chop the rest; set aside. Place crust on an ungreased 12-in. pizza pan. Spread beans over crust to within ½ in. of edges. Top with cheddar cheese and sliced onion.

2. Bake at 450° for 10-12 minutes or until cheese is melted. Top with lettuce, cheese blend, chopped onion, tomato, olives and tortilla chips.

30 Parmesan-Crusted Tilapia

I usually serve this crispy fish with tartar sauce and seasoned steamed veggies. It's like a Friday night fish fry without all the calories!

—**CHRISTI MCELROY** NEENAH, WISCONSIN

PREP/TOTAL TIME: 25 MINUTES **MAKES:** 4 SERVINGS

- ½ **cup all-purpose flour**
- 1 **egg, beaten**
- ½ **cup crushed butter-flavored crackers (about 10 crackers)**
- ¼ **cup grated Parmesan cheese**
- ½ **teaspoon salt**
- 4 **tilapia fillets (5 ounces each)**
- 2 **tablespoons olive oil**
  Lemon wedges

1. Place flour and egg in separate shallow bowls. In another shallow bowl, combine the crackers, cheese and salt. Dip fillets in the flour, egg, then cracker mixture.

2. In a large skillet, cook fillets in oil over medium heat for 3-5 minutes on each side or until golden brown and fish flakes easily with a fork. Serve with lemon wedges.

30 Onion-Dijon Pork Chops

Coated in a flavorful sauce, these chops are cooked to tender perfection. Serve with rice and carrots for a satisfying fall meal.

—**TASTE OF HOME TEST KITCHEN**

PREP/TOTAL TIME: 25 MINUTES **MAKES:** 4 SERVINGS

- 4 **boneless pork loin chops (5 ounces each)**
- ¼ **teaspoon salt**
- ¼ **teaspoon pepper**
- ¾ **cup thinly sliced red onion**
- ¼ **cup water**
- ¼ **cup cider vinegar**
- 3 **tablespoons brown sugar**
- 2 **tablespoons honey Dijon mustard**

1. Sprinkle pork chops with salt and pepper. In a large nonstick skillet coated with cooking spray, cook chops over medium heat for 4-6 minutes on each side or until lightly browned. Remove and keep warm.

2. Add the remaining ingredients to the skillet, stirring to loosen browned bits from pan. Bring to a boil; cook and stir for 2 minutes or until thickened. Return chops to the pan. Reduce heat; cover and simmer for 3-4 minutes or until a thermometer reads 145°. Let stand for 5 minutes before serving.

10 Mushroom Beef Tips with Rice

PREP/TOTAL TIME: 10 MINUTES
MAKES: 3 SERVINGS

- 1 **cup sliced fresh mushrooms**
- 2 **tablespoons butter**
- 1 **package (17 ounces) refrigerated beef tips with gravy**
- 1 **package (8.8 ounces) ready-to-serve long grain rice**
- ½ **cup sour cream**

1. In a large skillet, saute mushrooms in butter for 2 minutes. Add beef to pan; cook for 4-6 minutes or until heated through, stirring occasionally.

2. Meanwhile, cook rice according to package directions. Remove beef mixture from heat; stir in sour cream. Serve with rice.

20 Maple Pretzel Chicken

This unexpected combo delivers delicious results! The finer the pretzel crumb, the better.
—**TARA SZLAG** COLUMBUS, OHIO

PREP/TOTAL TIME: 20 MINUTES
MAKES: 4 SERVINGS

- 4 **boneless skinless chicken breast halves (5 ounces each)**
- 1 **egg**
- ½ **cup maple syrup**
- 1½ **cups crushed pretzels**
- ¼ **cup canola oil**

1. Flatten chicken to ½-in. thickness. In a bowl, whisk egg and syrup. Place pretzels in another bowl. Dip chicken in egg mixture; coat with pretzels.

2. In a large skillet, cook chicken in oil over medium heat for 5-6 minutes on each side or until juices run clear.

Here's a quick and simple version of the beef tips my husband loves. Think: savory Stroganoff flavor with only five ingredients!
—**PAMELA SHANK** PARKERSBURG, WEST VIRGINIA

30 ▶ Spinach Salmon Bundles

These elegant bundles turn weeknight dinner into a fancy occasion. Rich salmon and flaky golden-brown pastry will delight family and guests—and no one has to know how easy it is!
—**LARISSA GEDNEY** MYRTLE BEACH, SOUTH CAROLINA

PREP/TOTAL TIME: 30 MINUTES **MAKES:** 4 SERVINGS

- 2 **tubes (8 ounces each) refrigerated crescent rolls**
- 4 **salmon fillets (6 ounces each)**
- ¼ **teaspoon salt**
- ¼ **teaspoon pepper**
- ⅓ **cup garlic-herb spreadable cheese**
- 1 **package (10 ounces) frozen chopped spinach, thawed and squeezed dry**

1. Unroll crescent dough and separate into four rectangles; seal perforations. Place a salmon fillet in the center of each rectangle; sprinkle with salt and pepper. Spoon the spreadable cheese over each; top with spinach. Fold dough over filling and pinch edges to seal.

2. Place on an ungreased baking sheet. Bake at 400° for 20-25 minutes or until golden brown.

Editor's Note: *This recipe was tested with Alouette spreadable cheese.*

30 ▶ Crab Melt Loaf

Our family loves seafood, and this recipe is a nice switch from traditional sandwiches. I've served big slices of it for lunch, Sunday brunch and as a light dinner with salad.
—**LOUISE FAUTH** FOREMOST, ALBERTA

PREP/TOTAL TIME: 30 MINUTES **MAKES:** 8 SERVINGS

- 1 **pound imitation crabmeat, chopped**
- ½ **cup mayonnaise**
- ¼ **cup thinly sliced green onions**
- ¼ **cup diced celery**
- 2 **cups (8 ounces) shredded part-skim mozzarella cheese**
- ⅛ **teaspoon salt**
- ⅛ **teaspoon pepper**
- 1 **loaf (1 pound) unsliced French bread, split**

1. In a large bowl, combine the crab, mayonnaise, onions and celery. Stir in the cheese, salt and pepper. Spread over bread bottom; replace top.

2. Wrap in a large piece of heavy-duty foil. Place on an ungreased baking sheet. Bake at 400° for 20 minutes or until heated through. Cut into slices.

top tip Baked items depend on correct oven temperature to rise and cook properly. For best results, first check that oven racks are properly positioned. Then preheat the oven while you prepare the recipe.

For me, cooking is about more than putting food on the table; it's my primary hobby. And while I love to cook for myself, I sometimes just want to get in and out of the kitchen fast...especially after a long day at work.

So I rely on easy recipes that taste great and help me maximize my lazy time in the evening. Even though I'm cooking for one, I always make enough that I have plenty of leftovers. This saves cooking time, and it's especially great when I'm excited about what's on the menu.

This chicken recipe is my take on a classic **Hungarian chicken dish**. I serve it with **Smashed Potatoes alongside...perfect for soaking up the creamy sauce**. For a nutritious side dish that cooks hands-free while I prepare the rest of the meal, **Easy Roasted Asparagus** is perfect.

30 Smashed Potatoes

PREP/TOTAL TIME: 25 MINUTES **MAKES:** 4 SERVINGS

- 7 to 8 medium red potatoes (about 2 pounds), quartered
- ¼ cup sour cream
- ¼ cup milk
- 2 tablespoons butter
- ¼ teaspoon salt
- ¼ teaspoon pepper
  Pinch ground nutmeg

1. Place potatoes in a large saucepan and cover with water. Bring to a boil. Reduce heat; cover and cook for 10-15 minutes or until tender. Drain.

2. In a large bowl, mash potatoes with the sour cream, milk, butter, salt, pepper and nutmeg.

20 Easy Roasted Asparagus

PREP/TOTAL TIME: 15 MINUTES **MAKES:** 4 SERVINGS

- 1 pound fresh asparagus, trimmed
- 1 tablespoon olive oil
- ¼ teaspoon salt
- ⅛ teaspoon pepper

1. Place the asparagus on an ungreased baking sheet. Drizzle with oil. Sprinkle with salt and pepper; turn to coat. Bake at 425° for 10-15 minutes or until asparagus is tender.

30 Zippy Paprika Chicken

PREP/TOTAL TIME: 30 MINUTES **MAKES:** 4 SERVINGS

- 2 tablespoons paprika
- 1 to 2 tablespoons Southwest marinade mix
- ⅛ teaspoon salt
- ⅛ teaspoon pepper
- 4 boneless skinless chicken breast halves (4 ounces each)
- 2 tablespoons olive oil
- ¼ cup water
- 2 tablespoons soy sauce
- 5 teaspoons lemon juice
- ½ cup sour cream

1. In a large resealable plastic bag, combine the paprika, marinade mix, salt and pepper; add chicken. Seal bag and shake to coat; refrigerate for 10 minutes.

2. In a large skillet, cook the chicken in oil over medium heat for 5-6 minutes on each side or until a thermometer reads 170°. Remove and keep warm.

3. Add the water, soy sauce and lemon juice to skillet; cook for 1-2 minutes, stirring to loosen browned bits. Remove from the heat; stir in sour cream until blended. Serve with chicken.

Editor's Note: *This recipe was tested with McCormick Grill Mates Southwest Marinade seasoning packet.*

30 Speedy Salmon Patties

When I was a girl growing up on the farm, my mom often prepared these nicely seasoned patties when we were working late in the field. They're also tasty with chopped green peppers added to the mixture.

—**BONNIE EVANS** CAMERON, NORTH CAROLINA

PREP/TOTAL TIME: 25 MINUTES **MAKES:** 3 SERVINGS

- ⅓ **cup finely chopped onion**
- 1 **egg, beaten**
- 5 **saltines, crushed**
- ½ **teaspoon Worcestershire sauce**
- ¼ **teaspoon salt**
- ⅛ **teaspoon pepper**
- 1 **can (14¾ ounces) salmon, drained, bones and skin removed**
- 2 **teaspoons butter**

1. In a large bowl, combine the first six ingredients. Crumble salmon over mixture and mix well. Shape into six patties.

2. In a large skillet over medium heat, fry patties in butter for 3-4 minutes on each side or until set and golden brown.

30 Beer Pork Chops

These tender chops in a savory sauce are perfect for a hectic weeknight because they're so easy to prep. They use only five ingredients! Try them with hot buttery noodles.

—**JANA CHRISTIAN** FARSON, WYOMING

PREP/TOTAL TIME: 30 MINUTES **MAKES:** 4 SERVINGS

- 4 **boneless pork loin chops (4 ounces each)**
- ½ **teaspoon salt**
- ½ **teaspoon pepper**
- 1 **tablespoon canola oil**
- ¾ **cup beer or nonalcoholic beer**
- 3 **tablespoons ketchup**
- 2 **tablespoons brown sugar**

1. Sprinkle both sides of pork chops with salt and pepper. In a large skillet, brown chops in oil on both sides over medium heat.

2. Combine the beer, ketchup and brown sugar; pour over pork. Bring to a boil. Reduce heat; simmer, uncovered, for 12-15 minutes or until a thermometer reads 145°. Let stand for 5 minutes before serving.

30 Mock Stroganoff

I'm not a huge steak eater, but I love the flavor of Stroganoff. Using hamburger in this version made it more palatable for me, and it was an easy dish for our children to eat as toddlers.

—TERRI WETZEL ROSEBURG, OREGON

PREP/TOTAL TIME: 25 MINUTES **MAKES:** 4 SERVINGS

- 3 cups uncooked yolk-free noodles
- 1 pound ground beef
- ¼ cup chopped onion
- ¼ cup sliced fresh mushrooms
- 1½ cups water
- 2 envelopes brown gravy mix
- 2 cups (16 ounces) sour cream

1. Cook noodles according to package directions. Meanwhile, in a large skillet, cook the beef, onion and mushrooms over medium heat until meat is no longer pink; drain.

2. Stir in water and gravy mix. Bring to a boil; cook and stir for 2 minutes or until thickened. Remove from the heat; stir in sour cream. Drain noodles. Serve with meat mixture.

20 Crab Louis

I make this salad when it's hot outside and we're looking for something quick and simple for dinner. It's great with butter crackers and, perhaps, a little cheese.

—GAIL VANGUNDY PARKER, COLORADO

PREP/TOTAL TIME: 15 MINUTES **MAKES:** 2 SERVINGS

- 2 cups spring mix salad greens
- 1 can (6 ounces) lump crabmeat, drained
- 2 medium tomatoes, quartered
- 2 hard-cooked eggs, quartered
- 6 pitted ripe olives
- 3 tablespoons chili sauce
- 2 tablespoons mayonnaise
- ½ teaspoon finely chopped onion
- ¼ teaspoon sugar
- ⅛ teaspoon Worcestershire sauce

1. Divide the salad greens, crab, tomatoes, eggs and olives between two serving plates. In a small bowl, combine the remaining ingredients; drizzle over salads.

When we lived in Ohio and were just starting out, we were so busy with my husband's teaching schedule, my own work as a graduate assistant, our occasional taking or teaching of night classes, plus keeping up with our young son Ethan. I liked prepping our meals while Ethan napped, but since there were no guarantees as to how much time I'd have, quicker recipes were always better!

I made this meal once when my parents came to visit, and everyone raved. **Rosemary Lamb Chops feel extra special**, but they're really fast and easy to make. I tend to make them for special occasions, but they're quick enough for a nice weeknight dinner. My **couscous side dish starts with a boxed mix**; then it's just a matter of adding a few ingredients. I like to serve a green salad as an additional side dish.

Super-easy **Blueberry Crumble** is loaded with old-fashioned flavor, but it's hot out of the microwave in just a few minutes. It's so good paired with the cool creaminess of ice cream. Try it with other fruit, such as peaches, for variety.

20 Rosemary Lamb Chops

PREP/TOTAL TIME: 20 MINUTES **MAKES:** 4 SERVINGS

- 2 **teaspoons dried rosemary, crushed**
- 1 **teaspoon dried thyme**
- ½ **teaspoon salt**
- ¼ **teaspoon pepper**
- ¼ **cup olive oil**
- 8 **lamb loin chops (1 inch thick and 6 ounces each)**

1. Combine the rosemary, thyme, salt and pepper. Pour oil over both sides of lamb chops; rub with the herb mixture.

2. In a large skillet, cook chops over medium heat for 6-7 minutes on each side or until meat reaches desired doneness (for medium-rare, a thermometer should read 145°; medium, 160°; well-done, 170°).

20 Mediterranean Couscous

PREP/TOTAL TIME: 15 MINUTES **MAKES:** 4 SERVINGS

- 2 **tablespoons chopped onion**
- 2 **tablespoons olive oil, divided**
- 3 **teaspoons minced garlic**
- 1¼ **cups water**
- 1 **package (5.6 ounces) couscous with toasted pine nuts**
- 1½ **teaspoons chicken bouillon granules**
- ½ **cup cherry tomatoes, halved**
- 2 **tablespoons grated Parmesan cheese**

1. In a small skillet, saute onion in 1 tablespoon oil for 3-4 minutes or until tender. Add garlic; cook 1 minute longer.

2. Meanwhile, in a large saucepan, combine the water, contents of seasoning packet from couscous mix, bouillon and remaining oil. Bring to a boil.

3. Stir in onion mixture and couscous. Cover and remove from the heat; let stand for 5 minutes. Fluff with a fork. Stir in tomatoes and cheese.

20 Blueberry Crumble

PREP/TOTAL TIME: 15 MINUTES **MAKES:** 4 SERVINGS

- 3 **cups fresh or frozen blueberries**
- 3 **tablespoons sugar**
- 1 **tablespoon cornstarch**
- ⅓ **cup old-fashioned oats**
- ⅓ **cup packed brown sugar**
- 3 **tablespoons all-purpose flour**
- 2 **tablespoons chopped almonds**
- ⅛ **teaspoon ground cinnamon**
- 3 **tablespoons cold butter**
  Vanilla ice cream

1. In a greased 9-in. microwave-safe pie plate, combine the blueberries, sugar and cornstarch. Cover and microwave on high for 7-8 minutes or until thickened, stirring twice.

2. Meanwhile, in a small bowl, combine the oats, brown sugar, flour, almonds and cinnamon. Cut in butter until mixture resembles coarse crumbs. Sprinkle over blueberry mixture.

3. Microwave, uncovered, on high for 2-3 minutes or until butter is melted. Serve with ice cream.

Editor's Note: *This recipe was tested in a 1,100-watt microwave.*

30 Curry Scallops and Rice

Buttery scallops, crunchy peppers and rice with a hint of curry...what's not to love?

—TASTE OF HOME TEST KITCHEN

PREP/TOTAL TIME: 30 MINUTES
MAKES: 4 SERVINGS

- 1 **package (6¼ ounces) curry rice pilaf mix**
- ¼ **cup butter, divided**
- 1½ **pounds sea scallops**
- 1 **package (14 ounces) thawed pepper strips, chopped**
- ¼ **cup minced fresh parsley**
- ¼ **teaspoon salt**

1. Prepare pilaf mix according to package directions, using 1 tablespoon butter.

2. In a large skillet, saute scallops in remaining butter until firm and opaque. Remove and keep warm. In the same skillet, saute peppers until tender. Stir in the scallops, rice, parsley and salt.

30 Buffalo Chicken

Topped with gooey cheese and zesty buffalo wing sauce, these quick and easy chicken breasts have unforgettable flavor.

—JEANNE COLLINS CARY, NORTH CAROLINA

PREP/TOTAL TIME: 30 MINUTES **MAKES:** 4 SERVINGS

- 4 **boneless skinless chicken breast halves (5 ounces each)**
- ¼ **teaspoon salt**
- ¼ **teaspoon pepper**
- 2 **eggs**
- ½ **cup seasoned bread crumbs**
- 3 **tablespoons canola oil**
- ¼ **cup buffalo wing sauce**
- ¼ **cup shredded provolone cheese**
- ¼ **cup shredded part-skim mozzarella cheese**

1. Flatten chicken to ½-in. thickness. Sprinkle with salt and pepper. In a shallow bowl, whisk eggs. Place bread crumbs in another shallow bowl. Dip chicken in eggs, then coat with bread crumbs.

2. In a large skillet over medium heat, cook chicken in oil for 7-10 minutes on each side or until a thermometer reads 170°, adding wing sauce during the last 2 minutes. Turn chicken to coat with sauce; sprinkle with cheeses. Cover and cook until cheese is melted.

30 Chip-Crusted Chicken

Dijon-mayo and barbecue potato chips might sound strange together, but the flavors combine beautifully!

—MIKE TCHOU PEPPER PIKE, OHIO

PREP/TOTAL TIME: 30 MINUTES
MAKES: 6 SERVINGS

- ⅔ **cup Dijon-mayonnaise blend**
- 6 **cups barbecue potato chips, finely crushed**
- 6 **boneless skinless chicken breast halves (5 ounces each)**

1. Place mayonnaise blend and potato chips in separate shallow bowls. Dip chicken in mayonnaise blend, then coat with chips. Place on an ungreased baking sheet. Bake at 375° for 20-25 minutes or until juices run clear.

My husband, Tracy, spends long days on the road as a truck driver, and he really appreciates home cooking on his days off. So I've found some great ways to make us scrumptious, satisfying comfort food in very little time.

The **Turkey Cutlets with Pan Gravy** recipe is a great alternative to roasting a whole turkey when you want the taste of a homemade turkey dinner. I sometimes serve it with a boxed stuffing mix, cranberry sauce and veggies or salad. The vegetables in this menu get a crispy flavorful topping, which is **a great way to spark up frozen veggies**.

And a no-fail side dish like my **mashed potatoes** is one you'll reach for time and time again when you need to get dinner on quickly. The potatoes are dressed up with broth, rich sour cream, Parmesan cheese and crispy onions, yet they're on the table in under 20 minutes.

20 ▶ Turkey Cutlets with Pan Gravy

PREP/TOTAL TIME: 20 MINUTES **MAKES:** 4 SERVINGS

- 1 teaspoon poultry seasoning
- ½ teaspoon seasoned salt
- ¼ teaspoon pepper, divided
- 1 package (17.6 ounces) turkey breast cutlets
- 2 tablespoons canola oil
- 2 tablespoons butter
- ¼ cup all-purpose flour
- 2 cups chicken broth

1. Combine the poultry seasoning, seasoned salt and ⅛ teaspoon pepper. Sprinkle over turkey. In a large skillet, cook cutlets in batches in oil for 2-3 minutes on each side or until no longer pink. Remove to a serving platter and keep warm.

2. In the same skillet, melt butter; stir in flour until smooth. Gradually stir in broth. Bring to a boil; cook and stir for 2 minutes or until thickened. Season with remaining pepper. Serve with turkey.

20 ▶ Italian Vegetable Medley

PREP/TOTAL TIME: 15 MINUTES **MAKES:** 4 SERVINGS

- 1 package (16 ounces) frozen broccoli vegetable blend
- 2 tablespoons grated Parmesan cheese
- 1 tablespoon seasoned bread crumbs
- ⅛ teaspoon garlic powder
- ⅛ teaspoon seasoned salt
- ⅛ teaspoon pepper
- 1 tablespoon butter

1. Microwave vegetables according to package directions. Meanwhile, in a small bowl, combine the cheese, bread crumbs, garlic powder, seasoned salt and pepper. Drain vegetables; stir in butter. Sprinkle with cheese mixture.

20 ▶ Crunchy Mashed Potatoes

PREP/TOTAL TIME: 15 MINUTES **MAKES:** 5 SERVINGS

- 3 cups chicken broth
- 1 cup 2% milk
- 1 garlic clove, minced
- ¼ teaspoon pepper
- 3 cups mashed potato flakes
- ¼ cup sour cream
- 1½ cups cheddar French-fried onions
- ¼ cup grated Parmesan cheese

1. In a large saucepan, bring broth to a boil. Remove from heat. Add the milk, garlic and pepper. Whisk in potato flakes and sour cream until smooth.

2. Spoon potato mixture into a greased 9-in. square baking pan. Sprinkle with onions and cheese. Broil 4-6 in. from the heat for 20-30 seconds or until golden brown.

top tip Great Flavor from a Few Extra Steps

Margaret dresses up convenience items like frozen pre-cut veggies and instant potatoes to give them great homemade flavor. Broiling the potatoes takes just moments, but gives the Parmesan-onion topping a toasty added crunch. No one will guess this delicious turkey dinner—complete with homemade gravy!—clocks in at less than 30 minutes.

30 ▶ Tuna Veggie Macaroni

PREP/TOTAL TIME: 25 MINUTES
MAKES: 3 SERVINGS

- 1¼ cups uncooked elbow macaroni
- 5 ounces process cheese (Velveeta), cubed
- ½ cup milk
- 2 cups frozen peas and carrots, thawed
- 1 can (5 ounces) albacore white tuna in water
- ¼ teaspoon dill weed

1. Cook macaroni according to package directions; drain. Add cheese and milk; cook and stir over medium heat until cheese is melted. Stir in the vegetables, tuna and dill; heat through.

30 ▶ Oven-Baked Burgers

A crispy coating mix is the secret ingredient that dresses up these burgers you bake in the oven.

—MIKE GOLDMAN
ARDEN HILLS, MINNESOTA

PREP/TOTAL TIME: 30 MINUTES
MAKES: 4 SERVINGS

- ¼ cup steak sauce
- 2 tablespoons plus ⅓ cup seasoned coating mix, divided
- 1 pound ground beef
- 4 hamburger buns, split
- 4 lettuce leaves

1. In a bowl, combine steak sauce and 2 tablespoons of coating mix. Crumble beef over mixture and mix well. Shape into four 3½-in. patties. Dip both sides of patties in remaining coating. Place on an ungreased baking sheet.

2. Bake at 350° for 20 minutes or until a thermometer reads 160° and juices run clear, turning once. Serve on buns with lettuce.

After experimenting with many different versions, I came up with this super-delicious tuna mac recipe. My family can't get enough of it!
—**AL ROBBINS** CHANDLER, ARIZONA

30 Tortellini Marinara

My family loves tortellini with a loaf of crusty French bread and fresh green beans. I sometimes warm this easy supper in the slow cooker if I know it's going to be a super-busy day.

—**RITA PEREZ** ROSEVILLE, CALIFORNIA

PREP/TOTAL TIME: 25 MINUTES **MAKES:** 6 SERVINGS

- 1 **package (9 ounces) refrigerated cheese tortellini**
- 1 **pound bulk Italian sausage**
- 1 **package (15 ounces) refrigerated marinara sauce**
- 1 **can (14½ ounces) diced Italian tomatoes, undrained**
- ½ **pound sliced fresh mushrooms**
- 1 **cup (4 ounces) shredded part-skim mozzarella cheese**

1. Cook tortellini according to package directions.

2. Meanwhile, in a large skillet, cook sausage over medium heat until no longer pink; drain. Stir in marinara sauce, tomatoes and mushrooms. Bring to a boil. Reduce heat; cover and simmer for 5 minutes or until mushrooms are tender.

3. Drain tortellini; stir into skillet. Sprinkle with cheese. Remove from the heat; cover and let stand for 5 minutes or until cheese is melted.

30 Barbecued Monterey Chicken

It's easy to turn regular chicken into something special with barbecue sauce, crisp bacon and melted cheese. It gets even better with a sprinkling of fresh tomato and green onion.

—**LINDA COLEMAN** CEDAR RAPIDS, IOWA

PREP/TOTAL TIME: 25 MINUTES **MAKES:** 4 SERVINGS

- 4 **bacon strips**
- 4 **boneless skinless chicken breast halves (4 ounces each)**
- 1 **tablespoon butter**
- ½ **cup barbecue sauce**
- 3 **green onions, chopped**
- 1 **medium tomato, chopped**
- 1 **cup (4 ounces) shredded cheddar cheese**

1. Cut bacon strips in half widthwise. In a large skillet, cook bacon over medium heat until cooked but not crisp. Remove to paper towels to drain.

2. Drain drippings from skillet; cook chicken in butter over medium heat for 5-6 minutes on each side or until a thermometer reads 170°.

3. Top each chicken breast with the barbecue sauce, green onions, tomato and two reserved bacon pieces; sprinkle with cheese. Cover and cook for 5 minutes or until cheese is melted.

STEAKHOUSE DINNER ANY NIGHT AT ALL

BY KAROL CHANDLER-EZELL
NACOGDOCHES, TEXAS

I'm an anthropology professor at a local university. My husband, Alex, teaches high school science and has a long commute. Add a rambunctious baby girl to the mix and our schedules are chock-full. Luckily, I love the challenge of coming up with quick but satisfying meals for us that are healthy and well-balanced.

A butcher gave me great advice on cooking different types of meat. Broiling works really well on very lean cuts like sirloin. **Let the steaks stand** for a couple of minutes before serving to preserve their juiciness.

After I broil the steaks, I like to top the **Twice-Baked Deviled Potatoes** with shredded cheese and cracker crumbs and pop them under the broiler for a few minutes until they're lightly browned. But you can skip this step if you prefer. You can also make them a bit lighter by using turkey bacon and reduced-fat cheese. On the side, **Tomato-Stuffed Avocados** are a great way to get your veggies. Each bite has lots of garden-fresh flavor.

20 Broiled Sirloin Steaks

PREP/TOTAL TIME: 20 MINUTES **MAKES:** 4 SERVINGS

- 2 **tablespoons lime juice**
- 1 **teaspoon onion powder**
- 1 **teaspoon garlic powder**
- ¼ **teaspoon ground mustard**
- ¼ **teaspoon dried oregano**
- ¼ **teaspoon dried thyme**
- 4 **beef top sirloin steaks (5 ounces each)**
- 1 **cup sliced fresh mushrooms**

1. In a small bowl, combine the first six ingredients; rub over both sides of steaks.

2. Broil 4 in. from the heat for 7 minutes. Turn steaks; top with mushrooms. Broil 7-8 minutes longer or until meat reaches desired doneness (for medium-rare, a thermometer should read 145°; medium, 160°; well-done, 170°) and the mushrooms are tender.

30 Twice-Baked Deviled Potatoes

PREP/TOTAL TIME: 30 MINUTES **MAKES:** 4 SERVINGS

- 4 **small baking potatoes**
- ¼ **cup butter, softened**
- ¼ **cup milk**
- 1 **cup (4 ounces) shredded cheddar cheese**
- ⅓ **cup real bacon bits**
- 2 **green onions, chopped**
- 1 **teaspoon Dijon mustard**
   Dash paprika

1. Scrub and pierce potatoes; place on a microwave-safe plate. Microwave, uncovered, on high for 7-10 minutes or until tender, turning once. Let stand for 5 minutes. Cut a thin slice off the top of each potato and discard. Scoop out pulp, leaving a thin shell.

2. In a large bowl, mash the pulp with butter and milk. Stir in the cheese, bacon, onions, mustard and paprika. Spoon into potato shells. Return to the microwave-safe plate. Microwave, uncovered, on high for 1-2 minutes or until cheese is melted.

Editor's Note: *This recipe was tested in a 1,100-watt microwave.*

10 Tomato-Stuffed Avocados

PREP/TOTAL TIME: 10 MINUTES **MAKES:** 4 SERVINGS

- 2 **plum tomatoes, seeded and chopped**
- ¾ **cup thinly sliced red onion, quartered**
- 1 **teaspoon julienned fresh basil leaves**
- ½ **teaspoon salt**
- ¼ **teaspoon pepper**
- 2 **medium ripe avocados, halved and pitted**
- 2 **teaspoons lime juice**

1. In a small bowl, gently toss the tomatoes, onion, basil, salt and pepper.

2. Spoon mixture into avocado halves and drizzle with lime juice. Serve immediately.

30 Cinnamon-Apple Pork Chops

When I found this recipe online years ago, it quickly became a favorite. The ingredients are easy to keep on hand, and the one-pan cleanup is a bonus.

—CHRISTINA PRICE WHEELING, WEST VIRGINIA

PREP/TOTAL TIME: 25 MINUTES **MAKES:** 4 SERVINGS

- 4 **boneless pork loin chops (4 ounces each)**
- 2 **tablespoons reduced-fat butter, divided**
- 3 **tablespoons brown sugar**
- 1 **teaspoon ground cinnamon**
- ½ **teaspoon ground nutmeg**
- ¼ **teaspoon salt**
- 4 **medium tart apples, thinly sliced**
- 2 **tablespoons chopped pecans**

1. In a large skillet over medium heat, cook pork chops in 1 tablespoon butter for 4-5 minutes on each side or until a thermometer reads 145°. Meanwhile, in a small bowl, combine the brown sugar, cinnamon, nutmeg and salt.

2. Remove chops and keep warm. Add the apples, pecans, brown sugar mixture and remaining butter to the pan; cook and stir until apples are tender. Serve with chops.

Editor's Note: *This recipe was tested with Land O'Lakes light stick butter.*

30 Easy Chicken Strips

I came up with these crispy strips one night when I was looking for a fast new way to serve chicken. They make great appetizers, especially when served with barbecue or sweet-and-sour sauce for dunking. I've been told they taste like those served in a restaurant!

—CRYSTAL SHECKLES-GIBSON BEESPRING, KENTUCKY

PREP/TOTAL TIME: 30 MINUTES **MAKES:** 6 SERVINGS

- ¼ **cup all-purpose flour**
- ¾ **teaspoon seasoned salt**
- ⅓ **cup butter, melted**
- 1¼ **cups crushed cornflakes**
- 1½ **pounds boneless skinless chicken breasts, cut into 1-inch strips**

1. In a shallow bowl, combine flour and seasoned salt. Place cornflakes and butter in separate shallow bowls. Coat chicken with flour mixture, then dip in butter and coat with cornflakes.

2. Transfer to an ungreased baking sheet. Bake at 400° for 15-20 minutes or until no longer pink.

30 ▶ Crispy Herb-Coated Pork Chops

Having run out of my usual pork chop coating mix one night, I came up with this one. It just might become your new family favorite!

—ANN JOVANOVIC CHICAGO, ILLINOIS

PREP/TOTAL TIME: 25 MINUTES **MAKES:** 4 SERVINGS

- ⅓ cup butter, cubed
- ⅔ cup butter and herb-flavored mashed potato flakes
- ⅔ cup grated Parmesan cheese
- ¾ teaspoon garlic powder
- 4 bone-in center-cut pork loin chops
- 2 tablespoons canola oil

1. In a shallow bowl, melt butter. In a large resealable plastic bag, combine the potato flakes, cheese and garlic powder. Dip chops, one at a time, in butter, then place in bag; seal and shake to coat.

2. In a large skillet, cook the chops in oil over medium heat for 7-8 minutes on each side or until a thermometer reads 145°. Let stand for 5 minutes before serving.

30 ▶ Stovetop Beef 'n' Shells

As tasty as it is fast, this simple supper is great when I'm pressed for time. Team it with salad, bread and fruit for a satisfying meal.

—DONNA ROBERTS MANHATTAN, KANSAS

PREP/TOTAL TIME: 30 MINUTES **MAKES:** 4 SERVINGS

- 1½ cups uncooked medium pasta shells
- 1 pound lean ground beef (90% lean)
- 1 medium onion, chopped
- 1 garlic clove, minced
- 1 can (15 ounces) crushed tomatoes
- 1 can (8 ounces) tomato sauce
- 1 teaspoon sugar
- ½ teaspoon salt
- ½ teaspoon pepper

1. Cook pasta according to package directions. Meanwhile, in a large saucepan, cook beef and onion over medium heat until meat is no longer pink. Add garlic; cook 1 minute longer. Drain.

2. Stir in the tomatoes, tomato sauce, sugar, salt and pepper. Bring to a boil. Reduce heat; simmer, uncovered, for 10-15 minutes. Drain pasta; stir into beef mixture and heat through.

30 Lemon Teriyaki Chicken

My easy stovetop chicken features mild and delicate flavors. It's fantastic with rice and a green vegetable like broccoli. The whole family will love this one!

—CLARA COULSON MINNEY
WASHINGTON COURT HOUSE, OHIO

PREP/TOTAL TIME: 25 MINUTES
MAKES: 4 SERVINGS

- 4 **boneless skinless chicken breast halves (4 ounces each)**
- 2 **tablespoons all-purpose flour**
- 3 **tablespoons butter**
- ¼ **cup reduced-sodium teriyaki sauce**
- 2 **tablespoons lemon juice**
- ¾ **teaspoon minced garlic**
- ½ **teaspoon sugar**

1. Flatten chicken to ½-in. thickness; coat with flour.

2. In a large skillet, cook chicken in butter over medium heat for 4-5 minutes on each side or until a thermometer reads 170°. Remove and set aside.

3. Add teriyaki sauce, lemon juice, garlic and sugar to pan, stirring to loosen browned bits.

4. Return chicken to the pan and heat through.

30 Salisbury Steaks for 2

Sometimes I forget about this favorite recipe, so my husband will say, "How about Salisbury Steak for dinner?" He really likes it.

—TONI MARTIN BYRON CENTER, MICHIGAN

PREP/TOTAL TIME: 25 MINUTES **MAKES:** 2 SERVINGS

- 1 **egg**
- ¼ **cup 2% milk**
- ¼ **cup dry bread crumbs**
- 1 **envelope brown gravy mix, divided**
- 1 **teaspoon dried minced onion**
- ½ **pound lean ground beef (90% lean)**
- ½ **cup water**
- 1 **tablespoon prepared mustard**

1. In a large bowl, whisk egg and milk. Add the bread crumbs, 1 tablespoon gravy mix and onion. Crumble beef over mixture and mix well. Shape into two patties, about ¾ in. thick. Place in a small baking pan.

2. Broil 3-4 in. from the heat for 6-7 minutes on each side or until a thermometer reads 160° and juices run clear.

3. Place the remaining gravy mix in a small saucepan; stir in water and mustard. Bring to a boil; cook and stir until thickened. Serve with patties.

My husband, Howard, works far from home; he's at the Grand Canyon for his job most days. Though I like us to have special meals when he is home, I would rather spend time with him than in the kitchen.

This is one of our favorite go-to meals. Everyone who's tasted **my rich and creamy shrimp penne** thinks it must be difficult to make. But jarred spaghetti and Alfredo sauces make it come together fast. **I make the snap pea side dish** about once a month, as it complements so many entrees.

I created the little **Mud Pies** one day just putting together what I thought would make a great flavor combination. They're cute and feel special, and I love that they don't require any baking.

20 Creamy Tomato Shrimp with Penne

PREP/TOTAL TIME: 20 MINUTES **MAKES:** 4 SERVINGS

- 2 cups uncooked penne pasta
- 1 pound uncooked medium shrimp, peeled and deveined
- 1 teaspoon minced garlic
- ½ teaspoon crushed red pepper flakes
- 2 tablespoons olive oil
- 1½ cups spaghetti sauce
- 1 carton (10 ounces) refrigerated Alfredo sauce
- 2 tablespoons butter
- ¼ teaspoon salt
- ⅛ teaspoon pepper
- 2 tablespoons minced fresh parsley

1. Cook pasta according to package directions. Meanwhile, in a large skillet, saute the shrimp, garlic and pepper flakes in oil until shrimp turn pink. Stir in the spaghetti sauce, Alfredo sauce, butter, salt and pepper; heat through.

2. Drain pasta; serve with shrimp mixture. Sprinkle with parsley.

20 Pea Pods and Peppers

PREP/TOTAL TIME: 15 MINUTES **MAKES:** 4 SERVINGS

- ¾ pound fresh snow peas
- 1 medium sweet red pepper, julienned
- ½ small onion, sliced
- ¼ teaspoon garlic salt
- ⅛ teaspoon pepper
- 1 tablespoonolive oil
- 1 tablespoon butter

1. In a large skillet, saute the snow peas, red pepper, onion, garlic salt and pepper in oil and butter until vegetables are tender.

10 Mud Pies

PREP/TOTAL TIME: 10 MINUTES **MAKES:** 4 SERVINGS

- ⅔ cup Nutella
- 4 individual graham cracker tart shells
- 1 pint coffee ice cream
   Whipped cream and chocolate-covered coffee beans

1. Spoon Nutella into tart shells. Top each with ice cream; garnish with whipped cream and coffee beans.

30 Cheese Ravioli with Veggies

My sons ask for this ravioli all the time. I first served it when friends dropped by and stayed for dinner. I've since added vegetables to make it a complete meal. Peas, corn, broccoli or zucchini can be used alone or in any combination that you like instead of the vegetable medley used here.

—**AMY BURNS** CHARLESTON, ILLINOIS

PREP/TOTAL TIME: 25 MINUTES **MAKES:** 6 SERVINGS

- 1 package (16 ounces) frozen California-blend vegetables
- 1 package (25 ounces) frozen cheese ravioli
- ¼ cup butter, melted
- ¼ teaspoon salt-free seasoning blend
- ¼ cup shredded Parmesan cheese

1. Fill a Dutch oven two-thirds full with water; bring to a boil. Add the vegetables; cook for 5 minutes. Add the ravioli. Cook 5 minutes longer or until vegetables and ravioli are tender; drain.

2. Gently stir in butter. Sprinkle with the seasoning blend and cheese.

20 Chicken Caesar Wraps

I turned the classic salad into a refreshing sandwich with the recipe for these tasty wraps. They make an ideal summertime meal.

—**NANCY PRATT** LONGVIEW, TEXAS

PREP/TOTAL TIME: 15 MINUTES **MAKES:** 6 SERVINGS

- ¾ cup fat-free creamy Caesar salad dressing
- ¼ cup grated Parmesan cheese
- ½ teaspoon garlic powder
- ¼ teaspoon pepper
- 3 cups cubed cooked chicken breast
- 2 cups torn romaine
- ¾ cup Caesar salad croutons, coarsely chopped
- 6 whole wheat tortillas (8 inches), room temperature

1. In a large bowl, combine the dressing, cheese, garlic powder and pepper. Add the chicken, romaine and croutons. Spoon ⅔ cup chicken mixture down the center of each tortilla; roll up.

top tip

I have found that shredding cheese is much easier (and so is the cleanup!) when I spritz the cheese grater with cooking spray before I begin.

—**SHERRY B.** WHITTIER, CALIFORNIA

98

92

101

Slow Cooker & Bread Machine

❝My husband and I love barbecue ribs, but we rarely have time to fire up the grill. So we let the slow cooker do the work for us. By the time we get home from work, the ribs are tender, juicy and ready to devour.❞

KANDY BINGHAM GREEN RIVER, WYOMING
about her recipe, Sweet and Savory Ribs, on page 92

Tender Pork Roast

PREP: 5 MINUTES **COOK:** 8 HOURS
MAKES: 8 SERVINGS

- 1 **boneless pork loin roast (3 pounds)**
- 1 **can (8 ounces) tomato sauce**
- ¾ **cup soy sauce**
- ½ **cup sugar**
- 2 **teaspoons ground mustard**

1. Cut roast in half; place in a 5-qt. slow cooker. Combine remaining ingredients; pour over roast. Cover and cook on low for 8-9 hours or until meat is tender. Remove roast to a serving platter and keep warm. If desired, skim fat from cooking juices and thicken for gravy.

Soft Oatmeal Bread

My husband loves to make this bread. With its mild oat taste and soft texture, it's sure to be a hit with the whole family. Slices are great toasted up for breakfast, too.

—NANCY MONTGOMERY
PLAINWELL, MICHIGAN

PREP: 10 MINUTES **BAKE:** 3 HOURS
MAKES: 1 LOAF (2 POUNDS, 20 SLICES)

- 1½ **cups water (70° to 80°)**
- ¼ **cup canola oil**
- 1 **teaspoon lemon juice**
- ¼ **cup sugar**
- 2 **teaspoons salt**
- 3 **cups all-purpose flour**
- 1½ **cups quick-cooking oats**
- 2½ **teaspoons active dry yeast**

1. In bread machine pan, place all ingredients in order suggested by manufacturer. Select basic bread setting. Choose crust color and loaf size if available.

2. Bake according to bread machine directions (check dough after 5 minutes of mixing; add 1 to 2 tablespoons of water or flour if needed).

A fall-apart-tender pork roast is wonderful to serve to company. It never fails to please. Nothing could be easier when you're entertaining.

—LAVERN PETERSON MINNEAPOLIS, MINNESOTA

Raisin Bran Bread

You won't even realize you're getting bran cereal in your diet when you sample this yummy bread. It's moist and slightly sweet from raisins.
—**JEAN DAVIAU** SAN JACINTO, CALIFORNIA

PREP: 10 MINUTES **BAKE:** 3 HOURS
MAKES: 1 LOAF (1½ POUNDS, 16 SLICES)

- 1 cup plus 1 tablespoon water (70° to 80°)
- ¼ cup packed brown sugar
- 2 tablespoons butter, softened
- 1½ cups raisin bran
- ½ teaspoon salt
- ¼ teaspoon baking soda
- 2¼ cups bread flour
- 2¼ teaspoons active dry yeast
- ½ cup raisins

1. In bread machine pan, place the first eight ingredients in order suggested by manufacturer. Select basic bread setting. Choose crust color and loaf size if available.

2. Bake according to bread machine directions (check dough after 5 minutes of mixing; add 1 to 2 tablespoons of water or flour if needed). Just before the final kneading (your machine may audibly signal this), add the raisins.

Creamy Italian Chicken

Here's a recipe for tender chicken in a creamy sauce that gets fast flavor from salad dressing mix. Served over rice or pasta, it's rich, delicious and special enough for company.
—**MAURA MCGEE** TALLAHASSEE, FLORIDA

PREP: 15 MINUTES **COOK:** 4 HOURS **MAKES:** 4 SERVINGS

- 4 boneless skinless chicken breast halves (4 ounces each)
- 1 envelope Italian salad dressing mix
- ¼ cup water
- 1 package (8 ounces) cream cheese, softened
- 1 can (10¾ ounces) condensed cream of chicken soup, undiluted
- 1 can (4 ounces) mushroom stems and pieces, drained
  Hot cooked pasta or rice
  Fresh oregano leaves, optional

1. Place the chicken in a 3-qt. slow cooker. Combine salad dressing mix and water; pour over chicken. Cover and cook on low for 3 hours.

2. In a small bowl, beat cream cheese and soup until blended. Stir in mushrooms. Pour over chicken. Cook 1 hour longer or until chicken is tender. Serve with pasta or rice. Garnish with oregano if desired.

Red Pepper Chicken

PREP: 15 MINUTES **COOK:** 6 HOURS **MAKES:** 4 SERVINGS

- 4 boneless skinless chicken breast halves (4 ounces each)
- 1 can (15 ounces) black beans, rinsed and drained
- 1 can (14½ ounces) Mexican stewed tomatoes, undrained
- 1 jar (12 ounces) roasted sweet red peppers, drained and cut into strips
- 1 large onion, chopped
- ½ teaspoon salt
  Pepper to taste
  Hot cooked rice

1. Place the chicken in a 3-qt. slow cooker. In a bowl, combine the beans, tomatoes, red peppers, onion, salt and pepper. Pour over the chicken. Cover and cook on low for 6 hours or until chicken is tender. Serve with rice.

❝ Chicken is treated to black beans, red peppers and juicy tomatoes in this Southwestern supper. We love it served with rice cooked in chicken broth. ❞

—**PIPER SPIWAK** VIENNA, VIRGINIA

Slow-Cooked Tamale Casserole

I've been making tamale casserole for years because my family really likes it. It's great for busy days because you make it earlier in the day and just let it cook.

—**DIANA BRIGGS** VENETA, OREGON

PREP: 10 MINUTES **COOK:** 4 HOURS
MAKES: 6 SERVINGS

- 1 pound ground beef
- 1 egg, beaten
- 1½ cups milk
- ¾ cup cornmeal
- 1 can (15¼ ounces) whole kernel corn, drained
- 1 can (14½ ounces) diced tomatoes, undrained
- 1 can (2¼ ounces) sliced ripe olives, drained
- 1 envelope chili seasoning
- 1 teaspoon seasoned salt
- 1 cup (4 ounces) shredded cheddar cheese

1. In a skillet, cook beef over medium heat until no longer pink; drain. In a large bowl, combine the egg, milk and cornmeal until smooth. Add corn, tomatoes, olives, chili seasoning, seasoned salt and beef.

2. Transfer to a greased 3-qt. slow cooker. Cover and cook on high for 3 hours and 45 minutes. Sprinkle with cheese; cover and cook 15 minutes longer or until cheese is melted.

Sausage Pepper Sandwiches

Peppers and onions add a fresh taste to a classic sausage filling for sandwiches. My mother gave me this recipe that's fun to eat and serve, perfect for a casual night!
—SUZETTE GESSEL ALBUQUERQUE, NEW MEXICO

PREP: 15 MINUTES **COOK:** 6 HOURS **MAKES:** 6 SERVINGS

  6 **Italian sausage links (4 ounces each)**
  1 **medium green pepper, cut into 1-inch pieces**
  1 **large onion, cut into 1-inch pieces**
  1 **can (8 ounces) tomato sauce**
  ⅛ **teaspoon pepper**
  6 **hoagie or submarine sandwich buns, split**

1. In a large skillet, brown sausage links over medium heat. Cut into ½-in. slices; place in a 3-qt. slow cooker. Stir in the green pepper, onion, tomato sauce and pepper.

2. Cover and cook on low for 6-8 hours or until sausage is no longer pink and vegetables are tender. Use a slotted spoon to serve on buns.

Sausage Spanish Rice

My husband and I both work the midnight shift, so I'm always on the lookout for slow cooker recipes. This one couldn't be easier. We often enjoy it as a main course because it's so hearty, but it's also good as a side dish.
—MICHELLE MCKAY GARDEN CITY, MICHIGAN

PREP: 10 MINUTES **COOK:** 5 HOURS
MAKES: 6 SERVINGS

  1 **pound smoked kielbasa or Polish sausage, sliced**
  2 **cans (14½ ounces each) diced tomatoes, undrained**
  2 **cup water**
1½ **cups uncooked converted rice**
  1 **cup salsa**
  1 **medium onion**
  ½ **cup chopped green pepper**
  ½ **cup chopped sweet red pepper**
  1 **can (4 ounces) chopped green chilies**
  1 **envelope taco seasoning**

1. In a 3- or 4-qt. slow cooker, combine all ingredients. Cover and cook on low for 5-6 hours or until rice is tender.

Easy-Does-It Spaghetti

Combine ground beef, pasta, mushrooms and a handful of other ingredients in your slow cooker for a savory dish that will appeal to all ages. If you'd like, substitute ½ cup of chopped onion for the dried minced onion.

—GENEVIEVE HRABE
PLAINVILLE, KANSAS

PREP: 20 MINUTES **COOK:** 5 HOURS
MAKES: 6-8 SERVINGS

- 2 **pounds ground beef, cooked and drained**
- 1 **can (46 ounces) tomato juice**
- 1 **can (15 ounces) tomato sauce**
- 1 **can (8 ounces) mushroom stems and pieces, drained**
- 2 **tablespoons dried minced onion**
- 2 **teaspoon salt**
- 1 **teaspoon garlic powder**
- 1 **teaspoon ground mustard**
- ½ **teaspoon each ground allspice, mace and pepper**
- 1 **package (7 ounces) spaghetti, broken in half**

1. In a 5-qt. slow cooker, combine the beef, tomato juice, tomato sauce, mushrooms and seasonings. Cover and cook on high for 4-5 hours.

2. Stir in spaghetti. Cover and cook on high 1 hour longer or until spaghetti is tender.

Honey-Wheat Oatmeal Bread

Wholesome honey-sweetened bread is delicious straight out of the bread machine. Serve it with dinner or toasted for breakfast.

—WANNETTA EHNES EAGLE BEND, MINNESOTA

PREP: 10 MINUTES **BAKE:** 3 HOURS **MAKES:** 1 LOAF (2 POUNDS, 20 SLICES)

- 1¼ **cups water (70° to 80°)**
- ½ **cup honey**
- 2 **tablespoons canola oil**
- 1½ **teaspoons salt**
- 1½ **cups bread flour**
- 1½ **cups whole wheat flour**
- 1 **cup quick-cooking oats**
- 1 **package (¼ ounce) active dry yeast**

1. In bread machine pan, place all ingredients in order suggested by manufacturer. Select basic bread setting. Choose crust color and loaf size if available.

2. Bake according to bread machine directions (check dough after 5 minutes of mixing; add 1 to 2 tablespoons of water or flour if needed).

Corn Chowder

I combine and refrigerate the ingredients for this easy chowder the night before I serve it. In the morning, I start the slow cooker before I leave for work. And when I come home, a hot tasty meal awaits!

—**MARY HOGUE** ROCHESTER, PENNSYLVANIA

PREP: 10 MINUTES **COOK:** 6 HOURS
MAKES: 8 SERVINGS (2 QUARTS)

- 2½ cups 2% milk
- 1 can (14¾ ounces) cream-style corn
- 1 can (10¾ ounces) condensed cream of mushroom soup, undiluted
- 1¾ cups frozen corn
- 1 cup frozen shredded hash brown potatoes
- 1 cup cubed fully cooked ham
- 1 large onion, chopped
- 2 teaspoons dried parsley flakes
- 2 tablespoons butter
  Salt and pepper to taste

1. In a 3-qt. slow cooker, combine all ingredients. Cover and cook on low for 6 hours.

Chili Coney Dogs

Everyone in our family, from smallest kids to oldest adults, loves these dogs. They're so easy to throw together and heat in the slow cooker.

—**MICHELE HARRIS** VICKSBURG, MICHIGAN

PREP: 20 MINUTES **COOK:** 4 HOURS
MAKES: 8 SERVINGS

- 1 pound lean ground beef (90% lean)
- 1 can (15 ounces) tomato sauce
- ½ cup water
- 2 tablespoons Worcestershire sauce
- 1 tablespoon dried minced onion
- ½ teaspoon garlic powder
- ½ teaspoon ground mustard
- ½ teaspoon chili powder
- ½ teaspoon pepper
  Dash cayenne pepper
- 8 hot dogs
- 8 hot dog buns, split
  Shredded cheddar cheese, relish and chopped onion, optional

1. In a large skillet, cook beef over medium heat until no longer pink; drain. Stir in the tomato sauce, water, Worcestershire sauce, onion and spices.

2. Place hot dogs in a 3-qt. slow cooker; top with beef mixture. Cover and cook on low for 4-5 hours or until heated through. Serve on buns with cheese, relish and onion if desired.

I have been making burritos for years, changing the recipe here and there until I created this tasty version. It's a favorite of company and family alike. —**SHARON BELMONT** LINCOLN, NEBRASKA

Pork Burritos

PREP: 20 MINUTES **COOK:** 8 HOURS
MAKES: 14 SERVINGS

- 1 boneless pork sirloin roast (3 pounds)
- ¼ cup reduced-sodium chicken broth
- 1 envelope reduced-sodium taco seasoning
- 1 tablespoon dried parsley flakes
- 2 garlic cloves, minced
- ½ teaspoon pepper
- ¼ teaspoon salt
- 1 can (16 ounces) refried beans
- 1 can (4 ounces) chopped green chilies
- 14 flour tortillas (8 inches), warmed

  Optional toppings: shredded lettuce, chopped tomatoes, chopped green pepper, guacamole, reduced-fat sour cream and shredded reduced-fat cheddar cheese

1. Cut roast in half; place in a 4- or 5-qt. slow cooker. In a small bowl, combine the broth, taco seasoning, parsley, garlic, pepper and salt. Pour over roast. Cover and cook on low for 8-10 hours or until meat is very tender.

2. Remove pork from the slow cooker; cool slightly. Shred with two forks; set aside. Skim fat from the liquid; stir in beans and chilies. Return pork to the slow cooker; heat through.

3. Spoon ½ cup pork mixture down the center of each tortilla; add toppings of your choice. Fold sides and ends over filling and roll up.

Hot Chili Dip

I first made this yummy dip for my husband's birthday party. Everyone wanted the recipe!

—NIKKI ROSATI
FRANKSVILLE, WISCONSIN

PREP: 5 MINUTES **COOK:** 1 HOUR
MAKES: ABOUT 2 CUPS

- 1 jar (24 ounces) salsa
- 1 can (15 ounces) chili with beans
- 2 cans (2¼ ounces each) sliced ripe olives, drained
- 12 ounces process cheese (Velveeta), cubed
  Tortilla chips

1. In a 1½-qt. slow cooker, combine all ingredients. Cover and cook on low for 1-2 hours or until cheese is melted, stirring halfway through. Serve with chips.

Peach Pork Chops

Peaches add sweetness to pork chops in this time-tested favorite.

—ADELE DUROCHER
NEWPORT BEACH, CALIFORNIA

PREP: 15 MINUTES **COOK:** 6 HOURS
MAKES: 5 SERVINGS

- 1 can (29 ounces) peach halves
- 5 bone-in pork loin chops (1 inch thick)
- 1 tablespoon canola oil
- ¼ cup packed brown sugar
- ½ teaspoon ground cinnamon
- ¼ teaspoon ground cloves
- 1 can (8 ounces) tomato sauce
- ¼ cup cider vinegar

1. Drain peaches, reserving ¼ cup juice; set aside. In a large skillet, brown pork chops in oil; transfer to a 3-qt. slow cooker.

2. Combine brown sugar and spices. Add tomato sauce, vinegar and reserved peach juice; pour over chops. Top with peach halves. Cover and cook on low for 6-8 hours or until tender.

Parmesan Italian Loaf

This is one of my favorite breads. It goes with anything from bologna sandwiches to spaghetti.

—JAMI BLUNT HARDY, ARKANSAS

PREP: 10 MINUTES **BAKE:** 3 HOURS **MAKES:** 1 LOAF (1½ POUNDS, 16 SLICES)

- 1 cup water (70° to 80°)
- 2 tablespoons plus 1½ teaspoons butter, softened
- 1 tablespoon honey
- ⅔ cup grated Parmesan cheese
- 1½ teaspoons garlic powder
- ¾ teaspoon salt
- 3 cups bread flour
- 2¼ teaspoons active dry yeast

1. In bread machine pan, place all ingredients in order suggested by manufacturer. Select basic bread setting. Choose crust color and loaf size if available. Bake according to bread machine directions (check dough after 5 minutes of mixing; add 1 to 2 tablespoons of water or flour if needed).

Thai Pork

My husband and I both work long hours. This slow cooker recipe is large enough that the two of us can eat as much yummy pork as we like—and still have leftovers!

—DAWN SCHMIDT DURHAM, NORTH CAROLINA

PREP: 20 MINUTES **COOK:** 8 HOURS
MAKES: 8 SERVINGS

- 2 medium sweet red peppers, julienned
- 1 boneless pork shoulder butt roast (3 pounds)
- ⅓ cup reduced-sodium teriyaki sauce
- 3 tablespoons rice vinegar
- 2 garlic cloves, minced
- ½ teaspoon crushed red pepper flakes
- ¼ cup creamy peanut butter
- 4 cups hot cooked rice
- ½ cup chopped unsalted peanuts
- 4 green onions, sliced

1. Place peppers in a 3-qt. slow cooker. Cut roast in half; place on top of peppers. Combine the teriyaki sauce, vinegar and garlic; pour over roast. Sprinkle with pepper flakes. Cover and cook on low for 8-9 hours or until meat is tender.

2. Remove meat from slow cooker. When cool enough to handle, shred meat with two forks. Reserve 2 cups cooking juices; skim fat. Stir peanut butter into reserved juices. Return pork and cooking juices to slow cooker; heat through. Serve with cooked rice; sprinkle with peanuts and green onions.

Picante Beef Roast

I created this delicious recipe because I love the flavor of taco seasoning and think it shouldn't be reserved just for tacos! Preparation couldn't be easier, and it works great with a pork roast, too.

—MARGARET THIEL LEVITTOWN, PENNSYLVANIA

PREP: 15 MINUTES **COOK:** 8 HOURS **MAKES:** 8 SERVINGS

- 1 beef rump roast or bottom round roast (3 pounds), trimmed
- 1 jar (16 ounces) picante sauce
- 1 can (15 ounces) tomato sauce
- 1 envelope taco seasoning
- 3 tablespoons cornstarch
- ¼ cup cold water

1. Cut roast in half; place in a 5-qt. slow cooker. In a large bowl, combine the picante sauce, tomato sauce and taco seasoning; pour over roast.

2. Cover and cook on low for 8-9 hours or until meat is tender.

3. Remove meat to a serving platter; keep warm. Skim fat from cooking juices; transfer 3 cups to a small saucepan. Bring liquid to a boil.

4. Combine cornstarch and water until smooth. Gradually stir into pan. Bring to a boil; cook and stir for 2 minutes or until thickened. Slice roast; serve with gravy.

Buffet Meatballs

These always-popular bites come together with just a handful of ingredients, including convenient packaged meatballs. Grape juice and apple jelly are the secrets behind the sweet yet tangy sauce.

—JANET ANDERSON CARSON CITY, NEVADA

PREP: 10 MINUTES **COOK:** 4 HOURS
MAKES: ABOUT 10½ DOZEN

- **1 cup grape juice**
- **1 cup apple jelly**
- **1 cup ketchup**
- **1 can (8 ounces) tomato sauce**
- **1 package (64 ounces) frozen fully cooked Italian meatballs**

1. In a small saucepan, combine the juice, jelly, ketchup and tomato sauce. Cook and stir over medium heat until jelly is melted.

2. Place meatballs in a 5-qt. slow cooker. Pour sauce over the top and gently stir to coat. Cover and cook on low for 4-5 hours or until heated through.

Split Pea Soup

Slow cook your split pea soup while you are out for the day and a delicious dinner will be ready when you arrive back home! This is a real stick-to-your-ribs soup. The ham hocks lend a rich, smoky flavor.

—TASTE OF HOME TEST KITCHEN

PREP: 15 MINUTES **COOK:** 8 HOURS
MAKES: 7 SERVINGS (ABOUT 2 QUARTS)

- **1 can (49½ ounces) chicken broth**
- **1½ pounds smoked ham hocks**
- **2 cups each chopped onions, celery and carrots**
- **1 package (16 ounces) dried green split peas**
- **2 bay leaves**
- **Salad croutons, optional**

1. In a 4- or 5-qt. slow cooker, combine the broth, ham hocks, vegetables, peas and bay leaves. Cover and cook on low for 8-10 hours or until ham hocks and peas are tender.

2. Discard bay leaves. Remove meat from bones when cool enough to handle; cut ham into small pieces and set aside. Cool soup slightly.

3. In a blender, cover and process soup in batches until smooth. Return soup to slow cooker; stir in reserved ham. Heat through. Garnish with croutons if desired.

Jambalaya

Sausage, chicken and shrimp make jambalaya so satisfying. It's the perfect food for casual get-togethers.

—SHERRY HUNTWORK GRETNA, NEBRASKA

PREP: 20 MINUTES **COOK:** 6¼ HOURS
MAKES: 12 SERVINGS

- 1 pound smoked kielbasa or Polish sausage, sliced
- ½ pound boneless skinless chicken breasts, cut into 1-inch cubes
- 1 can (14½ ounces) beef broth
- 1 can (14½ ounces) diced tomatoes, undrained
- 2 celery ribs, chopped
- ⅓ cup tomato paste
- 4 garlic cloves, minced
- 1 tablespoon dried parsley flakes
- 1½ teaspoons dried basil
- 1 teaspoon cayenne pepper
- ½ teaspoon salt
- ½ teaspoon dried oregano
- 1 pound cooked medium shrimp, peeled and deveined
- 2 cups cooked rice

1. In a 4-qt. slow cooker, combine the first 12 ingredients. Cover and cook on low for 6-7 hours or until chicken is no longer pink.

2. Stir in shrimp and rice. Cover and cook 15 minutes longer or until heated through.

Beef in Mushroom Gravy

This is one of the best and easiest meals I've ever made. It has only four ingredients, and they all go into the pot at once. The well-seasoned meat makes its own gravy. It tastes wonderful over mashed potatoes!

—MARGERY BRYAN MOSES LAKE, WASHINGTON

PREP: 10 MINUTES **COOK:** 7 HOURS
MAKES: 6 SERVINGS

- 2 to 2½ pounds boneless beef round steak
- 1 to 2 envelopes onion soup mix
- 1 can (10¾ ounces) condensed cream of mushroom soup, undiluted
- ½ cup water
  Mashed potatoes, optional

1. Cut steak into six serving-size pieces; place in a 3-qt. slow cooker. Combine the soup mix, soup and water; pour over beef. Cover and cook on low for 7-8 hours or until meat is tender. Serve with mashed potatoes if desired.

Golden Wheat Bread

Fresh warm wheat bread is great alone or with a bowl of bean soup. Mine has a crispy golden crust. It's also perfect spread with butter or your favorite jam!

—**CINDY REAMS** PHILIPSBURG, PENNSYLVANIA

PREP: 10 MINUTES **BAKE:** 4 HOURS
MAKES: 1 LOAF (1½ POUNDS, 16 SLICES)

- 1 **cup plus 2 tablespoons water (70° to 80°)**
- ¼ **cup canola oil**
- 2 **tablespoons prepared mustard**
- 2 **tablespoons honey**
- 1 **teaspoon salt**
- 2½ **cups bread flour**
- 1 **cup whole wheat flour**
- 2¼ **teaspoons active dry yeast**

1. In bread machine pan, place all ingredients in order suggested by manufacturer. Select basic bread setting. Choose crust color and loaf size if available.

2. Bake according to bread machine directions (check dough after 5 minutes of mixing; add 1-2 tablespoons of water or flour if needed).

Home-Style Stew

My husband and I both work full time, so quick meals are important. Because this stew always tastes great, it's a regular menu item for us.

—**MARIE SHANKS** TERRE HAUTE, INDIANA

PREP: 20 MINUTES **COOK:** 6 HOURS
MAKES: 5 SERVINGS

- 2 **packages (16 ounces each) frozen vegetables for stew**
- 1½ **pounds beef stew meat, cut into 1-inch cubes**
- 1 **can (10¾ ounces) condensed cream of mushroom soup, undiluted**
- 1 **can (10¾ ounces) condensed tomato soup, undiluted**
- 1 **envelope reduced-sodium onion soup mix**

1. Place vegetables in a 5-qt. slow cooker. In a large nonstick skillet coated with cooking spray, brown beef on all sides.

2. Transfer to slow cooker. Combine the remaining ingredients; pour over the top.

3. Cover and cook on low for 6-8 hours or until meat is tender.

Creole Chicken Thighs

Cajun seasoning, fresh veggies and parsley add loads of taste and spice to this flavorful and easy-to-make meal. The slow cooker does the work so you don't have to!

—MATTHEW LAMAN
HUMMELSTOWN, PENNSYLVANIA

PREP: 30 MINUTES **COOK:** 7 HOURS
MAKES: 8 SERVINGS

- 8 bone-in chicken thighs (about 3 pounds), skin removed
- 3 tablespoons Cajun seasoning, divided
- 1 tablespoon canola oil
- 3½ cups chicken broth
- 1 can (16 ounces) red beans, rinsed and drained
- 1½ cups uncooked converted rice
- 2 medium tomatoes, finely chopped
- 1 medium green pepper, chopped
- 2 tablespoons minced fresh parsley

1. Sprinkle chicken with 1 tablespoon Cajun seasoning. In a large skillet, brown chicken in oil.

2. In a 5-qt. slow cooker, combine the broth, beans, rice, tomatoes, green pepper, parsley and remaining Cajun seasoning. Top with chicken.

3. Cover and cook on low for 7-8 hours or until chicken is tender.

Cola Barbecue Ribs

Enjoy the smoky goodness of a summer barbecue all year long by preparing these moist and tender ribs in your slow cooker— inclement weather or not.

—KAREN SHUCK EDGAR, NEBRASKA

PREP: 10 MINUTES **COOK:** 9 HOURS **MAKES:** 4 SERVINGS

- ¼ cup packed brown sugar
- 2 garlic cloves, minced
- 1 teaspoon salt
- ½ teaspoon pepper
- 3 tablespoons Liquid Smoke, optional
- 4 pounds pork spareribs, cut into serving-size pieces
- 1 medium onion, sliced
- ½ cup cola
- 1½ cups barbecue sauce

1. In a small bowl, combine the brown sugar, garlic, salt, pepper and Liquid Smoke if desired; rub over ribs.

2. Layer ribs and onion in a greased 5- or 6-qt. slow cooker; pour cola over ribs. Cover and cook on low for 8-10 hours or until ribs are tender. Drain liquid. Pour sauce over ribs and cook 1 hour longer.

Herbed Chicken and Tomatoes

I put a tangy spin on chicken by adding just a few easy ingredients. Recipes like this are really a plus when you work a full-time job but still want to have a healthy, satisfying meal on the table in short order.
—**REBECCA POPKE** LARGO, FLORIDA

PREP: 10 MINUTES **COOK:** 5 HOURS
MAKES: 4 SERVINGS

- 1 **pound boneless skinless chicken breasts, cut into 1½-inch pieces**
- 2 **cans (14½ ounces each) Italian diced tomatoes, undrained**
- 1 **envelope Lipton savory herb with garlic soup mix**
- ¼ **teaspoon sugar**
  Hot cooked pasta
  Shredded Parmesan cheese

1. In a 3-qt. slow cooker, combine the chicken, tomatoes, soup mix and sugar. Cover and cook on low for 5-6 hours or until chicken is no longer pink. Serve with pasta; sprinkle with cheese.

Cheddar Olive Loaf

Cheddar cheese gives this zesty bread an appealing pale orange tint. It smells so good while baking that I can hardly wait until it's done and cool enough to slice!
—**CATHERINE DAWE** KENT, OHIO

PREP: 10 MINUTES **BAKE:** 3 HOURS
MAKES: 1 LOAF (1½ POUNDS, 16 SLICES)

- 1 **cup water (70° to 80°)**
- 4 **teaspoons sugar**
- ¾ **teaspoon salt**
- 1¼ **cups shredded sharp cheddar cheese**
- 3 **cups bread flour**
- 2 **teaspoons active dry yeast**
- ¾ **cup pimiento-stuffed olives, well drained and sliced**

1. In bread machine pan, place the first six ingredients in order suggested by manufacturer. Select basic bread setting. Choose crust, color and loaf size if available. Bake according to bread machine directions (check dough after 5 minutes of mixing; add 1 to 2 tablespoons of water or flour if needed).

2. Just before the final kneading (your machine may audibly signal this), add the olives.

Editor's Note: *We recommend you do not use a bread machine's time-delay feature for this recipe.*

I usually have everything on hand for this hearty stew, so it's easy to load up the slow cooker any time. When I get home, dinner's ready and waiting. —MARGERY BRYAN MOSES LAKE, WASHINGTON

Hobo Meatball Stew

PREP: 20 MINUTES **COOK:** 6 HOURS
MAKES: 4 SERVINGS

- 1 **pound lean ground beef (90% lean)**
- 1½ **teaspoons salt or salt-free seasoning blend, divided**
- ½ **teaspoon pepper, divided**
- 4 **medium potatoes, peeled and cut into chunks**
- 4 **medium carrots, cut into chunks**
- 1 **large onion, cut into chunks**
- ½ **cup water**
- ½ **cup ketchup**
- 1½ **teaspoons cider vinegar**
- ½ **teaspoon dried basil**

1. In a bowl, combine the beef, 1 teaspoon salt and ¼ teaspoon pepper. Shape into 1-in. balls. In a skillet over medium heat, brown meatballs on all sides; drain.

2. Place the potatoes, carrots and onion in a 3-qt. slow cooker; top with meatballs. Combine the water, ketchup, vinegar, basil, and remaining salt and pepper; pour over meatballs.

3. Cover and cook on low for 6-8 hours or until the vegetables are tender.

Preparing meatballs in bulk cuts back on prep time. I often make as many as five dinners' worth of meatballs at once. Then I freeze the cooked meatballs for quick meals when needed.

—**CHRISTI G.** TULSA, OKLAHOMA

Lemony Turkey Breast

Lemon and a hint of garlic add a lovely touch to tender slices of slow-cooked turkey breast. I usually serve the gravy over a combination of white and brown rice, along with broccoli for a healthy meal.

—LYNN LAUX BALLWIN, MISSOURI

PREP: 10 MINUTES **COOK:** 5 HOURS
MAKES: 14 SERVINGS

- 1 **bone-in turkey breast (5 to 6 pounds)**
- 1 **medium lemon, halved**
- 1 **teaspoon salt-free lemon-pepper seasoning**
- 1 **teaspoon garlic salt**
- 4 **teaspoons cornstarch**
- ½ **cup reduced-sodium chicken broth**

1. Remove skin from turkey. Pat turkey dry with paper towels; spray turkey with cooking spray. Place breast side up in a 5-qt. slow cooker. Squeeze half of the lemon over turkey; sprinkle with lemon-pepper and garlic salt. Place lemon halves under turkey.

2. Cover and cook on low for 5-7 hours or until meat is tender. Remove turkey and keep warm. Discard lemon.

3. For gravy, pour cooking liquid into a measuring cup; skim fat. In a saucepan, combine cornstarch and broth until smooth. Gradually stir in cooking liquid. Bring to a boil; cook and stir for 2 minutes or until thickened. Serve with turkey.

Slow-Cooked Sloppy Joes

On hot summer days, this cooks without heating up the kitchen while I work on the rest of the meal. It's easy to double or triple for crowds, and if there are any leftovers, you can freeze them to enjoy later!

—CAROL LOSIER BALDWINSVILLE, NEW YORK

PREP: 20 MINUTES **COOK:** 3 HOURS **MAKES:** 8 SERVINGS

- 1½ **pounds ground beef**
- 1 **cup chopped celery**
- ½ **cup chopped onion**
- 1 **bottle (12 ounces) chili sauce**
- 2 **tablespoons brown sugar**
- 2 **tablespoons sweet pickle relish**
- 1 **tablespoon Worcestershire sauce**
- 1 **teaspoon salt**
- ⅛ **teaspoon pepper**
- 8 **hamburger buns, split**

1. In a large skillet, cook the beef, celery and onion over medium heat until meat is no longer pink; drain. Transfer to a 3-qt. slow cooker.

2. Stir in the chili sauce, brown sugar, pickle relish, Worcestershire sauce, salt and pepper. Cover and cook on low for 3-4 hours or until heated through. Spoon ½ cup beef mixture onto each bun.

Slow 'n' Easy Chili

What's nice about this recipe is that you can add virtually any extras, such as chopped bell peppers or sliced fresh mushrooms, to make your own specialty.

—**GINNY PUCKETT** LUTZ, FLORIDA

PREP: 15 MINUTES **COOK:** 6 HOURS
MAKES: 6-8 SERVINGS

- ½ **pound ground beef, cooked and drained**
- ½ **pound bulk pork sausage, cooked and drained**
- 1 **can (28 ounces) crushed tomatoes**
- 1 **can (16 ounces) chili beans, undrained**
- 1 **can (10¾ ounces) condensed tomato soup, undiluted**
- 1 **large onion, chopped**
- 2 **envelopes chili seasoning**
  Sour cream and shredded cheddar cheese

1. In a 3-qt. slow cooker, combine the first seven ingredients. Cover and cook on low for 6-8 hours or until heated through, stirring occasionally. Serve with sour cream and cheese.

Sweet and Savory Ribs

My husband and I love barbecue ribs, but we rarely have time to fire up the grill. So we let the slow cooker do the work for us. By the time we get home from work, the ribs are tender, juicy and ready to devour.

—**KANDY BINGHAM** GREEN RIVER, WYOMING

PREP: 10 MINUTES **COOK:** 8 HOURS
MAKES: 8 SERVINGS

- 1 **large onion, chopped**
- 4 **pounds boneless country-style pork ribs**
- 1 **bottle (18 ounces) honey barbecue sauce**
- ⅓ **cup maple syrup**
- ¼ **cup spicy brown mustard**
- ½ **teaspoon salt**
- ¼ **teaspoon pepper**

1. Place onion in a 5-qt. slow cooker. Top with the ribs. Combine the barbecue sauce, syrup, mustard, salt and pepper; pour over ribs. Cover and cook on low for 8-9 hours or until meat is tender.

Paprika Onion Bread

Paprika adds a hint of color to this aromatic bread that's just delicious spread with cream cheese. My family likes it served with goulash.

—JACKIE ROBBINS FLINT, MICHIGAN

PREP: 10 MINUTES **BAKE:** 3 HOURS
MAKES: 1 LOAF (1½ POUNDS, 16 SLICES)

- 1 cup water (70° to 80°)
- 2 tablespoons butter, softened
- ⅓ cup finely chopped onion
- 1½ teaspoons salt
- 1 teaspoon sugar
- 1 teaspoon paprika
- 3 cups bread flour
- 1 package (¼ ounce) active dry yeast

1. In bread machine pan, place all ingredients in order suggested by manufacturer. Select basic bread setting. Choose crust color and loaf size if available. Bake according to bread machine directions (check dough after 5 minutes of mixing; add 1 to 2 tablespoons water or flour if needed).

Soy-Garlic Chicken

PREP: 10 MINUTES **COOK:** 4 HOURS
MAKES: 6 SERVINGS

- 6 chicken leg quarters, skin removed
- 1 can (8 ounces) tomato sauce
- ½ cup soy sauce
- ¼ cup packed brown sugar
- 2 teaspoons minced garlic

1. With a sharp knife, cut leg quarters at the joints if desired. Place in a 4-qt. slow cooker.

2. In a small bowl, combine the tomato sauce, soy sauce, brown sugar and garlic; pour over chicken. Cover and cook on low for 4-5 hours or until the chicken is tender.

❝I'm a full-time mom and help my husband on our ranch, so I'm always looking for good hearty dinners I can easily make in the slow cooker. My family really likes this one.❞

—COLLEEN FABER BUFFALO, MONTANA

Vegetable Beef Soup

PREP: 10 MINUTES **COOK:** 8 HOURS
MAKES: 10 SERVINGS (2½ QUARTS)

- 1 **pound ground beef**
- 1 **can (46 ounces) tomato juice**
- 1 **package (16 ounces) frozen mixed vegetables, thawed**
- 2 **cups frozen cubed hash brown potatoes, thawed**
- 1 **envelope onion soup mix**

1. In a large skillet, cook beef over medium heat until no longer pink; drain. Transfer to a 5-qt. slow cooker. Stir in the tomato juice, mixed vegetables, potatoes and soup mix.

2. Cover and cook on low for 8-10 hours or until heated through.

Wonderful White Bread

Simply wonderful is how I describe a loaf of this home-style white bread. Its light texture makes it great for sandwiches or toast.

—KAREN KALOYDIS
FLUSHING, MICHIGAN

PREP: 10 MINUTES **BAKE:** 3 HOURS
MAKES: 1 LOAF (1½ POUNDS, 16 SLICES)

- 1 **cup plus 1 tablespoon water (70° to 80°)**
- 1 **egg**
- 4½ **teaspoons canola oil**
- ¼ **cup sugar**
- 1½ **teaspoons salt**
- 3¼ **cups bread flour**
- 1 **package (¼ ounce) active dry yeast**

1. In a bread machine pan, place all ingredients in order suggested by manufacturer. Select basic bread setting. Choose crust color and loaf size if available. Bake according to bread machine directions (check dough after 5 minutes of mixing; add 1 to 2 tablespoons of water or flour if needed).

Convenient frozen veggies and hash browns make this meaty soup a snap to mix up. Simply brown the ground beef, then stir everything together to simmer all day. It's fantastic served with bread and a salad. **—CAROL CALHOUN** SIOUX FALLS, SOUTH DAKOTA

Italian Sausage Dinner

My whole family loves this dish. It's easy to prepare before I go to work, and it makes the house smell so good at the end of the day.

—**KATHY KASPROWICZ** ARLINGTON HEIGHTS, ILLINOIS

PREP: 20 MINUTES **COOK:** 6 HOURS
MAKES: 5 SERVINGS

- 1 **pound small red potatoes**
- 2 **large zucchini, cut into 1-inch slices**
- 2 **large green peppers, cut into 1½-inch pieces**
- 1 **large onion, cut into wedges**
- ¼ **teaspoon salt**
- ¼ **teaspoon pepper**
- 1 **pound Italian sausage links, cut into 1½-inch pieces**
- 1 **tablespoon olive oil**
- ½ **cup white wine or chicken broth**
- 1 **tablespoon Italian seasoning**

1. Place the first six ingredients in a 6-qt. slow cooker. In a large skillet, brown sausages in oil. Reduce heat. Add wine and Italian seasoning, stirring to loosen browned bits from pan. Transfer to slow cooker. Cover and cook on low for 6-8 hours or until potatoes are tender.

Ham with Cherry Sauce

I often make my easy cherry ham for church breakfasts. It's such a favorite that I've even served it at Easter dinners and at a friend's wedding brunch.

—**CAROL LEE JONES** TAYLORS, SOUTH CAROLINA

PREP: 20 MINUTES **COOK:** 4 HOURS
MAKES: 10-12 SERVINGS

- 1 **boneless fully cooked ham (3 to 4 pounds)**
- ½ **cup apple jelly**
- 2 **teaspoons prepared mustard**
- ⅔ **cup ginger ale, divided**
- 1 **can (21 ounces) cherry pie filling**
- 2 **tablespoons cornstarch**

1. Score surface of ham, making diamond shapes ½ in. deep. In a small bowl, combine the jelly, mustard and 1 tablespoon ginger ale; rub over scored surface of ham. Cut ham in half; place in a 5-qt. slow cooker.

2. Cover and cook on low for 4-5 hours or until a thermometer reads 140°, basting with cooking juices near the end of cooking time.

3. For sauce, place pie filling in a saucepan. Combine cornstarch and remaining ginger ale; stir into pie filling until blended. Bring to a boil; cook and stir for 2 minutes or until thickened. Serve over ham.

Hawaiian Sausage Subs

If you're looking for a different way to use kielbasa, the sweet and mildly spicy flavor of these sandwiches makes a nice change of pace.

—JUDY DAMES BRIDGEVILLE, PENNSYLVANIA

PREP: 15 MINUTES **COOK:** 3 HOURS
MAKES: 12 SERVINGS

  3   **pounds smoked kielbasa or Polish sausage, cut into 3-inch pieces**
  2   **bottles (12 ounces each) chili sauce**
  1   **can (20 ounces) pineapple tidbits, undrained**
  ¼   **cup packed brown sugar**
 12   **hoagie buns, split**

1. Place kielbasa in a 3-qt. slow cooker. Combine the chili sauce, pineapple and brown sugar; pour over kielbasa. Cover and cook on low for 3-4 hours or until heated through. Serve on buns.

Corned Beef Dinner

This flavorful meal is a must for St. Patrick's Day, but it's great any time of the year. Don't forget to serve it with fresh crusty rye bread!

—MICHELLE RHODES FORT BLISS, TEXAS

PREP: 25 MINUTES **COOK:** 8 HOURS
MAKES: 8 SERVINGS

  4   **to 5 medium red potatoes, quartered**
  2   **cups fresh baby carrots, halved lengthwise**
  3   **cups chopped cabbage**
  1   **corned beef brisket with spice packet (3½ pounds)**
  3   **cups water**
  1   **tablespoon caraway seeds**

1. Place the potatoes, carrots and cabbage in a 5-qt. slow cooker. Cut brisket in half; place over vegetables. Add the water, caraway seeds and contents of spice packet. Cover and cook on low for 8-10 hours or until the meat and vegetables are tender.

top tip For best results, a slow cooker should be from one-half to two-thirds full. Unless directed to stir the food or to add ingredients during cooking, avoid lifting the lid. Lifting the lid extends cooking time.

Family-Favorite Beef Roast

Just a few ingredients are all you'll need for a tangy beef roast that feeds a bunch. The gravy is tasty on mashed potatoes, too, so make plenty.

—JEANIE BEASLEY TUPELO, MISSISSIPPI

PREP: 10 MINUTES **COOK:** 6 HOURS
MAKES: 8 SERVINGS

- 1 boneless beef chuck roast (3 to 4 pounds)
- 1 can (14½ ounces) stewed tomatoes, cut up
- 1 can (10¾ ounces) condensed cream of mushroom soup, undiluted
- 1 envelope Lipton beefy onion soup mix
- ¼ cup cornstarch
- ½ cup cold water

1. Cut roast in half. Transfer to a 5-qt. slow cooker. In a small bowl, combine the tomatoes, soup and soup mix; pour over meat. Cover and cook on low for 6-8 hours or until meat is tender.

2. Remove meat to a serving platter; keep warm. Skim fat from cooking juices; transfer to a large saucepan. Bring liquid to a boil. Combine cornstarch and water until smooth; gradually stir into the pan. Bring to a boil; cook and stir for 2 minutes or until thickened. Serve with roast.

Chocolate Walnut Bread

I let my bread machine do the work when making this lightly sweet and tender loaf. Its quick prep time and indulgent flavor will make it a favorite in your home, too.

—MARGARET BEYERSDORF KISSIMMEE, FLORIDA

PREP: 10 MINUTES **BAKE:** 3 HOURS
MAKES: 1 LOAF (1½ POUNDS, 16 SLICES)

- ⅔ cup warm milk (70° to 80°)
- ⅓ cup water (70° to 80°)
- 5 tablespoons butter, softened
- ⅓ cup packed brown sugar
- 5 tablespoons baking cocoa
- 1 teaspoon salt
- 3 cups bread flour
- 2¼ teaspoons active dry yeast
- ⅔ cup chopped walnuts, toasted

1. In bread machine pan, place the first eight ingredients in order suggested by manufacturer. Select basic bread setting. Choose crust color and loaf size if available.

2. Bake according to bread machine directions (check dough after 5 minutes of mixing; add 1 to 2 tablespoons of water or flour if needed).

3. Just before the final kneading (your bread machine may audibly signal this), add the walnuts.

Editor's Note: *We recommend you do not use a bread machine's time-delay feature for this recipe.*

Warm Christmas Punch

PREP: 5 MINUTES **COOK:** 2 HOURS
MAKES: 8 SERVINGS (2 QUARTS)

- 1 **bottle (32 ounces) cranberry juice**
- 5 **cans (6 ounces each) unsweetened pineapple juice**
- ⅓ **cup red-hot candies**
- 1 **cinnamon stick (3½ inches)**

1. In a 3-qt. slow cooker, combine all ingredients.

2. Cover and cook on low for 2-4 hours or until heated through and candies are dissolved. Discard cinnamon stick before serving.

Cranberry Meatballs

Whether you serve them as appetizers or the main course, these tasty meatballs are always popular.
—**NINA HALL** SPOKANE, WASHINGTON

PREP: 20 MINUTES **COOK:** 6 HOURS
MAKES: 6 SERVINGS

- 2 **eggs, beaten**
- 1 **cup dry bread crumbs**
- ⅓ **cup minced fresh parsley**
- 2 **tablespoons finely chopped onion**
- 1½ **pounds lean ground beef (90% lean)**
- 1 **can (14 ounces) jellied cranberry sauce**
- 1 **bottle (12 ounces) chili sauce**
- ⅓ **cup ketchup**
- 2 **tablespoons brown sugar**
- 1 **tablespoon lemon juice**

1. Combine first four ingredients. Crumble beef over mixture; mix well. Shape into 1½-in. balls. Place in a 3-qt. slow cooker.

2. Combine the remaining ingredients. Pour over meatballs. Cover and cook on low for 6 hours or until meat is no longer pink.

Red-hot candies add rich color and spiciness to this festive punch, and the cranberry juice gives it a little tang. —**JULIE STERCHI** JACKSON, MISSOURI

Onion Meat Loaf

My husband and I really enjoy this hearty and delicious, yet oh-so-simple, meat loaf. Just five ingredients and into the slow cooker!

—RHONDA COWDEN
QUINCY, ILLINOIS

PREP: 15 MINUTES **COOK:** 5 HOURS
MAKES: 8 SERVINGS

- 2 eggs, beaten
- ¾ cup quick-cooking oats
- ½ cup ketchup
- 1 envelope onion soup mix
- 2 pounds ground beef

1. Cut three 20-in. x 3-in. strips of heavy-duty foil; crisscross so they resemble spokes of a wheel. Place strips on the bottom and up the sides of a 3-qt. slow cooker. Coat strips with cooking spray.

2. In a large bowl, combine the eggs, oats, ketchup and soup mix. Crumble beef over mixture and mix well. Shape into a loaf. Place loaf in the center of the strips.

3. Cover and cook on low for 5-6 hours or until a thermometer reads 160°.

4. Using foil strips as handles, remove meat loaf to a platter.

Reuben Spread

My daughter shared this recipe with me for a hearty spread that tastes just like a Reuben sandwich. Serve it from a slow cooker set to low so that it stays tasty and warm.

—ROSALIE FUCHS PAYNESVILLE, MINNESOTA

PREP: 5 MINUTES **COOK:** 2 HOURS **MAKES:** 3½ CUPS

- 1 can (14 ounces) sauerkraut, rinsed and well drained
- 1 package (8 ounces) cream cheese, cubed
- 2 cups (8 ounces) shredded Swiss cheese
- 1 package (3 ounces) deli corned beef, chopped
- 3 tablespoons prepared Thousand Island salad dressing
  Snack rye bread or crackers

1. In a 1½-qt. slow cooker, combine the first five ingredients. Cover and cook on low for 2-3 hours or until cheeses are melted; stir to blend. Serve warm with bread or crackers.

Tomato Hamburger Soup

As a full-time teacher, I only have time to cook from scratch a few nights each week. This recipe makes a big enough batch to feed my family for two nights.

—JULIE KRUGER ST. CLOUD, MINNESOTA

PREP: 10 MINUTES **COOK:** 4 HOURS
MAKES: 12 SERVINGS (3 QUARTS)

- 1 can (46 ounces) V8 juice
- 2 packages (16 ounces each) frozen mixed vegetables
- 1 pound ground beef, cooked and drained
- 1 can (10¾ ounces) condensed cream of mushroom soup, undiluted
- 2 teaspoons dried minced onion
  Salt and pepper to taste

1. In a 5-qt. slow cooker, combine the first five ingredients. Cover and cook on high for 4-5 hours or until heated through. Season with salt and pepper.

Simple Chicken Tagine

I like to sprinkle this stew with toasted almonds or cashews and serve it with hot couscous. With a touch of sweetness from cinnamon and dried apricots, it tastes like you spent all day in the kitchen!

—ANGELA BUCHANAN LONGMONT, COLORADO

PREP: 15 MINUTES **COOK:** 6 HOURS **MAKES:** 6 SERVINGS

- 2¼ pounds bone-in chicken thighs, skin removed
- 1 large onion, chopped
- 2 medium carrots, sliced
- ¾ cup unsweetened apple juice
- 1 garlic clove, minced
- 1 teaspoon salt
- ½ teaspoon ground cinnamon
- ½ teaspoon pepper
- 1 cup chopped dried apricots
  Hot cooked couscous

1. Place the chicken, onion and carrots in a 3- or 4-qt. slow cooker coated with cooking spray. In a small bowl, combine the apple juice, garlic, salt, cinnamon and pepper; pour over vegetables.

2. Cover and cook on low for 6-8 hours or until chicken is tender.

3. Remove chicken from slow cooker; shred meat with two forks. Skim fat from cooking juices; stir in apricots. Return shredded chicken to slow cooker; heat though. Serve with couscous.

> My grandchildren really like this hearty loaf's crunchy crust and chewy interior. I like how nutritious it is, containing more fiber than many other loaves. —**JOHN REED** LEE'S SUMMIT, MISSOURI

Three-Grain Bread

PREP: 10 MINUTES **BAKE:** 3 HOURS
MAKES: 1 LOAF (2 POUNDS, 20 SLICES)

- 1½ cups water (70° to 80°)
- ½ cup honey
- 1½ teaspoons salt
- 2 cups bread flour
- 1 cup whole wheat flour
- ¾ cup rye flour
- ¾ cup cornmeal
- 2¼ teaspoons active dry yeast

1. In bread machine pan, place all ingredients in order suggested by manufacturer. Select basic bread setting. Choose crust color and loaf size if available.

2. Bake according to bread machine directions (check dough after 5 minutes of mixing; add 1 to 2 tablespoons of water or flour if needed).

Chicken with Stuffing

With just a few ingredients, you can create a comforting home-style meal of chicken and corn bread stuffing.
—**SUSAN KUTZ**
STILLMAN VALLEY, ILLINOIS

PREP: 5 MINUTES **COOK:** 4 HOURS
MAKES: 4 SERVINGS

- 4 boneless skinless chicken breast halves (4 ounces each)
- 1 can (10¾ ounces) condensed cream of chicken soup, undiluted
- 1¼ cups water
- ¼ cup butter, melted
- 1 package (6 ounces) corn bread stuffing mix

1. Place chicken in a greased 3-qt. slow cooker. Top with soup. In a bowl, combine the water, butter and stuffing mix; spoon over the chicken. Cover and cook on low for 4 hours or until chicken is tender.

Pork Chop Dinner

Canned soup creates an easy gravy for tender pork and potatoes in this simple supper idea. Feel free to vary the amount of onion soup mix in the recipe to suit your family's tastes.

—MIKE AVERY
BATTLE CREEK, MICHIGAN

PREP: 10 MINUTES **COOK:** 6 HOURS
MAKES: 4 SERVINGS

- 6 to 8 medium carrots (1 pound), coarsely chopped
- 3 to 4 medium potatoes, cubed
- 4 boneless pork loin chops (¾ inch thick)
- 1 large onion, sliced
- 1 envelope onion soup mix
- 2 cans (10¾ ounces each) condensed cream of mushroom soup, undiluted

1. Place carrots and potatoes in a 3-qt. slow cooker. Top with the pork chops, onion, soup mix and cream of mushroom soup.

2. Cover and cook on low for 6-8 hours or until meat and vegetables are tender.

Slow-Cooked Stuffed Peppers

What an easy way to fix stuffed peppers without parboiling! Light and packed with Southwest flavor, they also come with 8 grams of fiber per serving. How can you go wrong?

—MICHELLE GURNSEY LINCOLN, NEBRASKA

PREP: 15 MINUTES **COOK:** 3 HOURS **MAKES:** 4 SERVINGS

- 4 medium sweet red peppers
- 1 can (15 ounces) black beans, rinsed and drained
- 1 cup (4 ounces) shredded pepper Jack cheese
- ¾ cup salsa
- 1 small onion, chopped
- ½ cup frozen corn
- ⅓ cup uncooked converted long grain rice
- 1¼ teaspoons chili powder
- ½ teaspoon ground cumin
  Reduced-fat sour cream, optional

1. Cut tops off peppers and remove seeds; set aside. In a large bowl, combine the beans, cheese, salsa, onion, corn, rice, chili powder and cumin; spoon into peppers. Place in a 5-qt. slow cooker coated with cooking spray.

2. Cover and cook on low for 3-4 hours or until peppers are tender and filling is heated through. Serve with sour cream if desired.

Curried Lentil Soup

PREP: 15 MINUTES **COOK:** 8 HOURS
MAKES: 10 SERVINGS (2½ QUARTS)

- 4 **cups water**
- 1 **can (28 ounces) crushed tomatoes**
- 3 **medium potatoes, peeled and diced**
- 3 **medium carrots, thinly sliced**
- 1 **cup dried lentils, rinsed**
- 1 **large onion, chopped**
- 1 **celery rib, chopped**
- 4 **teaspoons curry powder**
- 2 **bay leaves**
- 2 **garlic cloves, minced**
- 1½ **teaspoons salt, optional**

1. In a 4- or 5-qt. slow cooker, combine the first 10 ingredients. Cover and cook on low for 8 hours or until lentils are tender. Add salt if desired. Discard bay leaves.

Creamy Beef and Pasta

When the kids were young, I often made this meal when my husband and I went out for date night.

—CAROL LOSIER
BALDWINSVILLE, NEW YORK

PREP: 15 MINUTES **COOK:** 6 HOURS
MAKES: 4-6 SERVINGS

- 2 **cans (10¾ ounces each) condensed cream of mushroom soup, undiluted**
- 2 **cups (8 ounces) shredded cheddar or part-skim mozzarella cheese**
- 1 **pound ground beef, cooked and drained**
- 2 **cups uncooked small pasta**
- 2 **cups milk**
- ½ **to 1 teaspoon onion powder**
- ½ **to 1 teaspoon salt**
- ¼ **to ½ teaspoon pepper**

1. In a 3-qt. slow cooker, combine all ingredients. Cover and cook on low for 6-8 hours or until the pasta is tender.

Curry gives sensational flavor to this hearty vegetarian soup. It's delicious with a dollop of sour cream. My family is so excited every time I make it. **—CHRISTINA TILL** SOUTH HAVEN, MICHIGAN

Oatmeal Molasses Bread

Here's a lightly sweet bread with good texture and a nice crunchy crust.

—RUTH ANDREWSON LEAVENWORTH, WASHINGTON

PREP: 10 MINUTES **BAKE:** 3 HOURS
MAKES: 1 LOAF (2 POUNDS, 20 SLICES)

- 1 **cup warm water (70° to 80°)**
- ½ **cup molasses**
- 1 **tablespoon canola oil**
- 1 **teaspoon salt**
- 3 **cups bread flour**
- 1 **cup quick-cooking oats**
- 1 **package (¼ ounce) active dry yeast**

1. In bread machine pan, place all ingredients in order suggested by manufacturer. Select basic bread setting. Choose crust color and loaf size if available.

2. Bake according to bread machine directions (check dough after 5 minutes of mixing; add 1 to 2 tablespoons of water or flour if needed).

So-Easy Southwest Chicken

Prepared salsa and convenient canned corn and beans add fun color, texture and flavor to chicken breasts. I usually serve this with salad and white rice. Our children love it!

—KAREN WATERS LAUREL, MARYLAND

PREP: 10 MINUTES **COOK:** 6 HOURS
MAKES: 6 SERVINGS

- 2 **cans (15¼ ounces each) whole kernel corn, drained**
- 1 **can (15 ounces) black beans, rinsed and drained**
- 1 **jar (16 ounces) chunky salsa, divided**
- 6 **boneless skinless chicken breast halves (4 ounces each)**
- 1 **cup (4 ounces) shredded cheddar cheese**

1. In a 5-qt. slow cooker, combine the corn, black beans and ½ cup of salsa. Top with chicken; pour the remaining salsa over chicken.

2. Cover and cook on low for 6-8 hours or until meat is tender. Sprinkle with cheese. Cover and cook 5 minutes longer or until cheese is melted.

top tip

Canned beans often stick to the bottom of the can and require a spoon to remove. So I open the bottom of the can instead of the top. With a little shake, the contents come right out.

—TAMMY B. UNION CENTER, SOUTH DAKOTA

Slow-Cooked Mac 'n' Cheese

The name of this recipe alone is enough to make mouths water. This is comfort food at its finest: rich, hearty and extra-cheesy. It serves nine as a side dish, though you might just want to make it your main course!

—SHELBY MOLINA WHITEWATER, WISCONSIN

PREP: 25 MINUTES **COOK:** 2¾ HOURS **MAKES:** 9 SERVINGS

- 2 cups uncooked elbow macaroni
- 1 can (12 ounces) reduced-fat evaporated milk
- 1½ cups fat-free milk
- ⅓ cup egg substitute
- 1 tablespoon butter, melted
- 8 ounces reduced-fat process cheese (Velveeta), cubed
- 2 cups (8 ounces) shredded sharp cheddar cheese, divided

1. Cook macaroni according to package directions; drain and rinse in cold water. In a large bowl, combine the evaporated milk, milk, egg substitute and butter. Stir in the process cheese, 1½ cups sharp cheddar cheese and macaroni.

2. Transfer to a 3-qt. slow cooker coated with cooking spray. Cover and cook on low for 2-3 hours or until center is set, stirring once. Sprinkle with remaining sharp cheddar cheese.

Teriyaki Pulled Pork Sandwiches

The aroma of pork roast slowly cooking in pineapple juice and teriyaki sauce is wonderful when you come home after a busy day!

—TASTE OF HOME TEST KITCHEN

PREP: 10 MINUTES **COOK:** 8 HOURS **MAKES:** 8 SERVINGS

- 1 boneless pork shoulder butt roast (3 pounds)
- 2 teaspoons olive oil
- 1 cup finely chopped onion
- 1 cup reduced-sodium teriyaki sauce, divided
- ½ cup unsweetened pineapple juice
- 3 tablespoons all-purpose flour
- 8 whole wheat hamburger buns, split
- 1 can (20 ounces) sliced pineapple, drained

1. Cut roast in half. In a large skillet, brown roast in oil; place in a 5-qt. slow cooker. Add the onion, ½ cup teriyaki sauce and pineapple juice. Cover and cook on low for 7-9 hours or until meat is tender.

2. Remove roast; set aside. In a small bowl, combine flour and remaining teriyaki sauce until smooth; stir into cooking juices. Cover and cook on high for 30-40 minutes or until thickened.

3. Shred meat with two forks; return to the slow cooker and heat through. Spoon ½ cup onto each bun; top with a pineapple slice.

Butterscotch Dip

If you like the sweetness of butterscotch chips, you'll enjoy this warm rum-flavored fruit dip. I serve it with apple and pear wedges. It holds up for up to 2 hours in the slow cooker.

—JEAUNE HADL VAN METER LEXINGTON, KENTUCKY

PREP: 5 MINUTES **COOK:** 45 MINUTES
MAKES: ABOUT 3 CUPS

- 2 packages (10 to 11 ounces each) butterscotch chips
- ⅔ cup evaporated milk
- ⅔ cup chopped pecans
- 1 tablespoon rum extract
  Apple and pear wedges

1. In a 1½-qt. slow cooker, combine butterscotch chips and milk. Cover and cook on low for 45-50 minutes or until chips are softened; stir until smooth. Stir in pecans and extract. Serve warm with fruit.

Favorite Italian Beef Sandwiches

I'm a paramedic and firefighter, and slow-cooked recipes like this one suit my unpredictable schedule. My husband, children and the hungry bunch at the firehouse love these robust sandwiches that have just a little zip.

—KRIS SWIHART PERRYSBURG, OHIO

PREP: 20 MINUTES **COOK:** 8 HOURS
MAKES: 10-12 SERVINGS

- 1 jar (11½ ounces) pepperoncini
- 1 boneless beef chuck roast (3½ to 4 pounds)
- ¼ cup water
- 1¾ teaspoons dried basil
- 1½ teaspoons garlic powder
- 1½ teaspoons dried oregano
- 1¼ teaspoons salt
- ¼ teaspoon pepper
- 1 large onion, sliced and quartered
- 10 to 12 hard rolls, split

1. Drain the pepperoncini, reserving liquid. Remove and discard stems of peppers; set peppers aside. Cut roast into large chunks; place a third of the meat in a 5-qt. slow cooker. Add water.

2. In a small bowl, combine the seasonings; sprinkle half over beef. Layer with half of the remaining meat, then the onion and pepperoncini. Pour pepperoncini liquid over the top. Add remaining meat to slow cooker; sprinkle with remaining seasonings.

3. Cover and cook on low for 8-9 hours or until meat is tender. Shred beef with two forks. Using a slotted spoon, serve beef and peppers on rolls.

Editor's Note: *Look for pepperoncinis (pickled peppers) in the pickle and olive section.*

111

120

119

Sides & Salads

“With only four ingredients, you'll have rich, cheesy, irresistible fettucine in no time. Try it with steak for a super treat!”

SUNDRA HAUCK BOGALUSA, LOUISIANA
about her recipe, Parmesan Fettuccine, on page 120

20 Grilled Corn Medley

Who knew a store-bought dressing could add so much flavor? This medley tastes delightful with garden-fresh veggies. Feel free to sub in your favorites and let the grill and the dressing do the rest!

—TASTE OF HOME TEST KITCHEN

PREP/TOTAL TIME: 20 MINUTES
MAKES: 8 SERVINGS

- 3 **medium ears sweet corn, cut into 2-inch pieces**
- 1 **medium sweet red pepper, cut into 1-inch pieces**
- 1 **medium zucchini, sliced**
- 20 **small fresh mushrooms**
- ¼ **cup creamy Caesar salad dressing**
- ¼ **teaspoon salt**
- ¼ **teaspoon pepper**

1. In a large bowl, combine all ingredients; toss to coat. Transfer to a disposable foil pan.

2. Grill, covered, over medium-hot heat for 5 minutes; stir. Grill 3-5 minutes longer or until vegetables are tender.

30 Party Tortellini Salad

Here's an easy tortellini salad with plenty of crowd-pleasing flavors. With its light vinaigrette dressing, it's a wonderful addition to cookouts and picnics.

—MARY WILT IPSWICH, MASSACHUSETTS

PREP/TOTAL TIME: 25 MINUTES **MAKES:** 10 SERVINGS

- 1 **package (19 ounces) frozen cheese tortellini**
- 2 **cups fresh broccoli florets**
- 1 **medium sweet red pepper, chopped**
- ½ **cup pimiento-stuffed olives, halved**
- ¾ **cup reduced-fat red wine vinaigrette**
- ½ **teaspoon salt**

1. Cook tortellini according to package directions; drain and rinse in cold water.

2. In a large bowl, combine the tortellini, broccoli, red pepper and olives. Drizzle with dressing and sprinkle with salt; toss to coat. Cover and refrigerate until serving.

10 Golden Garlic Bread

PREP/TOTAL TIME: 10 MINUTES **MAKES:** 6-8 SERVINGS

- ⅓ cup butter, softened
- ¼ cup grated Parmesan cheese
- 1 to 2 garlic cloves, minced
- 1 teaspoon dried basil
- 1 loaf (1 pound) French bread, halved lengthwise

1. Combine the butter, cheese, garlic and basil; spread over cut sides of bread. Place on an ungreased baking sheet. Broil 4 in. from the heat until golden brown, about 3 minutes. Cut into 3-in. pieces.

"You can have hot homemade garlic bread any time—just top crusty bread with this buttery spread and broil for a couple of minutes."

—ANNETTE SELF JUNCTION CITY, OHIO

20 Taco Salad

Here's a fun and fresh-tasting salad that's perfect with burritos or other Mexican fare. It's nice to have taco salad for a side dish when it's as easy as this.

—KATHY YBARRA ROCK SPRINGS, WYOMING

PREP/TOTAL TIME: 15 MINUTES **MAKES:** 4-6 SERVINGS

- 6 cups chopped iceberg lettuce
- ½ cup finely chopped onion
- ¾ to 1 cup canned kidney beans, rinsed and drained
- 1½ cups (6 ounces) shredded cheddar cheese
- 1 medium tomato, chopped
- 4 cups nacho tortilla chips
- ½ cup Thousand Island salad dressing

1. In a large bowl, layer the first five ingredients in order listed. Just before serving, add chips and salad dressing; toss to coat.

 top tip When you don't have fresh garlic, substitute ¼ teaspoon of garlic powder for each clove that is called for in the recipe. You can also use ½ teaspoon jarred minced garlic instead of one clove.

20 Tomato-Green Bean Salad

Feta cheese adds a salty kick to this fuss-free salad. It tastes even better the next day, when the flavors all have a chance to blend.

—ESTELLE LAULETTA BOSTON, MASSACHUSETTS

PREP/TOTAL TIME: 20 MINUTES **MAKES:** 4 SERVINGS

- ½ **pound fresh green beans, trimmed**
- 1½ **cups cherry tomatoes, halved**
- ¾ **cup pitted ripe olives, halved**
- ¼ **cup Italian salad dressing**
- ⅔ **cup crumbled feta cheese**

1. Place beans in a large saucepan and cover with water. Bring to a boil. Cook, uncovered, for 8-10 minutes or until crisp-tender. Drain and immediately place beans in ice water. Drain and pat dry.

2. In a large bowl, combine the beans, tomatoes and olives. Drizzle with dressing; toss to coat. Chill until serving. Just before serving, sprinkle with cheese.

10 Sweet Sesame Salad

I jazz up salad greens with tomatoes, mandarin oranges and sesame seeds, then top it off with honey vinaigrette for a sweet and fruity sensation the whole family loves.

—KRISTINE MARRA CLIFTON PARK, NEW YORK

PREP/TOTAL TIME: 10 MINUTES **MAKES:** 6 SERVINGS

- 1 **package (10 ounces) ready-to-serve salad greens**
- 1 **medium tomato, cut into thin wedges**
- ⅔ **cup balsamic vinaigrette**
- 2 **teaspoons honey**
- 1 **can (11 ounces) mandarin oranges, drained**
- 1 **teaspoon sesame seeds, toasted**

1. In a salad bowl, combine greens and tomato; set aside. Whisk vinaigrette and honey; drizzle over greens. Sprinkle with oranges and sesame seeds; toss to coat. Serve immediately.

10 ▶ Carrot Raisin Salad

PREP/TOTAL TIME: 10 MINUTES
MAKES: 8 SERVINGS

- 4 **cups shredded carrots**
- ¾ **to 1½ cups raisins**
- ¼ **cup mayonnaise**
- 2 **tablespoons sugar**
- 2 **to 3 tablespoons 2% milk**

1. Place carrots and raisins in a large bowl. In a small bowl, combine the mayonnaise, sugar and enough milk to achieve dressing consistency. Pour over carrot mixture; toss to coat.

20 ▶ Microwave Broccoli and Rice

Broccoli and instant rice make a versatile side that's perfect with most entrees, and the microwave makes it super-fast!

—SHIRLEY TOCKEY
CLEVELAND, OKLAHOMA

PREP/TOTAL TIME: 15 MINUTES
MAKES: 2 SERVINGS

- ½ **cup water**
- ½ **cup uncooked instant rice**
- 2 **teaspoons butter, cut up**
- ¾ **teaspoon reduced-sodium chicken bouillon granules or ½ vegetable bouillon cube**
- ⅛ **teaspoon pepper**
- 2 **cups fresh broccoli florets**

1. In a 3-cup microwave-safe bowl, combine the water, rice, butter, bouillon and pepper. Top with broccoli florets. Cover and microwave on high for 2½ to 3 minutes or until the broccoli is tender. Let stand for 5 minutes. Stir before serving.

Editor's Note: *This recipe was tested in a 1,100-watt microwave.*

This traditional salad is one of my mother-in-law's favorites. It's fun to eat because of its crunchy texture, and the raisins give it a slightly sweet flavor. **—DENISE BAUMERT** DALHART, TEXAS

20 Speedy Sweet Potatoes

I discovered this yummy sweet potato recipe years ago. There's no need for lots of butter and sugar because the pineapple and marshmallows provide plenty of sweetness. It's a holiday favorite at our house.
—**BETH BUHLER** LAWRENCE, KANSAS

PREP/TOTAL TIME: 15 MINUTES **MAKES:** 6 SERVINGS

- 2 **cans (15¾ ounces each) sweet potatoes, drained**
- ½ **teaspoon salt**
- 1 **can (8 ounces) crushed pineapple, drained**
- ¼ **cup coarsely chopped pecans**
- 1 **tablespoon brown sugar**
- 1 **cup miniature marshmallows, divided**
  Ground nutmeg

1. In a 1½-qt. microwave-safe dish, layer sweet potatoes, salt, pineapple, pecans, brown sugar and ½ cup marshmallows. Cover and microwave on high for 3 to 6 minutes or until bubbly around the edges. Top with the remaining marshmallows.

2. Microwave, uncovered, on high for 1-2 minutes or until marshmallows puff. Sprinkle with nutmeg.

Editor's Note: *This recipe was tested in a 1,100-watt microwave.*

30 Roasted Potatoes with Thyme and Gorgonzola

Creamy Gorgonzola cheese turns this basic potato recipe into a spectacular side! Try pairing this with all your favorite entrees.
—**VIRGINIA STURM** SAN FRANCISCO, CALIFORNIA

PREP/TOTAL TIME: 30 MINUTES **MAKES:** 2 SERVINGS

- ½ **pound small red potatoes, halved**
- 1½ **teaspoons olive oil**
- 1½ **teaspoons minced fresh thyme or ½ teaspoon dried thyme**
- ⅛ **teaspoon salt**
- ⅛ **teaspoon pepper**
- 3 **tablespoons crumbled Gorgonzola cheese**

1. In a large bowl, combine the first five ingredients. Place in a greased 15-in. x 10-in. x 1-in. baking pan.

2. Bake, uncovered, at 425° for 20-25 minutes or until potatoes are tender, stirring once. Sprinkle with cheese.

20 ▶ Spicy Tomato Pasta

This zesty angel hair with fresh tomato is a great way to round out almost any meal. Pump up the Cajun seasoning to whatever level you prefer. Here's a great side to accompany grilled meat or seafood.

—**MANDI SMITH** KNOXVILLE, TENNESSEE

PREP/TOTAL TIME: 20 MINUTES **MAKES:** 5 SERVINGS

        8 ounces uncooked angel hair pasta
        1 medium tomato, chopped
        2 tablespoons olive oil
        1 tablespoon lemon juice
        ½ teaspoon Cajun seasoning
        ¼ teaspoon salt
        ¼ teaspoon pepper

1. Cook pasta according to package directions. Meanwhile, in a small bowl, combine the tomato, oil, lemon juice, Cajun seasoning, salt and pepper. Drain pasta; transfer to a serving bowl. Add tomato mixture; toss to coat.

20 ▶ Sesame Breadsticks

Try these dressed-up refrigerated breadsticks..they have a mild flavor that goes great with pasta. The family will love them, and you'll love the quick preparation.

—**TASTE OF HOME TEST KITCHEN**

PREP/TOTAL TIME: 20 MINUTES **MAKES:** 1 DOZEN

        1 tube (11 ounces) refrigerated breadsticks
        1 tablespoon butter, melted
        1 tablespoon sesame seeds, toasted
        1 to 2 teaspoons dried basil
        ¼ to ½ teaspoon cayenne pepper

1. Unroll and separate breadsticks. Twist each breadstick two to three times and place on an ungreased baking sheet; brush with butter. Combine the sesame seeds, basil and cayenne; sprinkle over breadsticks.

2. Bake at 375° for 10-12 minutes or until golden brown. Serve warm.

A refreshing medley of summer vegetables is the perfect complement to zesty dishes like barbecued meats and poultry.
—**FLORINE BRUNS** FREDERICKSBURG, TEXAS

10 Tomato Cucumber Salad

PREP/TOTAL TIME: 10 MINUTES
MAKES: 4 SERVINGS

> 2 medium cucumbers, sliced
> 1 large tomato, cut into wedges
> 1 small red onion, cut into thin strips
> ¼ cup Italian salad dressing or salad dressing of your choice

1. In a large bowl, combine the vegetables. Add salad dressing; toss to coat.

20 Creamy Italian Noodles

These zesty noodles are so rich and creamy! They're special enough to make for company, yet they're ready in just 20 minutes.
—**LINDA HENDRIX**
MOUNDVILLE, MISSOURI

PREP/TOTAL TIME: 20 MINUTES
MAKES: 4-6 SERVINGS

> 4 cups uncooked egg noodles
> ¼ cup butter, melted
> ½ cup heavy whipping cream, half-and-half cream or evaporated milk
> ¼ cup grated Parmesan cheese
> 2¼ teaspoons Italian salad dressing mix

1. Cook noodles according to package directions; drain and place in a large bowl. Drizzle with butter. Add the remaining ingredients; toss to coat.

20 Tropical Fruit Salad

PREP/TOTAL TIME: 15 MINUTES
MAKES: 6 SERVINGS

- 2 cans (15¼ ounces each) mixed tropical fruit, drained
- 1 can (11 ounces) mandarin oranges, drained
- 1 medium banana, sliced
- 1 cup miniature marshmallows
- 1½ cups (12 ounces) vanilla yogurt
- ¼ cup flaked coconut
- ¼ cup slivered almonds, toasted

1. In a large bowl, combine the tropical fruit, oranges, banana and marshmallows. Add yogurt; toss gently to coat. Sprinkle with coconut and almonds. Refrigerate until serving.

20 Macaroni Salad

This tasty dish proves you don't have to feed a crowd to enjoy that delicious picnic salad flavor. Hard-cooked egg makes it nice and hearty.
—**RUTH WIMMER** BLAND, VIRGINIA

PREP/TOTAL TIME: 20 MINUTES
MAKES: 2 SERVINGS

- 1 cup uncooked elbow macaroni
- ¼ cup mayonnaise
- 1 teaspoon sugar
- 1 teaspoon cider vinegar
- ½ teaspoon salt
- ½ teaspoon prepared mustard
  Dash pepper
- 1 celery rib, chopped
- 2 tablespoons chopped onion
- 1 hard-cooked egg, chopped

1. Cook macaroni according to package directions; drain and rinse in cold water.

2. In a small bowl, combine the mayonnaise, sugar, vinegar, salt, mustard and pepper. Stir in celery and onion. Fold in macaroni and egg. Refrigerate until serving.

When I needed a speedy salad for a luncheon, I used what I had available and everyone loved the results! Light, fluffy and full of fruit, this salad could double as a healthy dessert. You can also tuck it into the kids' lunch boxes for a fun treat.
—**TERI LINDQUIST** GURNEE, ILLINOIS

20 Creamy Mashed Potatoes

Here's an easy way to make flavorful potatoes with a melted cheese top. The potatoes are extra-creamy, thanks to the addition of cream cheese. Try it with different flavors of potatoes and cheese to create your own signature dish!

—DEBBIE PATAKY
LOOKOUT MOUNTAIN, GEORGIA

PREP/TOTAL TIME: 15 MINUTES
MAKES: 6 SERVINGS

- 3 **cups water**
- 1 **cup 2% milk**
- 1 **package (7.6 ounces) roasted garlic instant mashed potatoes**
- 4 **ounces cream cheese, cubed**
- 1 **cup (4 ounces) shredded Mexican cheese blend**

1. In a large saucepan, bring water and milk to a rolling boil. Remove from the heat. Add the contents of both envelopes from the potato package. Let stand for 1 minute; whip with a fork.

2. Place the cream cheese in a microwave-safe bowl; cover and heat at 70% power for 30 seconds or until softened. Stir into the potato mixture.

3. Transfer to a greased 1-qt. baking dish. Sprinkle with cheese. Broil 4 in. from the heat for 3-4 minutes or until cheese is melted.

Editor's Note: *This recipe was tested in a 1,100-watt microwave.*

20 Asparagus with Sesame Seeds

Dress up crisp asparagus with reduced-sodium soy sauce and sesame seeds for a simple side to complement your favorite dinner entree.

—TASTE OF HOME TEST KITCHEN

PREP/TOTAL TIME: 15 MINUTES **MAKES:** 2 SERVINGS

- ½ **pound fresh asparagus, trimmed**
- 2 **tablespoons water**
- 1 **teaspoon reduced-sodium soy sauce**
- 1 **teaspoon olive oil**
- ⅛ **teaspoon salt**
  Dash pepper
- 1 **teaspoon sesame seeds, toasted**

1. Place the asparagus in a steamer basket; place in a saucepan over 1 in. of water. Bring to a boil; cover and steam for 4-5 minutes or until crisp-tender. Transfer to a serving dish. Combine the water, soy sauce, oil, salt and pepper; drizzle over asparagus. Sprinkle with sesame seeds.

20 Parmesan Fettuccine

With only four ingredients, you'll have rich, cheesy, irresistible fettucine in no time. Try it with steak for a super treat!

—**SUNDRA HAUCK** BOGALUSA, LOUISANNA

PREP/TOTAL TIME: 20 MINUTES **MAKES:** 4 SERVINGS

- 8 **ounces uncooked fettuccine**
- ⅓ **cup butter, cubed**
- ⅓ **cup grated Parmesan cheese**
- ⅛ **teaspoon pepper**

1. Cook the fettuccine according to package directions; drain.

2. In a large skillet, melt butter over low heat. Add fettuccine and stir until coated. Sprinkle with cheese and pepper; toss to coat.

30 Cheesy Zucchini Casserole

Tender zucchini gets pleasant flavor from a creamy sauce and cracker-crumb topping. This yummy casserole is a great way to use up that bumper crop of zucchini.

—**KATHI GRENIER** AUBURN, MAINE

PREP/TOTAL TIME: 30 MINUTES **MAKES:** 6 SERVINGS

- 2½ **pounds zucchini, cubed**
- 1 **cup diced process cheese (Velveeta)**
- 2 **tablespoons butter**
- ½ **teaspoon salt**
- ⅛ **teaspoon pepper**
- ⅓ **cup crushed saltines (about 10 crackers)**

1. Place zucchini in a saucepan and cover with water; cook over medium heat until tender, about 8 minutes. Drain well. Add cheese, butter, salt and pepper; stir until the cheese is melted.

2. Transfer to a greased shallow 1½-qt. baking dish. Sprinkle with cracker crumbs. Bake, uncovered, at 400° for 10-15 minutes or until lightly browned.

10 Honey-Glazed Carrots

My mother used sugar in her glazed carrots, but a local man who keeps bees on our farm shares honey with us, so I use that instead. Sweet!

—JUDIE ANGLEN RIVERTON, WYOMING

PREP/TOTAL TIME: 10 MINUTES **MAKES:** 4 SERVINGS

- 1 **package (16 ounces) baby carrots**
- 1 **tablespoon water**
- 2 **tablespoons butter**
- 2 **tablespoons honey**
- 1 **tablespoon lemon juice**

1. Place carrots and water in a 1½-qt. microwave-safe dish. Cover and microwave on high for 3-5 minutes or until crisp-tender.

2. Meanwhile, melt butter in a skillet; stir in honey and lemon juice. Cook over low heat for 3½ minutes, stirring constantly. Add carrots; cook and stir for 1 minute or until glazed.

Editor's Note: *This recipe was tested in a 1,100-watt microwave.*

20 Favorite Crab Pasta Salad

Wanda, a friend at work, made this for a party and boy, did it catch on fast! It's especially wonderful for summer picnics and barbecues.

—CHERYL SEWERYN LEMONT, ILLINOIS

PREP/TOTAL TIME: 20 MINUTES **MAKES:** 7 SERVINGS

- 3 **cups uncooked medium pasta shells**
- 1 **pound creamy coleslaw**
- ½ **cup mayonnaise**
- 1 **tablespoon chopped onion**
- 1 **teaspoon dill weed**
  Dash salt
- 2 **cups chopped imitation crabmeat**

1. Cook pasta according to package directions. Meanwhile, in a large serving bowl, combine the coleslaw, mayonnaise, onion, dill and salt. Stir in crab.

2. Drain pasta and rinse in cold water. Add to coleslaw mixture; toss to coat. Chill until serving.

30 Mom's Potato Pancakes

Old-fashioned potato pancakes are fluffy inside and crispy outside. Mom got this recipe from Grandma, so we've enjoyed it for years.

—**DIANNE ESPOSITE** NEW MIDDLETOWN, OHIO

PREP/TOTAL TIME: 30 MINUTES **MAKES:** 6 SERVINGS

    4 cups shredded peeled potatoes (about 4 large
       potatoes)
    1 egg, lightly beaten
    3 tablespoons all-purpose flour
    1 tablespoon grated onion
    1 teaspoon salt
  ¼ teaspoon pepper
       Canola oil

1. Rinse potatoes in cold water; drain well. Place in a large bowl. Stir in the egg, flour, grated onion, salt and pepper.

2. In a skillet, heat ¼ in. of oil over medium heat. Drop batter by ⅓ cupfuls into hot oil. Flatten to form a pancake. Fry in batches until both sides are golden brown. Drain on paper towels. Serve immediately.

10 Snap Peas 'n' Mushrooms

Here's a nice change of pace from your usual green vegetable. It's delicious with chicken or glazed pork.

—**MARIE HATTRUP** SPARKS, NEVADA

PREP/TOTAL TIME: 10 MINUTES **MAKES:** 4 SERVINGS

  ½ pound fresh sugar snap peas
  1¾ cups sliced fresh mushrooms
    1 tablespoon canola oil
    1 tablespoon reduced-sodium teriyaki sauce

1. In a small skillet, stir-fry the peas and mushrooms in oil and teriyaki sauce until crisp-tender.

top tip

Leftover mashed potatoes make great potato pancakes. I blend the potatoes with one or two eggs, chopped onion, salt and pepper. Then I shape the mixture into patties and brown in oil.

—**CHRISTY C.** DEERFIELD, MICHIGAN

Put a special spin on golden crescents by filling them with Swiss cheese, green onions and Dijon mustard. Just tucking those few ingredients inside makes them feel extra-special.

—**JOY MCMILLAN** THE WOODLANDS, TEXAS

30 Swiss Onion Crescents

PREP/TOTAL TIME: 30 MINUTES
MAKES: 8 ROLLS

- 1 **tube (8 ounces) refrigerated crescent rolls**
- 3 **tablespoons shredded Swiss cheese, divided**
- 2 **tablespoons chopped green onion**
- 1½ **teaspoons Dijon mustard**

1. Unroll crescent dough and separate into eight triangles. Combine 2 tablespoons of Swiss cheese, the green onion and mustard; spread about 1 teaspoon over each triangle.

2. Roll up from the short side. Place point side down on an ungreased baking sheet and curve into a crescent shape. Sprinkle with remaining cheese. Bake at 375° for 11-13 minutes or until golden brown.

10 Easy Cran-Apple Sauce

I often whip up this sweet-tart combination as a side dish for turkey breast or roasted chicken. It's also delicious after dinner if you top each serving with a dollop of whipped cream.

—**ROMAINE WETZEL**
RONKS, PENNSYLVANIA

PREP/TOTAL TIME: 5 MINUTES
YIELD: 4-6 SERVINGS

- 1 **can (8 ounces) jellied cranberry sauce**
- 1 **jar (24 ounces) applesauce**
  Whipped cream, optional

1. In a bowl, break apart cranberry sauce with a fork. Stir in applesauce. Chill until serving. Dollop each serving with whipped cream if desired.

🔲30 Garlic Mashed Red Potatoes

PREP/TOTAL TIME: 30 MINUTES **MAKES:** 6 SERVINGS

- 8 **medium red potatoes, quartered**
- 3 **garlic cloves, peeled**
- 2 **tablespoons butter**
- ½ **cup fat-free milk, warmed**
- ½ **teaspoon salt**
- ¼ **cup grated Parmesan cheese**

1. Place potatoes and garlic in a large saucepan; cover with water. Bring to a boil. Reduce heat; cover and simmer for 15-20 minutes or until potatoes are very tender.

2. Drain well. Add the butter, milk and salt; mash. Stir in cheese.

❝ These creamy garlic mashed potatoes are so good, you can serve them plain—no butter or gravy is needed. This is the only way I make my mashed potatoes anymore. ❞

—**VALERIE MITCHELL** OLATHE, KANSAS

🔲20 Elegant Broccoli

My broccoli is extremely easy to make in the microwave, and that's especially useful when the main dish is more elaborate. Everyone who's tried it loves it!

—**SARAH SMITH** EDGEWOOD, KENTUCKY

PREP/TOTAL TIME: 15 MINUTES **MAKES:** 4 SERVINGS

- 1½ **pounds fresh broccoli, cut into florets**
- ¼ **cup water**
- ⅓ **cup mayonnaise**
- ¼ **cup shredded cheddar cheese**
- 1 **tablespoon lemon juice**
- 1 **tablespoon Dijon mustard**
  Dash cayenne pepper

1. Place broccoli and water in a large microwave-safe bowl. Cover and microwave on high for 3-4 minutes or until tender; drain and keep warm.

2. For sauce, in a microwave-safe bowl, combine the remaining ingredients. Cover and microwave on high for 1-2 minutes or until warmed, stirring once. Serve over broccoli.

Editor's Note: *This recipe was tested in a 1,100-watt microwave.*

20 Garlic Parmesan Asparagus

Pair my garlicky asparagus with any entree for a memorable meal. We especially enjoy this with a simple baked salmon.

—TARA ERNSPIKER FALLING WATERS, WEST VIRGINIA

PREP/TOTAL TIME: 15 MINUTES **MAKES:** 4 SERVINGS

- ½ cup water
- 1 pound fresh asparagus, trimmed
- 1 teaspoon minced garlic
- 2 tablespoons butter, melted
- 1 tablespoon grated Parmesan cheese

1. In a large skillet, bring water to a boil. Add asparagus and garlic. Cover and cook for 5-7 minutes or until crisp-tender; drain. Drizzle with butter. Sprinkle with cheese; gently toss to coat.

30 Like-Homemade Baked Beans

Looking for a speedy way to jazz up canned pork and beans? Try giving them homemade flavor with bacon, onion, and brown sugar. This dish is a real people-pleaser at picnics and backyard barbecues.

—SUE THOMAS CASA GRANDE, ARIZONA

PREP/TOTAL TIME: 25 MINUTES **MAKES:** 3 SERVINGS

- 2 bacon strips, diced
- ½ cup chopped onion
- 1 can (15¾ ounces) pork and beans
- 2 tablespoons brown sugar
- 1½ teaspoons Worcestershire sauce
- ½ teaspoon ground mustard

1. In a large skillet, cook bacon until crisp. Add onion; cook until tender. Add remaining ingredients. Reduce heat; cook and stir for 10 minutes or until heated through.

10 Pesto Corn

This is one of my very favorite comfort foods. The bright flavor of pesto brings out the natural sweetness of corn.

—LAURIE BOCK LYNDEN, WASHINGTON

PREP/TOTAL TIME: 10 MINUTES **MAKES:** 3 SERVINGS

- 1 package (16 ounces) frozen corn, thawed
- ¾ cup shredded sharp cheddar cheese
- 1 tablespoon prepared pesto

1. In a small microwave-safe dish, combine all ingredients. Cover and cook on high for 2-3 minutes or until heated through.

Editor's Note: *This recipe was tested in a 1,100-watt microwave.*

10 Dijon-Walnut Spinach Salad

This favorite of ours has a great fresh taste, lots of different textures, and can be tossed together in a heartbeat. For variety, change up the dressing to a flavor of your choice.

—CHRIS DEMONTRAVEL
MOHEGAN LAKE, NEW YORK

PREP/TOTAL TIME: 10 MINUTES
MAKES: 13 SERVINGS

- 1 **package (9 ounces) fresh baby spinach**
- 1 **package (4 ounces) crumbled feta cheese**
- 1 **cup dried cranberries**
- 1 **cup walnut halves, toasted**
- ½ **cup honey Dijon vinaigrette**

1. In a salad bowl, combine the spinach, cheese, cranberries and walnuts. Drizzle with vinaigrette; toss to coat. Serve immediately.

30 Golden Potatoes

I like to serve this fancy-looking side dish to company because it looks like I fussed to make it.

—CARLA CAGLE
MARCELINE, MISSOURI

PREP/TOTAL TIME: 30 MINUTES
MAKES: 4-6 SERVINGS

- 2 **cans (15 ounces each) whole white potatoes, drained**
- ¼ **cup butter, melted**
- ½ **teaspoon seasoned salt**
- 2 **to 3 tablespoons grated Parmesan cheese**
- 1 **tablespoon minced fresh parsley**

1. Place potatoes in an ungreased 8-in. square baking dish. Pour butter over potatoes. Sprinkle with seasoned salt, cheese and parsley. Bake, uncovered, at 350° for 25 minutes or until potatoes are golden brown.

30 Parmesan Corn on the Cob

Here's an easy way to season fresh corn on the cob. Try it with steaks or your favorite grilled sausages. Your family will enjoy it.

—SUZANNE MCKINLEY LYONS, GEORGIA

PREP/TOTAL TIME: 25 MINUTES **MAKES:** 4 SERVINGS

- ¼ **cup butter, melted**
- ¼ **cup grated Parmesan cheese**
- ½ **teaspoon Italian seasoning**
- 4 **ears corn on the cob**
- ¼ **cup water**
  Salt to taste

1. In a small bowl, combine the butter, cheese and Italian seasoning; set aside. Remove husks and silk from corn; place in a shallow microwave-safe dish. Add water. Cover and microwave on high for 7-10 minutes, turning once. Let stand for 5 minutes; drain. Brush with butter mixture; sprinkle with salt.

Editor's Note: *This recipe was tested in a 1,100-watt microwave.*

20 Black-Eyed Pea Salad

PREP/TOTAL TIME: 15 MINUTES
MAKES: 4 SERVINGS

- 1 can (15½ ounces) black-eyed peas, rinsed and drained
- 1 celery rib, chopped
- 1 tablespoon finely chopped onion
- 1 tablespoon canola oil
- 1 tablespoon cider vinegar
- 1 tablespoon reduced-fat mayonnaise
- ¼ teaspoon salt
  Dash cayenne pepper
- 1 medium tomato, chopped

1. In a large bowl, combine the peas, celery and onion.

2. In a small bowl, whisk the oil, vinegar, mayonnaise, salt and cayenne. Stir into vegetable mixture. Chill until serving. Stir in tomato just before serving.

10 Tomatoes with Feta Cheese

I make this no-fuss side salad at least once a month. It's a great way to use up summer tomatoes and fresh basil from the garden.
—RUTH LEE TROY, ONTARIO

PREP/TOTAL TIME: 5 MINUTES
MAKES: 4 SERVINGS

- 8 slices tomato
- 2 tablespoons crumbled feta cheese
- 1 tablespoon balsamic vinegar
- 2 tablespoons minced fresh basil
  Pepper to taste

1. Arrange tomato slices on a serving plate. Sprinkle with feta cheese. Drizzle with vinegar; sprinkle with basil and pepper.

A homemade dressing marries the flavors of my unique salad. It's a nice contribution to a spring luncheon or barbeque buffet in the summertime. **—OLIVE FOEMMEL** CHILI, WISCONSIN

30▶ Skillet Sweet Potatoes

These delicious sweet potatoes bring a bright citrusy flavor to your plate. Their subtle, more delicate sweetness is a refreshing change from candied yams.

—TASTE OF HOME TEST KITCHEN

PREP/TOTAL TIME: 25 MINUTES **MAKES:** 3 SERVINGS

- 1 **pound sweet potatoes, peeled and cut into ½-inch slices**
- ½ **cup orange juice**
- 1 **tablespoon butter**
- ½ **teaspoon grated orange peel**
- ¼ **teaspoon pumpkin pie spice**

1. Place sweet potatoes in a small saucepan and cover with water. Bring to a boil. Reduce heat; cover and simmer for 4-6 minutes or just until tender.

2. Meanwhile, in a small skillet, bring the orange juice, butter, orange peel and pie spice to a boil. Reduce heat; simmer, uncovered, for 3-4 minutes or until thickened. Drain sweet potatoes; return to pan. Pour glaze over potatoes and stir gently to coat.

20▶ Couscous with Mushrooms

I use couscous a lot because it cooks quickly and is so versatile—you can add almost any vegetable to it.

—CLAUDIA RUISS MASSAPEQUA, NEW YORK

PREP/TOTAL TIME: 15 MINUTES **MAKES:** 4 SERVINGS

- 1¼ **cups water**
- 2 **tablespoons butter**
- 2 **teaspoons chicken bouillon granules**
- ¼ **teaspoon salt**
- ¼ **teaspoon pepper**
- 1 **cup uncooked couscous**
- 1 **can (7 ounces) mushroom stems and pieces, drained**

1. In a large saucepan, bring the water, butter, bouillon, salt and pepper to a boil. Stir in couscous and mushrooms.

2. Cover and remove from the heat; let stand for 5 minutes. Fluff with a fork.

20 Vegetables with Cheese Sauce

Even picky eaters like vegetables in yummy cheese sauce. The sauce is great with other veggies, too, like summer squash or potatoes.

—CRYSTAL SHECKLES-GIBSON BEESPRING, KENTUCKY

PREP/TOTAL TIME: 15 MINUTES **MAKES:** 6 SERVINGS

- **2 packages (16 ounces each) frozen California-blend vegetables**
- **1 package (8 ounces) process cheese (Velveeta), cubed**
- **3 tablespoons milk**

1. Microwave vegetable blend according to package directions. In a small saucepan, combine cheese and milk. Cook and stir over low heat until melted. Serve with vegetables.

20 Dilled Noodles

I tried these noodles the first year I had an herb garden, when I was looking for recipes that call for fresh herbs. We even like the noodles with hot dogs and hamburgers.

—ANNA PRENNI SALTSBURG, PENNSYLVANIA

PREP/TOTAL TIME: 20 MINUTES **MAKES:** 2 SERVINGS

- **1½ cups uncooked egg noodles**
- **½ cup 4% cottage cheese**
- **1 to 2 tablespoons snipped fresh dill or 1 to 2 teaspoons dill weed**
- **¼ teaspoon salt**
  Dash pepper

1. In a large saucepan, cook noodles according to package directions. Meanwhile, combine the remaining ingredients. Drain noodles; add to cottage cheese mixture and toss gently.

135

141

180

Gatherings

❝ I've been making this recipe for as long as I can remember...and every time that I have a party. It's simple, doesn't take a lot of ingredients or preparation, and is always a favorite with guests.❞

CAREN ADAMS FONTANA, CALIFORNIA
about her recipe, Grilled Jerk Chicken Wings, on page 141

Chocolate Fudge Cake

I first made this cake in my junior high home economics class. I've changed the recipe through the years to make the cake a little richer, and the homemade chocolate frosting is my own creation.

—**KATARINA GREER** VICTORIA, BRITISH COLUMBIA

PREP: 30 MINUTES **BAKE:** 25 MINUTES + COOLING
MAKES: 16-20 SERVINGS

- ½ cup butter, softened
- 1¼ cups packed brown sugar
- 1 egg
- 1 teaspoon vanilla extract
- 1½ cups all-purpose flour
- 6 tablespoons baking cocoa
- 1½ teaspoons cream of tartar
- 1 teaspoon baking soda
- 1 teaspoon baking powder
- ¼ teaspoon salt
- ¾ cup water
- ½ cup milk

FROSTING

- ½ cup butter, softened
- 1 cup confectioners' sugar
- ¼ cup baking cocoa
- 1 to 2 tablespoons milk
- 1 can (16 ounces) vanilla frosting

1. Grease a 13-in. x 9-in. baking pan; line with parchment paper. Grease the paper; set aside. In a large bowl, cream butter and brown sugar. Beat in egg and vanilla. Combine the flour, cocoa, cream of tartar, baking soda, baking powder and salt; add to creamed mixture alternately with water and milk, beating well after each addition.

2. Pour into prepared pan. Bake at 350° for 22-27 minutes or until a toothpick inserted near the center comes out clean. Cool for 10 minutes before inverting onto a wire rack. Discard parchment paper. Cool cake completely.

3. For frosting, in a large bowl, beat the butter, confectioners' sugar and cocoa until smooth. Beat in enough milk to achieve spreading consistency. Transfer cake to a serving platter. Spread with chocolate frosting; decorate with vanilla frosting.

Basketball Cake

You don't need a special pan to make this fun cake. It scored big points at a dinner held for the church basketball team my husband coached!

—**LONNA LICCINI** CLIFTON, VIRGINIA

PREP: 20 MINUTES **BAKE:** 1 HOUR + COOLING
MAKES: 12-16 SERVINGS

- 1 package (18¼ ounces) chocolate cake mix
- 1½ cups canned vanilla frosting
  Orange paste food coloring
- 4 pieces black shoestring licorice

1. Prepare cake batter according to package directions. Pour into a greased and floured 2½-qt. ovenproof bowl.

2. Bake at 350° for 60-70 minutes or until a toothpick inserted near the center comes out clean. Cool for 10 minutes before removing from bowl to a wire rack to cool completely.

3. In a small bowl, combine frosting and food coloring. Place cake on a serving plate. Spread with frosting. Gently press a meat mallet into frosting so texture resembles a basketball. For seams, gently press licorice into frosting.

Brownie-filled ice cream cones are a fun addition to any summer get-together. They appeal to the child in everyone! —**MITZI SENTIFF** ANNAPOLIS, MARYLAND

Brownie Cones

PREP: 10 MINUTES
BAKE: 25 MINUTES + COOLING
MAKES: 17 SERVINGS

- 1 package fudge brownie mix (13-inch x 9-inch pan size)
- 17 ice cream cake cones (about 3 inches tall)
- 1 cup (6 ounces) semisweet chocolate chips
- 1 tablespoon shortening
  Colored sprinkles

1. Prepare brownie batter according to package directions, using 3 eggs. Place the ice cream cones in muffin cups; spoon about 3 tablespoons batter into each cone.

2. Bake at 350° for 25-30 minutes or until a toothpick comes out clean and tops are dry (do not overbake). Cool completely.

3. In a microwave, melt chocolate chips and shortening; stir until smooth. Dip tops of brownies in melted chocolate; allow excess to drip off. Decorate with sprinkles.

Editor's Note: *This recipe was tested with Keebler ice cream cups. These brownie cones are best served the day they're prepared.*

Cream-Filled Cupcakes

These chocolate cupcakes have a fun filling and shiny chocolate frosting that make them extra-special.

—KATHY KITTELL LENEXA, KANSAS

PREP: 20 MINUTES
BAKE: 15 MINUTES + COOLING
MAKES: 2 DOZEN

- 1 **package (18¼ ounces) devil's food cake mix**
- 2 **teaspoons hot water**
- ¼ **teaspoon salt**
- 1 **jar (7 ounces) marshmallow creme**
- ½ **cup shortening**
- ⅓ **cup confectioners' sugar**
- ½ **teaspoon vanilla extract**

GANACHE FROSTING
- 1 **cup (6 ounces) semisweet chocolate chips**
- ¾ **cup heavy whipping cream**

1. Prepare and bake cake batter according to package directions for cupcakes. Cool for 5 minutes before removing from pans to wire racks to cool completely.

2. For filling, in a small bowl, combine water and salt until salt is dissolved. Cool. In a small bowl, beat the marshmallow creme, shortening, confectioners' sugar and vanilla until light and fluffy; beat in salt mixture.

3. Cut a small hole in the corner of a pastry or plastic bag; insert round pastry tip. Fill the bag with cream filling. Push the tip through the bottom of paper liner to fill each cupcake.

4. Place chocolate chips in a small bowl. In a saucepan, bring cream just to a boil. Pour over chocolate; whisk until smooth. Cool, stirring occasionally, to room temperature or until dipping consistency.

5. Dip cupcake tops in ganache; chill for 20 minutes or until set. Store in the refrigerator.

Butterfly Cake

The colorful cake we created will set taste buds aflutter and give your next warm-weather gathering a bright lift!

—TASTE OF HOME TEST KITCHEN

PREP: 30 MINUTES **BAKE:** 25 MINUTES + STANDING **MAKES:** 8 SERVINGS

- 1 **package (18¼ ounces) yellow cake mix**
- 1 **individual cream-filled sponge cake**
- 1 **can (16 ounces) chocolate frosting**
   Red shoestring licorice
   Assorted candies of your choice

1. Prepare cake batter according to package directions, using two greased and floured 9-in. round baking pans. Bake at 350° for 25-30 minutes or until a toothpick inserted near the center comes out clean. Cool for 10 minutes before removing cakes from pans to wire racks to cool completely.

2. Cut one cake in half widthwise. (Save the second cake for another use.) Cut a notch from the center of each cut side to define outer edges of wings. Cut corners of wings so they are slightly rounded. Let cake stand for 2 hours.

3. On a serving platter, position cake halves on each side of sponge cake. Frost top and sides of butterfly with chocolate frosting. Cut licorice into two small pieces; push ends into top of sponge cake for antennae. Decorate with candies.

Caramel Apple Cupcakes

Bring these extra-special cupcakes to your next event and watch how quickly they disappear! Kids will go for the fun appearance and tasty toppings, while adults will appreciate the tender spice cake underneath.

—DIANE HALFERTY CORPUS CHRISTI, TEXAS

PREP: 25 MINUTES **BAKE:** 20 MINUTES + COOLING
MAKES: 1 DOZEN

- 1 **package (18¼ ounces) spice cake mix or 1 package (18 ounces) carrot cake mix**
- 2 **cups chopped peeled tart apples**
- 20 **caramels**
- 3 **tablespoons 2% milk**
- 1 **cup finely chopped pecans, toasted**
- 12 **Popsicle sticks**

1. Prepare cake batter according to package directions; fold in apples.

2. Fill 12 greased or paper-lined jumbo muffin cups three-fourths full. Bake at 350° for 20 minutes or until a toothpick inserted near the center comes out clean. Cool for 10 minutes before removing from pans to wire racks to cool completely.

3. In a small saucepan, cook the caramels and milk over low heat until smooth. Spread over cupcakes. Sprinkle with pecans. Insert a wooden stick into the center of each cupcake.

Circus Cake

Ideal for a child's party, this whimsical cake steals the show with its fluffy cotton-candy topping and cute cookie-laced sides.

—TASTE OF HOME TEST KITCHEN

PREP: 30 MINUTES **BAKE:** 25 MINUTES + COOLING
MAKES: 12 SERVINGS

- 1 **package (18¼ ounces) white cake mix**
- 1 **can (16 ounces) vanilla frosting**
  Nerds candies
  Miniature chocolate cream-filled chocolate sandwich cookies
  Frosted animal crackers
  Miniature marshmallows
  Cotton candy
  Lollipops

1. Prepare and bake cake according to package directions, using two greased 9-in. round baking pans. Cool for 10 minutes before removing from pans to wire racks to cool completely.

2. Spread frosting between layers and over top and sides of cake. Lightly press the Nerds, sandwich cookies and animal crackers onto sides of cake. Arrange marshmallows along edge of cake. Just before serving, arrange cotton candy and lollipops on top of cake.

This popular taco soup offers a bright assortment of colors and flavors. Garnish with shredded cheese, sour cream or sliced jalapenos if you like.
—**JENNIFER VILLARREAL** TEXAS CITY, TEXAS

30 Taco Soup

PREP/TOTAL TIME: 25 MINUTES
MAKES: 8 SERVINGS (ABOUT 2 QUARTS)

> 1½ **pounds ground beef**
> 1 **envelope taco seasoning**
> 2 **cans (15¼ ounces each) whole kernel corn, undrained**
> 2 **cans (15 ounces each) Ranch Style beans (pinto beans in seasoned tomato sauce)**
> 2 **cans (14½ ounces each) diced tomatoes, undrained**
>   **Tortilla chips and shredded cheddar cheese**

1. In a Dutch oven, cook beef over medium heat until no longer pink; drain. Stir in the taco seasoning, corn, beans and tomatoes. Cook and stir until heated through.

2. Place tortilla chips in soup bowls; ladle soup over top. Sprinkle with cheese.

10 Beer Margaritas

There's nothing more refreshing than this cool combination of two popular drinks, beer and margaritas.
—**TASTE OF HOME TEST KITCHEN**

PREP/TOTAL TIME: 10 MINUTES
MAKES: 4 SERVINGS

> ¾ **cup thawed limeade concentrate**
> 1 **bottle (12 ounces) beer**
> ¾ **cup vodka**
> ¾ **cup water**
>   **Ice cubes, optional**
> **GARNISH**
>   **Lime slices**

1. In a pitcher, combine the limeade concentrate, beer, vodka and water. Serve over ice if desired in pilsner or highball glasses. Garnish as desired.

Editor's Note: *This recipe was tested with Corona beer.*

10 Pumpernickel Turkey Hero

A friend brought this loaf to a sandwich luncheon. I asked for the recipe so I could serve it to my family, and they liked it, too!

—**MILDRED SHERRER** BAY CITY, TEXAS

PREP/TOTAL TIME: 10 MINUTES
MAKES: 6 SERVINGS

- 1 loaf (1 pound) unsliced pumpernickel bread
- ⅓ cup Thousand Island salad dressing
- 6 lettuce leaves
- 2 medium tomatoes, sliced
- 3 slices red onion, separated into rings
- 6 slices Swiss cheese
- 1 package (12 ounces) thinly sliced deli turkey

1. Cut bread in half horizontally; spread salad dressing over cut sides. On the bottom half, layer the lettuce, tomatoes, onion, half of the cheese and half of the turkey. Top with remaining cheese and turkey. Replace bread top. Cut sandwich into wedges.

Picnic Fruit Punch

This fruity cooler is delicious and thirst-quenching on a warm day.

—**MARION LOWERY**
MEDFORD, OREGON

PREP: 10 MINUTES + CHILLING
MAKES: 5 QUARTS

- 8 cups cranberry juice
- 3 cups pineapple juice
- 3 cups orange juice
- ¼ cup lemon juice
- 1 liter ginger ale, chilled
- 1 medium navel orange, sliced

1. In a large container, combine juices; refrigerate until chilled. Just before serving, stir in ginger ale and orange slices.

10 Beer Dip

Here's a rich and cheesy dip that's made to go with pretzels. It's one of those snacks that when you start eating it, you just can't stop!

—**MICHELLE LONG** NEW CASTLE, COLORADO

PREP/TOTAL TIME: 5 MINUTES **MAKES:** 3½ CUPS

- 2 packages (8 ounces each) cream cheese, softened
- ⅓ cup beer or nonalcoholic beer
- 1 envelope ranch salad dressing mix
- 2 cups (8 ounces) shredded cheddar cheese
  Pretzels

1. In a large bowl, beat the cream cheese, beer and dressing mix until smooth. Stir in cheddar cheese. Serve with pretzels.

10 Beary Good Snack Mix

My family loves to hike and be outdoors, and we take this snack mix along for a boost of energy.

—DORIS WEDIG ELKHORN, WISCONSIN

PREP/TOTAL TIME: 10 MINUTES **MAKES:** 10 CUPS

- 1 **package (10 ounces) honey bear-shaped crackers (about 4 cups)**
- 1 **package (7 ounces) dried banana chips (about 2 cups)**
- 2 **cups M&M's**
- 1 **cup salted peanuts**
- 1 **cup dried cranberries**

1. In a large bowl, combine all ingredients. Store in an airtight container.

30 Vegetarian Sloppy Joes

The meat won't even be missed in this tangy vegetarian version of sloppy joes.

—LINDA WINTER OAK HARBOR, WASHINGTON

PREP/TOTAL TIME: 25 MINUTES **MAKES:** 6 SERVINGS

- 1 **small onion, finely chopped**
- 2 **teaspoons butter**
- 1 **package (12 ounces) frozen vegetarian meat crumbles**
- ½ **teaspoon pepper**
- 2 **tablespoons all-purpose flour**
- 1 **can (8 ounces) no-salt-added tomato sauce**
- ⅔ **cup ketchup**
- 6 **hamburger buns, split and toasted**

1. In a large nonstick skillet coated with cooking spray, saute onion in butter until tender. Stir in meat crumbles and pepper; heat through.

2. Sprinkle flour over mixture and stir until blended. Stir in tomato sauce and ketchup. Bring to a boil; cook and stir for 1-2 minutes or until thickened. Spoon ½ cup onto each bun.

Editor's Note: *Vegetarian meat crumbles are a nutritious protein source made from soy. Look for them in the natural foods freezer section.*

> I've been making this recipe for as long as I can remember...and every time that I have a party. It's simple, doesn't take a lot of ingredients or preparation, and is always a favorite with guests.
> —**CAREN ADAMS** FONTANA, CALIFORNIA

30 Grilled Jerk Chicken Wings

PREP/TOTAL TIME: 30 MINUTES
MAKES: ABOUT 2 DOZEN

- ½ cup Caribbean jerk seasoning
- 2½ pounds chicken wingettes and drumettes
- 2 cups honey barbecue sauce
- ⅓ cup packed brown sugar
- 2 teaspoons prepared mustard
- 1 teaspoon ground ginger

1. Place jerk seasoning in a large resealable plastic bag; add chicken, a few pieces at a time, and shake to coat. In a small bowl, combine the barbecue sauce, brown sugar, mustard and ginger; set aside.

2. Moisten a paper towel with cooking oil; using long-handled tongs, lightly coat the grill rack. Grill chicken wings, covered, over medium heat or broil 4 in. from the heat for 12-16 minutes, turning occasionally.

3. Brush with sauce mixture. Grill or broil 8-10 minutes longer or until juices run clear, basting and turning several times.

Editor's Note: *Caribbean jerk seasoning may be found in the spice aisle of your grocery store.*

30 Deluxe Nachos

Topped with a warm, cheesy sauce, fresh veggies and sour cream, my quick nacho platters will delight family and friends.

—**JENNIFER PARHAM** BROWNS SUMMIT, NORTH CAROLINA

PREP/TOTAL TIME: 30 MINUTES
MAKES: 8 SERVINGS

- 2 **cans (10¾ ounces each) condensed cheddar cheese soup, undiluted**
- 1 **cup salsa**
- 2 **packages (10 ounces each) tortilla chips**
- 2 **to 4 plum tomatoes, chopped**
- 1 **medium green pepper, chopped**
- 1 **medium sweet red pepper, chopped**
- 4 **to 6 green onions, sliced**
- 2 **cans (2¼ ounces each) sliced ripe olives, drained**
- 1 **cup (8 ounces) sour cream**

1. In a small saucepan, combine soup and salsa; heat through. Arrange tortilla chips on two serving platters; top with soup mixture. Sprinkle with the tomatoes, peppers, onions and olives. Top with sour cream. Serve immediately.

30 Chicken Artichoke Pizzas

PREP/TOTAL TIME: 25 MINUTES
MAKES: 2 PIZZAS (12 SLICES EACH)

- 1 **can (14 ounces) water-packed artichoke hearts, rinsed, drained and chopped**
- 3 **cups (12 ounces) shredded pepper jack cheese, divided**
- 1½ **cups cubed cooked chicken breast**
- 1 **can (4 ounces) chopped green chilies**
- ¼ **cup mayonnaise**
- ¼ **cup sour cream**
- 1 **envelope Italian salad dressing mix**
- 2 **prebaked 12-inch thin pizza crusts**

1. In a large bowl, combine the artichokes, 1 cup cheese, chicken, chilies, mayonnaise, sour cream and salad dressing mix. Place crusts on pizza pans; spread with artichoke mixture. Sprinkle remaining cheese over the tops.

2. Bake at 450° for 10-14 minutes or until bubbly.

30 Reuben Roll-Ups

This recipe turns the popular Reuben sandwich into an interesting and hearty snack. We love these roll-ups at our house.

—**PATRICIA KILE** ELIZABETHTOWN, PENNSYLVANIA

PREP/TOTAL TIME: 30 MINUTES **MAKES:** 8 ROLL-UPS

- 1 **tube (13.8 ounces) refrigerated pizza crust**
- 1 **cup sauerkraut, well drained**
- 1 **tablespoon Thousand Island salad dressing**
- 4 **slices corned beef, halved**
- 4 **slices Swiss cheese, halved**

1. Roll dough into a 12-in. x 9-in. rectangle. Cut into eight 3-in. x 4½-in. rectangles. Combine sauerkraut and salad dressing. Place a slice of beef on each rectangle. Top with about 2 tablespoons of the sauerkraut mixture and a slice of cheese. Roll up.

2. Place seam side down on a greased baking sheet. Bake at 425° for 12-14 minutes or until golden.

66 Your guests will love the cheesy goodness of this pleasing pizza. Pepper jack cheese and green chilies give it a little kick. 99

—**PAULA GYLLAND** BROOKFIELD, WISCONSIN

20 Orange-Glazed Smokies

I can whip up these tasty sausages in a matter of minutes for parties, and the tangy citrus sauce is an instant conversation starter.

—JUDY WILSON SUN CITY WEST, ARIZONA

PREP/TOTAL TIME: 15 MINUTES
MAKES: ABOUT 4 DOZEN

  1 **cup packed brown sugar**
  1 **tablespoon all-purpose flour**
  ¼ **cup thawed orange juice concentrate**
  2 **tablespoons prepared mustard**
  1 **tablespoon cider vinegar**
  1 **package (16 ounces) miniature smoked sausages**

1. In a large microwave-safe bowl, combine the first five ingredients. Add sausages; stir to coat.

2. Cover and microwave on high for 3-4 minutes or until bubbly, stirring three times.

Editor's Note: *This recipe was tested in a 1,100-watt microwave.*

20 Mini Ham 'n' Cheese Pizzas

With ham, cheese and creamy Alfredo sauce, our little pizzas are sure to please. Best of all, they're kid-friendly!

—TASTE OF HOME TEST KITCHEN

PREP/TOTAL TIME: 20 MINUTES
MAKES: 4 SERVINGS

  ¼ **cup refrigerated Alfredo sauce**
  4 **pita breads (6 inches)**
  1 **cup (4 ounces) shredded Swiss cheese**
1¾ **cups cubed fully cooked ham**
  ½ **cup shredded part-skim mozzarella cheese**
  1 **tablespoon minced chives**

1. Spread Alfredo sauce over pita breads. Top with Swiss cheese, ham, mozzarella cheese and chives.

2. Place on an ungreased baking sheet. Bake at 350° for 10-15 minutes or until cheese is melted.

10 ▶ Topsy-Turvy Sangria

Sangria is the perfect drink for casual get-togethers. It's even better if you make it the night before and let the flavors blend. But be careful—it goes down easy!

—TRACY FIELD
BREMERTON, WASHINGTON

PREP/TOTAL TIME: 10 MINUTES
MAKES: 10 SERVINGS (¾ CUP EACH)

- 1 bottle (750 milliliters) merlot
- 1 cup sugar
- 1 cup orange liqueur
- ½ to 1 cup brandy
- 3 cups lemon-lime soda, chilled
- 1 cup sliced fresh strawberries
- 1 medium lemon, sliced
- 1 medium orange, sliced
- 1 medium peach, sliced
  Ice cubes

1. In a pitcher, stir the wine, sugar, orange liqueur and brandy until sugar is dissolved. Stir in soda and fruit. Serve over ice.

20 ▶ Greek Garden Appetizer

This impressive dip is perfect for summer gatherings. It's a snap to whip up and tastes great with pita pockets.

—DEL MASON MARTENSVILLE, SASKATCHEWAN

PREP/TOTAL TIME: 15 MINUTES **YIELD:** 4 CUPS

- 1 carton (8 ounces) spreadable garden vegetable cream cheese
- 2 cups (8 ounces) crumbled feta cheese
- ¼ cup plain yogurt
- ½ teaspoon minced garlic
- ¼ teaspoon dried oregano
- ¼ teaspoon pepper
- 1½ cups chopped cucumber
- 1 cup chopped seeded tomatoes
- ¼ cup chopped green onions
- 2 tablespoons sliced ripe olives
  Miniature pita pockets

top tip

Be sure to allow cheese balls and dips and spreads that contain cream cheese to stand at room temperature for 15 minutes before serving time. They will be easier to spread and will have a more pronounced flavor.

1. In a large bowl, combine the cream cheese, feta, yogurt, garlic, oregano and pepper. Spread into a 9-in. pie plate. Sprinkle the cucumber, tomatoes, onions and olives over the cream cheese mixture. Serve with pita bread. Refrigerate leftovers.

30 Game-Day Bratwurst

PREP/TOTAL TIME: 25 MINUTES
MAKES: 6 SERVINGS

- 6 **fully cooked bratwurst links**
- ¾ **cup sauerkraut, rinsed and well drained**
- 6 **tablespoons French salad dressing**
- 6 **tablespoons shredded Monterey Jack cheese**
- 6 **brat buns, split**

1. Make a lengthwise slit three-fourths of the way through each bratwurst to within ½ in. of each end. Fill with sauerkraut; top with dressing and cheese.

2. Place bratwurst in buns; wrap each in a double thickness of foil. Grill, covered, over medium-hot heat 15 minutes or until heated through.

20 Hot Dogs with the Works

These grilled hot dogs are easy and fun to take anywhere.

MARIA REGAKIS
SOMERVILLE, MASSACHUSETTS

PREP/TOTAL TIME: 15 MINUTES
MAKES: 8 SERVINGS

- 1½ **cups (6 ounces) shredded pepper jack cheese**
- ¾ **cup chopped tomato**
- 3 **tablespoons chopped onion**
- 2 **tablespoons pickle relish**
- 8 **hot dogs**
- 8 **hot dog buns**

1. Combine cheese, tomato, onion and relish. Place hot dogs in buns; top with cheese mixture.

2. Wrap each hot dog in a double thickness of foil. Grill, covered, over medium-hot heat for 8-10 minutes or until heated through. Open foil carefully to allow steam to escape.

Looking for a twist on the usual tailgate fare? With French dressing and Monterey Jack cheese, these brats kick things up a notch! Instead of bratwurst, you can make the recipe with cooked Italian sausage links if you prefer. —**LAURA MCDOWELL** LAKE VILLA, ILLINOIS

30 Buffalo-Style Snack Mix

I like to dress up popcorn with corn chips and peanuts. The hot sauce adds a little kick that no one can resist.
—**DEIRDRE DEE COX** KANSAS CITY, KANSAS

PREP/TOTAL TIME: 25 MINUTES **MAKES:** 2½ QUARTS

- 2½ quarts popped popcorn, divided
- 2 cups corn chips
- 1 cup dry roasted peanuts
- ¼ cup butter, cubed
- 2 tablespoons Louisiana-style hot sauce
- 1 teaspoon celery seed

1. In a large bowl, combine 2 cups popcorn, corn chips and peanuts. In a small saucepan, melt butter; add hot sauce and celery seed. Remove from the heat. Pour over popcorn mixture and toss to coat.

2. Transfer to a greased 15-in. x 10-in. x 1-in. baking pan. Bake at 350° for 10-15 minutes or until crisp. Place in a large bowl; add remaining popcorn and toss to coat. Store in an airtight container.

20 Snackers

These crispy, chewy treats pack lots of peanut flavor. They're our favorite travel snack. I always make a double batch so we have some left when we reach our destination.
—**W.H. GREGORY** ROANOKE, VIRGINIA

PREP/TOTAL TIME: 20 MINUTES
MAKES: ABOUT 1½ DOZEN

- 3 cups Crispix cereal
- ½ cup salted peanuts
- ⅓ cup packed brown sugar
- ⅓ cup corn syrup
- ¼ cup peanut butter

1. In a large bowl, combine cereal and peanuts; set aside. In a microwave-safe bowl, combine brown sugar and corn syrup. Microwave on high for 30-60 seconds or until sugar is dissolved, stirring several times. Immediately stir in peanut butter until smooth. Pour over cereal mixture and toss to coat. Drop by rounded tablespoonfuls onto waxed paper. Let stand until set.

Editor's Note: *This recipe was tested in a 1,100-watt microwave.*

30 Chipotle Sliders

Here is the ultimate in fast-fixing mini burgers! Creamy mayo, cheese and sweet Hawaiian rolls help tame the heat of the chipotle peppers.

—**SHAWN SINGLETON** VIDOR, TEXAS

PREP/TOTAL TIME: 30 MINUTES
MAKES: 10 SLIDERS

- 1 package (12 ounces) Hawaiian sweet rolls, divided
- 1 teaspoon salt
- ½ teaspoon pepper
- 8 teaspoons minced chipotle peppers in adobo sauce, divided
- 1½ pounds ground beef
- 10 slices pepper jack cheese
- ½ cup mayonnaise

1. Place 2 rolls in a food processor; process until crumbly. Transfer to a large bowl; add the salt, pepper and 6 teaspoons chipotle peppers. Crumble beef over mixture and mix well. Shape into 10 patties.

2. Grill burgers, covered, over medium heat for 3-4 minutes on each side or until a thermometer reads 160° and juices run clear. Top with cheese. Grill 1 minute longer or until cheese is melted.

3. Split remaining rolls and grill, cut side down, over medium heat for 30-60 seconds or until toasted. Combine mayonnaise and remaining chipotle peppers; spread over roll bottoms. Top each with a burger. Replace roll tops.

20 Shrimp Spread

People will never know that you used lighter ingredients in this rich and crowd-pleasing shrimp appetizer.

—**NORENE WRIGHT** MANILLA, INDIANA

PREP/TOTAL TIME: 15 MINUTES **MAKES:** 20 SERVINGS

- 1 package (8 ounces) reduced-fat cream cheese
- ½ cup reduced-fat sour cream
- ¼ cup reduced-fat mayonnaise
- 1 cup seafood cocktail sauce
- 2 cups (8 ounces) shredded part-skim mozzarella cheese
- 1 can (6 ounces) small shrimp, rinsed and drained
- 3 green onions, sliced
- 1 medium tomato, finely chopped
  Sliced Italian bread or assorted crackers

1. In a small bowl, beat the cream cheese, sour cream and mayonnaise until smooth. Spread onto a 12-in. round serving plate; top with seafood sauce. Sprinkle with cheese, shrimp, onions and tomato.

2. Chill until serving. Serve with bread or crackers.

30 ▶ Waffle Fry Nachos

My husband and two grown sons really enjoy these appetizers when we're camping. They can devour a platter of them in no time. They're also fun to make when friends come over.

—**DEBRA MORGAN** IDAHO FALLS, INDIANA

PREP/TOTAL TIME: 25 MINUTES
MAKES: 6-8 SERVINGS

      1 **package (22 ounces) frozen waffle fries**
     10 **bacon strips, cooked and crumbled**
      3 **green onions, sliced**
      1 **can (6 ounces) sliced ripe olives, drained**
      2 **medium tomatoes, seeded and chopped**
    ⅔ **cup salsa**
    1½ **cups (6 ounces) shredded cheddar cheese**
    1½ **cups (6 ounces) shredded Monterey Jack cheese**
        Sour cream

1. Bake fries according to package directions. Transfer to a 10-in. ovenproof skillet. Top with the bacon, onions, olives, tomatoes, salsa and cheeses. Return to the oven for 5 minutes or until cheese is melted. Serve with sour cream.

30 ▶ Antipasto Pizza

A prebaked crust and ready-made pizza sauce cut the prep time for this deliciously different and versatile pizza. It's great as either an entree or hot appetizer.

—**MINDEE CURTIS** OMAHA, NEBRASKA

PREP/TOTAL TIME: 25 MINUTES **MAKES:** 8 SLICES

      1 **prebaked 12-inch pizza crust**
    ¾ **cup pizza sauce**
      2 **cups (8 ounces) shredded part-skim mozzarella cheese, divided**
    ½ **cup roasted sweet red peppers, drained and cut into strips**
    ½ **cup marinated quartered artichoke hearts, drained**
    ¼ **pound thinly sliced hard salami, julienned**
    ¼ **pound sliced deli ham, julienned**
    ¼ **cup minced fresh basil**

1. Place crust on an ungreased pizza pan. Spread sauce over crust; sprinkle with 1 cup cheese. Top with red peppers, artichokes, salami and ham; sprinkle with remaining cheese.

2. Bake at 450° for 10-12 minutes or until cheese is melted. Sprinkle with basil.

20 ▶ Paul's Burgers

My wife, Julie, sometimes jokes that she married me for better, for worse and for my cooking! I spent a lot of time in the kitchen while I was growing up and still enjoy doing so today.

—**PAUL MILLER** GREEN BAY, WISCONSIN

PREP/TOTAL TIME: 20 MINUTES **MAKES:** 4 SERVINGS

    ¼ **cup finely chopped onion**
    ¼ **cup ketchup**
      2 **teaspoons Italian seasoning**
      1 **teaspoon garlic powder**
    ½ **teaspoon salt**
      1 **pound ground beef**
      4 **hamburger buns, split**
        Lettuce leaves and tomato slices, optional

1. Combine the first five ingredients in a small bowl; crumble beef over mixture and mix well. Shape into four patties. Grill over medium heat for 4-5 minutes on each side or until a thermometer reads 160° and juices run clear. Serve on buns; top with lettuce and tomato if desired.

> I love the convenience of make-ahead recipes, and Overnight French Toast is one I use all the time. I like to sprinkle it with cinnamon and sugar after baking.
> —**STEPHANIE WEAVER** SLIGO, PENNSYLVANIA

Overnight French Toast

PREP: 15 MINUTES + CHILLING
BAKE: 45 MINUTES
MAKES: 12 SERVINGS

- 1 loaf (1 pound) cinnamon-raisin bread, cubed
- 1 package (8 ounces) cream cheese, cubed
- 8 eggs, lightly beaten
- 1½ cups half-and-half cream
- ½ cup sugar
- ½ cup maple syrup
- 2 tablespoons vanilla extract
- 1 tablespoon ground cinnamon
- ⅛ teaspoon ground nutmeg

1. Place half of the bread cubes in a greased 13-in. x 9-in. baking dish. Top with cream cheese and remaining bread.

2. In a large bowl, whisk the remaining ingredients until blended. Pour over the top. Cover and refrigerate overnight.

3. Remove from the refrigerator 30 minutes before baking. Cover and bake at 350° for 30 minutes.

4. Uncover; bake 15-20 minutes longer or until a knife inserted near the center comes out clean.

10 Strawberry Banana Smoothies

These refreshing smoothies are great to serve at breakfast or brunch. When he was little, my son would always come running when he heard the blender going!

—LINDA HENDRIX MOUNDVILLE, MISSOURI

PREP/TOTAL TIME: 5 MINUTES **MAKES:** 4 SERVINGS

- 1 **cup milk**
- 1 **cup water**
- 1 **package (10 ounces) frozen sweetened sliced strawberries, partially thawed**
- 1 **medium firm banana, cut into chunks**
- 1 **teaspoon vanilla extract**
- 6 **ice cubes**

1. In a blender, combine all of the ingredients. Cover and process until smooth. Pour into chilled glasses; serve immediately.

20 Cream-Topped Grapes

PREP/TOTAL TIME: 15 MINUTES **MAKES:** 8 SERVINGS

- 4 **ounces cream cheese, softened**
- ¼ **cup sugar**
- ½ **teaspoon vanilla extract**
- ½ **cup sour cream**
- 3 **cups seedless green grapes**
- 3 **cups seedless red grapes**

1. In a small bowl, beat the cream cheese, sugar and vanilla. Add the sour cream; mix well. Divide grapes among individual serving bowls; dollop with topping.

❝ I dress up bunches of red and green grapes with a decadent dressing that comes together in no time. You can also dollop the heavenly four-ingredient sauce over your favorite combination of fruit. ❞

—VIODA GEYER UHRICHSVILLE, OHIO

30 Raspberry Cheese Danish

Your guests will think you made these yummy rolls from scratch...or bought them from a bakery. No one needs to know the recipe calls for easy refrigerated dough!

—KAREN WEIR LITCHFIELD, CONNECTICUT

PREP/TOTAL TIME: 25 MINUTES **MAKES:** 8 SERVINGS

- 4 **ounces cream cheese, softened**
- ¼ **cup plus ½ cup confectioners' sugar, divided**
- 1 **can (8 ounces) refrigerated crescent rolls**
- ½ **cup seedless raspberry jam**
- 2 **teaspoons 2% milk**

1. In a small bowl, beat cream cheese and ¼ cup confectioners' sugar until smooth. Unroll crescent dough and separate into four rectangles; seal perforations. Cut each rectangle in half, making eight squares.

2. Transfer squares to a parchment paper-lined baking sheet. Spread 1 tablespoon cream cheese mixture diagonally across each square. Top with 1 tablespoon jam. Bring two opposite corners of dough over filling; pinch together firmly to seal.

3. Bake at 375° for 10-12 minutes or until golden brown. Combine the milk and remaining confectioners' sugar; drizzle over pastries. Serve warm. Refrigerate leftovers.

Bacon 'n' Egg Potato Bake

Frozen hash browns make this yummy recipe simple to prepare. Featuring bacon and cheddar cheese, it's tasty breakfast or brunch fare. You can even make it the night before, keep it in the fridge and bake it the next morning—so convenient!

—CHERYL JOHNSON PLYMOUTH, MINNESOTA

PREP: 20 MINUTES **BAKE:** 45 MINUTES
MAKES: 8 SERVINGS

- 1 **package (32 ounces) frozen cubed hash brown potatoes, thawed**
- 1 **pound bacon strips, cooked and crumbled**
- 1 **cup (4 ounces) shredded cheddar cheese, divided**
- ¼ to ½ **teaspoon salt**
- 8 **eggs**
- 2 **cups milk**
  Paprika

1. In a large bowl, combine the hash browns, bacon, ½ cup cheese and salt. Spoon into a greased 13-in. x 9-in. baking dish. In another large bowl, beat eggs and milk until blended; pour over hash brown mixture. Sprinkle with paprika.

2. Bake, uncovered, at 350° for 45-50 minutes or until a knife inserted near the center comes out clean. Sprinkle with remaining cheese.

Broccoli Hash Brown Quiche

Since we have six children, I rely on quick and nutritious dishes like this easy-prep quiche. I like to vary it by adding ham or bacon. It's great for breakfast or dinner.

—JOY VINCENT
GOLDSBORO, NORTH CAROLINA

PREP: 15 MINUTES
BAKE: 55 MINUTES
MAKES: 6 SERVINGS

- 3 **cups frozen shredded hash brown potatoes, thawed**
- 1½ **cups frozen broccoli cuts, thawed**
- 4 **eggs**
- 1 **cup (8 ounces) sour cream**
- ½ **teaspoon salt**
- 1 **cup (4 ounces) shredded Colby-Monterey Jack cheese**

1. Press the hash browns onto the bottom and up the sides of a greased 9-in. pie plate, forming a shell. Sprinkle with broccoli.

2. In a bowl, beat the eggs, sour cream and salt; stir in cheese. Pour over broccoli.

3. Bake at 350° for 55-65 minutes or until a knife inserted near the center comes out clean. Let stand for 5 minutes before cutting.

Brunch Enchiladas

When I have company for brunch, this tried-and-true casserole is usually on the menu. With ham, eggs and plenty of cheese, the enchiladas are hearty and fun. I like that I can assemble them the day before.

—GAIL SYKORA MENOMONEE FALLS, WISCONSIN

PREP: 15 MINUTES + CHILLING **BAKE:** 40 MINUTES + STANDING
MAKES: 10 ENCHILADAS

- 2 **cups cubed fully cooked ham**
- ½ **cup chopped green onions**
- 10 **flour tortillas (8 inches)**
- 2 **cups (8 ounces) shredded cheddar cheese, divided**
- 1 **tablespoon all-purpose flour**
- 2 **cups half-and-half cream**
- 6 **eggs, lightly beaten**
- ¼ **teaspoon salt, optional**

1. In a large bowl, combine ham and onions; place about ¼ cup down the center of each tortilla. Top with 2 tablespoons cheese. Roll up and place seam side down in a greased 13-in. x 9-in. baking dish.

2. In another large bowl, combine the flour, cream, eggs and salt if desired until smooth. Pour over tortillas. Cover and refrigerate for 8 hours or overnight.

3. Remove from the refrigerator 30 minutes before baking. Cover and bake at 350° for 25 minutes. Uncover; bake for 10 minutes. Sprinkle with remaining cheese; bake 3 minutes longer or until the cheese is melted. Let stand for 10 minutes before serving.

A standard offering at brunches, mimosas are as pretty as they are tasty. Make sure the Champagne is extra-dry or dry (not brut) for the best flavor. —**TASTE OF HOME TEST KITCHEN**

10 Mimosa

PREP/TOTAL TIME: 5 MINUTES
MAKES: 1 SERVING

- 2 **ounces Champagne or other sparkling wine, chilled**
- ½ **ounce Triple Sec**
- 2 **ounces orange juice**

GARNISH

Orange slice

1. Pour the Champagne into a champagne flute or wine glass. Pour the Triple Sec and orange juice into the glass. Garnish as desired.

Editor's Note: *To make a batch of mimosas (12 servings), slowly pour one bottle (750 ml) chilled Champagne into a pitcher. Stir in 3 cups orange juice and ¾ cup of Triple Sec.*

10 Creamy Smoked Salmon Spread

With its mild herb and rich salmon flavor, this creamy spread is wonderful on miniature bagels as part of a spring brunch.

—**FAITH AGNEW**
SPOTSWOOD, NEW JERSEY

PREP/TOTAL TIME: 10 MINUTES
MAKES: 1½ CUPS

- ½ **pound smoked salmon fillet**
- 1 **package (6½ ounces) garlic-herb spreadable cheese**
- ¼ **cup minced fresh parsley**
  Miniature bagels, split and toasted

1. Flake salmon into small pieces. In a small bowl, combine the spreadable cheese, parsley and salmon. Serve on bagels.

Eggs Benedict Casserole

Here's a casserole as tasty as Eggs Benedict, but without the hassle. Simply assemble the dish ahead, and bake it the next morning for an elegant brunch.

—SANDIE HEINDEL
LIBERTY, MISSOURI

PREP: 25 MINUTES + CHILLING
BAKE: 45 MINUTES
MAKES: 12 SERVINGS (1⅔ CUPS SAUCE)

- ¾ **pound Canadian bacon, chopped**
- 6 **English muffins, split and cut into 1-inch pieces**
- 8 **eggs**
- 2 **cups 2% milk**
- 1 **teaspoon onion powder**
- ¼ **teaspoon paprika**

SAUCE
- 4 **egg yolks**
- ½ **cup heavy whipping cream**
- 2 **tablespoons lemon juice**
- 1 **teaspoon Dijon mustard**
- ½ **cup butter, melted**

1. Place half of the bacon in a greased 13-in. x 9-in. baking dish; top with English muffins and remaining bacon. In a large bowl, whisk the eggs, milk and onion powder; pour over the top. Cover and refrigerate overnight.

2. Remove from the refrigerator 30 minutes before baking. Sprinkle with paprika. Cover and bake at 375° for 35 minutes. Uncover; bake 10-15 minutes longer or until a knife inserted near the center comes out clean.

3. In a double boiler or metal bowl over simmering water, constantly whisk the egg yolks, cream, lemon juice and mustard until mixture is thick enough to coat the back of a spoon. Reduce heat to low. Slowly drizzle in warm melted butter, whisking constantly. Serve immediately with casserole.

Mustard-Glazed Ham

My mom was known as the best cook around. This glazed ham was in her collection of handwritten recipes. I laminated the ones I use most often, including her ham. It's so easy, yet very special.

—DOROTHY SMITH EL DORADO, ARKANSAS

PREP: 5 MINUTES **BAKE:** 2 HOURS **MAKES:** 12-15 SERVINGS

- 1 **fully cooked boneless ham (4 to 5 pounds)**
- ¾ **to 1 cup water**
- ¼ **cup orange marmalade**
- ¼ **cup prepared mustard**
- ¼ **teaspoon ground ginger**

1. Place ham in a shallow roasting pan; add water to pan. Bake, uncovered, at 325° for 1 hour.

2. In a small bowl, combine the marmalade, mustard and ginger. Brush some over the ham. Bake 1 hour longer or until a thermometer reads 140°, brushing occasionally with glaze.

Herbed Asparagus Salad

PREP: 20 MINUTES + CHILLING **MAKES:** 6-8 SERVINGS

- 2 pounds fresh asparagus, cut into 1-inch pieces
- ¾ cup canola oil
- ½ cup lemon juice
- 1½ teaspoons sugar
- 1 teaspoon salt
- ½ teaspoon dried oregano
- ½ teaspoon dried tarragon
- ½ teaspoon coarsely ground pepper
- 1 garlic clove, minced
- 8 cups torn mixed salad greens
- 3 hard-cooked eggs, sliced

1. In a large saucepan, bring ½ in. of water to a boil. Add asparagus; cover and boil for 3 minutes. Drain and immediately place asparagus in ice water. Drain and pat dry. Place in a large bowl.

2. In a small bowl, whisk the oil, lemon juice, sugar, salt, oregano, tarragon, pepper and garlic. Pour over asparagus; cover and refrigerate for at least 2 hours.

3. Place salad greens on a serving platter. With a slotted spoon, arrange asparagus over greens. Garnish with egg slices.

20 ▶ Dill Deviled Eggs

My family says these deviled eggs are the best. I like them because they're a cinch to prepare. They make a popular contribution to a brunch—or picnic.

—CARRIE LONG CALEDONIA, WISCONSIN

PREP/TOTAL TIME: 15 MINUTES **MAKES:** 1 DOZEN

- 6 hard-cooked eggs
- ¼ cup mayonnaise
- 1 teaspoon white wine vinegar
- 1 teaspoon Dijon mustard
- ½ teaspoon dill weed
- ¼ teaspoon garlic powder
- ⅛ teaspoon salt
    Fresh dill sprigs, optional

1. Slice eggs in half lengthwise; remove yolks and set whites aside. In a small bowl, mash yolks. Add the mayonnaise, vinegar, mustard, dill, garlic powder and salt.

2. Spoon into egg whites. Garnish with dill sprigs if desired. Refrigerate until serving.

❝ Here's a wonderful way to serve fresh-cut asparagus. The tarragon and oregano are a nice surprise in the lemony vinaigrette, and sliced cooked eggs make a pretty garnish.❞

—DAWN SZALAI EDWARDSBURG, MICHIGAN

These little hot dogs are all wrapped up in Halloween fun. Kids really enjoy them!
—TASTE OF HOME TEST KITCHEN

30 Mummies on a Stick

PREP/TOTAL TIME: 30 MINUTES
MAKES: 10 SERVINGS

- 1 **tube (11 ounces) refrigerated breadsticks**
- 10 **Popsicle sticks**
- 10 **hot dogs**
   Prepared mustard

1. Separate dough; roll 10 pieces into 24-in. ropes. Insert a Popsicle stick into each hot dog. Starting at the stick end, wrap one dough rope around each hot dog, leaving 2 in. of the hot dog uncovered at the top for the mummy head.

2. Place mummies 1 in. apart on a greased baking sheet. Place remaining breadsticks on another baking sheet.

3. Bake at 350° for 18-20 minutes. Add dots of mustard for eyes. Save the leftover breadsticks for another use.

10 Halloween Snack Mix

I created this easy, fall-inspired snack mix on the spur of the moment. It's easy to toss together for a Halloween party or to package in individual bags for a fall bake sale.

—**BARBARA ROBERTS**
MIDDLETON, WISCONSIN

PREP/TOTAL TIME: 5 MINUTES
MAKES: ABOUT 2 QUARTS

- 6 **cups caramel corn**
- 2 **cups salted cashews or peanuts**
- 1½ **cups candy corn**
- ⅓ **cup raisins**

1. In a large bowl, combine all ingredients. Store snack mix in an airtight container.

Pizza Snake

Once this snake is filled, rolled and shaped, let the kids paint it. The bread will bake up colorful, yummy and just creepy enough to satisfy the boys and ghouls!

—**JEN SPAETH** OZARK, MISSOURI

PREP: 20 MINUTES
BAKE: 25 MINUTES
MAKES: 5 SERVINGS

- 1 tube (11 ounces) refrigerated crusty French loaf
- 1 jar (14 ounces) pizza sauce, divided
- 1 cup (4 ounces) shredded part-skim mozzarella cheese
- 1 cup sliced fresh mushrooms
- 25 slices pepperoni
- 1 egg, lightly beaten
  Assorted food coloring
  New paintbrushes

1. Unroll the French loaf dough into a large rectangle; spread with 1 cup pizza sauce to within 1 in. of edges. Sprinkle with cheese and mushrooms. Cut a forked tongue from a pepperoni slice; refrigerate. Layer remaining pepperoni over cheese and mushrooms.

2. Roll up jelly-roll style, starting with a long side; pinch seam to seal and tuck ends under. Place seam side down on a greased baking sheet and shape like an "S".

3. Divide egg among several small bowls; tint with food coloring as desired. Paint snake as desired with egg wash.

4. Bake at 350° for 25-30 minutes or until golden brown. Cut a small hole for the mouth; insert pepperoni tongue. Warm remaining pizza sauce; serve on the side.

Peanut Butter Popcorn Balls

Trick-or-treaters are always happy to receive these tasty popcorn balls. I love making them as well as eating them!

—**BETTY CLAYCOMB** ALVERTON, PENNSYLVANIA

PREP: 20 MINUTES + STANDING **MAKES:** 10 POPCORN BALLS

- 5 cups popped popcorn
- 1 cup dry roasted peanuts
- ½ cup sugar
- ½ cup light corn syrup
- ½ cup chunky peanut butter
- ½ teaspoon vanilla extract

1. Place popcorn and peanuts in a large bowl; set aside. In a large heavy saucepan over medium heat, bring sugar and corn syrup to a rolling boil, stirring occasionally. Remove from the heat; stir in peanut butter and vanilla. Quickly pour over popcorn mixture and mix well.

2. When cool enough to handle, quickly shape into ten 2½-in. balls. Let stand at room temperature until firm; wrap in plastic wrap.

With my easy recipe, even someone who has never made homemade gravy before can be assured of success.
—**PHYLLIS SCHMALZ** KANSAS CITY, KANSAS

20 Creamy Turkey Gravy

PREP/TOTAL TIME: 15 MINUTES
MAKES: 2⅓ CUPS

- 2 tablespoons cornstarch
- 2 tablespoons turkey or chicken drippings
- 2 cups chicken broth
- ¼ cup milk
- ⅛ teaspoon each salt and pepper

1. In a small saucepan, whisk cornstarch and drippings until smooth. Gradually stir in the broth, milk, salt and pepper. Bring to a boil; cook and stir for 2 minutes or until thickened. Serve with turkey or chicken.

30 Sour Cream Mashed Potatoes

I accidentally overcooked my potatoes once, and they were too soft for the recipe I had planned. So I added sour cream and seasonings to the pot and invented these melt-in-your-mouth mashed potatoes!
—**CAROLINE SPERRY** ALLENTOWN, MICHIGAN

PREP/TOTAL TIME: 30 MINUTES
MAKES: 5 SERVINGS

- 2 pounds red potatoes, quartered
- 1 cup (8 ounces) sour cream
- 2 tablespoons minced fresh parsley
- 1 teaspoon salt
- ½ teaspoon garlic powder
- ½ teaspoon pepper

1. Place potatoes in a large saucepan and cover with water. Bring to a boil. Reduce heat; cover and simmer for 15-20 minutes or until tender.

2. Drain and transfer to a large bowl. Add the remaining ingredients; mash until blended.

Green Bean Casserole

This has always been one of my favorite holiday foods because it can be prepared ahead and refrigerated until ready to bake.

—**ANNA BAKER** BLAINE, WASHINGTON

PREP: 15 MINUTES **BAKE:** 35 MINUTES
MAKES: 10 SERVINGS

- 2 **cans (10¾ ounces each) condensed cream of mushroom soup, undiluted**
- 1 **cup milk**
- 2 **teaspoons soy sauce**
- ⅛ **teaspoon pepper**
- 2 **packages (16 ounces each) frozen green beans, cooked and drained**
- 1 **can (6 ounces) French-fried onions, divided**

1. In a bowl, combine soup, milk, soy sauce and pepper. Gently stir in beans. Spoon half of the mixture into a 13-in. x 9-in. baking dish. Sprinkle with half of the onions. Spoon remaining bean mixture over the top.

2. Bake at 350° for 30 minutes or until heated through. Sprinkle with remaining onions. Bake 5 minutes longer or until the onions are brown and crispy.

10 Pineapple-Orange Cranberry Sauce

PREP/TOTAL TIME: 5 MINUTES **MAKES:** 2¾ CUPS

- 1 **can (14 ounces) whole-berry cranberry sauce**
- 1 **can (11 ounces) mandarin oranges, well drained**
- 1 **can (8 ounces) crushed pineapple, well drained**
- ¼ **cup chopped pecans, toasted**

1. In a small serving bowl, combine the cranberry sauce, oranges and pineapple. Stir in pecans just before serving.

❝This delicious side dish comes together in no time at all! Quick and versatile, it's excellent with any meat.❞

—**ADRIENNE NICCHIO** NORTH MERRICK, NEW YORK

Roasted Turkey Breast

My family always requests this turkey at family gatherings. The Italian dressing adds zip and moistness that you don't find in other recipes. If you'd like, you can make gravy from the pan drippings.

—**CINDY CARLSON** INGLESIDE, TEXAS

PREP: 10 MINUTES **BAKE:** 2 HOURS + STANDING **MAKES:** 12-14 SERVINGS

- 1 **bone-in turkey breast (about 7 pounds)**
- 1 **teaspoon garlic powder**
- ½ **teaspoon onion powder**
- ½ **teaspoon salt**
- ¼ **teaspoon pepper**
- 1½ **cups Italian dressing**

1. Place turkey breast in a greased 13-in. x 9-in. baking dish. Combine the seasonings; sprinkle over turkey. Pour dressing over the top.

2. Cover and bake at 325° for 2 to 2½ hours or until a thermometer reads 170°, basting occasionally with pan drippings. Let stand for 10 minutes before slicing.

Roasted Turkey: *Combine 1¾ teaspoons garlic powder, ¾ teaspoon each onion powder and salt, and ½ teaspoon pepper; sprinkle over a 12- to 14-pound turkey. Place in a roasting pan; top with 2½ cups Italian dressing. Cover and bake at 325° for 3 to 3½ hours or until a thermometer inserted in thigh reads 180°, basting occasionally with pan drippings. Let stand for 20 minutes before carving.*

20 Glazed Acorn Squash

With brown sugar, butter and honey, what's not to love about this sweet and yummy side dish? It's ready in no time from the microwave.

—**KARA DE LA VEGA**
SANTA ROSA, CALIFORNIA

PREP/TOTAL TIME: 20 MINUTES
MAKES: 4 SERVINGS

- 2 **medium acorn squash**
- ¼ **cup packed brown sugar**
- 2 **tablespoons butter**
- 4 **teaspoons honey**
- ¼ **teaspoon salt**
- ¼ **teaspoon pepper**

1. Cut squash in half; discard seeds. Place squash cut side down in a microwave-safe dish. Cover and microwave on high for 10-12 minutes or until tender.

2. Turn squash cut side up. Fill centers of squash with brown sugar, butter and honey; sprinkle with salt and pepper.

3. Cover and microwave on high for 2-3 minutes or until heated through.

Editor's Note: *This recipe was tested in a 1,100-watt microwave.*

Unstuffing Side Dish

With sausage, mushrooms, celery and the perfect blend of seasonings, this dressing is irresistible. I like to call it "unstuffing" since it bakes separately from the turkey, which I do on the grill.

—**KEN CHURCHES** KAILUA-KONA, HAWAII

PREP: 20 MINUTES **BAKE:** 40 MINUTES
MAKES: 8 SERVINGS

- ½ **pound bulk Italian sausage**
- ¼ **cup butter, cubed**
- ½ **pound sliced fresh mushrooms**
- ¾ **cup chopped celery**
- 1 **medium onion, chopped**
- 1 **teaspoon poultry seasoning**
- ½ **teaspoon salt**
- ¼ **teaspoon pepper**
- 6 **cups unseasoned stuffing cubes or dry cubed bread**
- 2½ **to 3 cups chicken broth**

1. In a large skillet, cook sausage until no longer pink; drain. Add the butter, mushrooms, celery and onion; cook for 3-5 minutes or until onion is tender. Stir in the poultry seasoning, salt and pepper. Transfer to a large bowl; add stuffing cubes and enough broth to moisten.

2. Place in a greased 2-qt. baking dish. Cover and bake at 350° for 30 minutes. Uncover and bake 10 minutes longer or until browned.

Eggnog Pumpkin Pie

My mom's pumpkin pie is the absolute best I have ever tasted. Eggnog is the special ingredient in the creamy custard filling.

—**TERRI GONZALEZ** ROSWELL, NEW MEXICO

PREP: 10 MINUTES **BAKE:** 1 HOUR + COOLING
MAKES: 6-8 SERVINGS

- 1 **can (15 ounces) solid-pack pumpkin**
- 1¼ **cups eggnog**
- ⅔ **cup sugar**
- 3 **eggs**
- 1½ **teaspoons pumpkin pie spice**
- ¼ **teaspoon salt**
- 1 **unbaked pastry shell (9 inches)**

1. In a large bowl, combine the pumpkin, eggnog, sugar, eggs, pumpkin pie spice and salt. Pour into pastry shell.

2. Bake at 375° for 60-65 minutes or until a knife inserted near the center comes out clean. Cool on a wire rack. Refrigerate until serving.

Editor's Note: *This recipe was made with commercially prepared eggnog.*

This sweet and savory brisket is a great complement to zesty horseradish potatoes. The rich color of the meat makes it an elegant holiday option. —**RACELLE SCHAEFER** STUDIO CITY, CALIFORNIA

Cranberry Brisket with Horseradish Mashed Potatoes

PREP: 20 MINUTES **BAKE:** 3 HOURS
MAKES: 8 SERVINGS (1⅔ CUPS GRAVY)

- 1 **fresh beef brisket (3 to 4 pounds)**
- 1 **can (14 ounces) whole-berry cranberry sauce**
- 1 **can (12 ounces) ginger ale**
- ½ **cup dried cranberries**
- 1 **envelope onion soup mix**
- 8 **medium potatoes, peeled and quartered**
- ⅓ **cup milk**
- ¼ **cup butter, cubed**
- 2 **tablespoons prepared horseradish**

1. Place brisket in a greased 13-in. x 9-in. baking dish. Combine the cranberry sauce, ginger ale, cranberries and soup mix; pour over meat. Cover and bake at 375° for 2 hours.

2. Uncover; bake brisket 1 hour longer or until meat is tender, basting occasionally.

3. Meanwhile, place potatoes in a Dutch oven; cover with water. Bring to a boil. Reduce the heat; cover and cook for 15-20 minutes or until tender.

4. Drain potatoes; mash with milk, butter and horseradish. Let brisket stand for 5 minutes before thinly slicing across the grain. Serve with cooking juices and mashed potatoes.

Editor's Note: *This is a fresh beef brisket, not corned beef.*

10 Easy Tossed Salad

There's amazing crunch and nutrition galore in this simple salad!

—KATIE WOLLGAST
FLORISSANT, MISSOURI

PREP/TOTAL TIME: 10 MINUTES
MAKES: 4 SERVINGS

- 8 **cups torn mixed salad greens**
- 1 **large apple, sliced**
- ½ **cup sliced almonds, toasted**
- ½ **cup dried cranberries**
- ½ **cup fat-free poppy seed salad dressing**

1. In a salad bowl, combine the salad greens, apple, almonds and cranberries. Drizzle with dressing; toss to coat. Serve immediately.

20 Glazed Dijon Carrots

I not only serve these sweet glazed carrots during the holidays, but many times throughout the year as well.

—TERI LINDQUIST GURNEE, ILLINOIS

PREP/TOTAL TIME: 20 MINUTES
MAKES: 4-6 SERVINGS

- 1 **package (16 ounces) baby carrots**
- ½ **cup water**
- 3 **tablespoons butter**
- 2 **tablespoons brown sugar**
- 1 **tablespoon Dijon mustard**
- ½ **teaspoon ground ginger**
- ¼ **teaspoon salt**

1. In a saucepan, bring carrots and water to a boil. Reduce heat; cover and cook for 10-12 minutes or until tender. Drain.

2. Place carrots in a serving dish and keep warm. In the same pan, melt butter. Add brown sugar, mustard, ginger and salt; cook and stir over medium heat until sugar is dissolved. Pour over carrots and toss to coat.

20 Parmesan Sticks

You'll like how easy these are to make and how good they smell while baking. Plus, they look so festive on the table. Change up the herbs to suit your own menu and tastes.

—TIM AILPORT WEST LAKELAND, MINNESOTA

PREP/TOTAL TIME: 20 MINUTES **MAKES:** 20 BREADSTICKS

- 1 **package (17.3 ounces) frozen puff pastry, thawed**
- 1 **egg, lightly beaten**
- 1½ **cups grated Parmesan cheese**
- 1 **tablespoon dried rosemary, crushed**

1. Brush one side of each puff pastry sheet with egg; sprinkle with cheese and rosemary. Cut each sheet into ten 1-in. strips. Place 1 in. apart on greased baking sheets.

2. Bake at 400° for 10-13 minutes or until golden brown.

Perfect Prime Rib

If you've never made prime rib before, you can't go wrong with this simple recipe. It comes from a chef at one of my favorite restaurants.

—PAULINE WAASDORP
FERGUS FALLS, MINNESOTA

PREP: 5 MINUTES + MARINATING
BAKE: 2½ HOURS + STANDING
MAKES: 8-10 SERVINGS

- ½ cup Worcestershire sauce
- 3 teaspoons garlic salt
- 3 teaspoons seasoned salt
- 3 teaspoons coarsely ground pepper
- 1 bone-in beef rib roast (5 to 6 pounds)

1. In a small bowl, combine the first four ingredients; rub half over the roast.

2. Place the roast in a large resealable plastic bag; seal and refrigerate overnight, turning often. Cover and refrigerate remaining marinade.

3. Drain and discard marinade. Place roast fat side up in a large roasting pan; pour reserved marinade over roast. Tent with foil. Bake at 350° for 1 hour.

4. Uncover and bake 1½ hours longer or until meat reaches desired doneness (for medium-rare, a thermometer should read 145°; medium, 160°; well-done 170°). Let stand for 15 minutes before slicing.

Gumdrop Fudge

Making candy is one of my favorite things to do during the holidays. This sweet white fudge is as easy to put together as it is beautiful to serve.

—JENNIFER SHORT OMAHA, NEBRASKA

PREP: 20 MIN. + CHILLING **MAKES:** ABOUT 3 POUNDS

- 1½ pounds white candy coating, coarsely chopped
- 1 can (14 ounces) sweetened condensed milk
- ⅛ teaspoon salt
- 1½ teaspoons vanilla extract
- 1½ cups chopped gumdrops

1. Line a 9-in. square pan with foil; set aside. In a heavy saucepan, combine the candy coating, milk and salt. Cook and stir over low heat until candy coating is melted. Remove from the heat; stir in the vanilla and gumdrops.

2. Spread into prepared pan. Cover and refrigerate until firm. Using foil, remove fudge from the pan; cut into 1-in. squares. Store in an airtight container at room temperature.

> My family loves any dessert that tastes like apple pie, and this one's so easy, the children can help make it. My four grandchildren love helping MawMaw in the kitchen to make treats like this. —**JUDY TAYLOR** KENNA, VIRGINIA

Quick Crescent Apple Dessert

PREP: 25 MINUTES
BAKE: 20 MINUTES + COOLING
MAKES: 12 SERVINGS

- 1 **tube (8 ounces) refrigerated crescent rolls**
- 1 **cup chopped walnuts**
- ¾ **cup sugar**
- ½ **teaspoon ground cinnamon**
- ¼ **teaspoon ground nutmeg**
- 1 **can (21 ounces) apple pie filling, chopped**

TOPPING

- ½ **cup all-purpose flour**
- ½ **cup packed brown sugar**
- ¼ **cup cold butter**
- 1 **cup flaked coconut**
- ¼ **cup chopped walnuts**

1. Unroll crescent dough into an ungreased 13-in. x 9-in. baking pan; seal seams and perforations. Bake at 375° for 10 minutes.

2. Combine the walnuts, sugar, cinnamon and nutmeg; sprinkle over crust. Spread with pie filling.

3. In a small bowl, combine flour and brown sugar; cut in butter until mixture resembles coarse crumbs. Stir in coconut and walnuts. Sprinkle over filling.

4. Bake at 375° for 18-22 minutes or until golden brown. Cool on a wire rack.

30 Baklava Tartlets

PREP/TOTAL TIME: 25 MINUTES
MAKES: 45 TARTLETS

- 2 cups finely chopped walnuts
- ¾ cup honey
- ½ cup butter, melted
- 1 teaspoon ground cinnamon
- 1 teaspoon lemon juice
- ¼ teaspoon ground cloves
- 3 packages (1.9 ounces each) frozen miniature phyllo tart shells

1. In a small bowl, combine the first six ingredients; spoon 2 teaspoonfuls into each tart shell. Refrigerate until serving.

10 Mock Champagne Punch

Of all the punch recipes I've tried, I keep coming back to this pretty one that's also nonalcoholic.

—BETTY CLAYCOMB
ALVERTON, PENNSYLVANIA

PREP/TOTAL TIME: 10 MINUTES
MAKES: 2 QUARTS

- 1 quart white grape juice, chilled
- 1 quart ginger ale, chilled
  Strawberries or raspberries

1. Combine grape juice and ginger ale; pour into a punch bowl or glasses. Garnish with berries.

Want a quick treat that's delicious and easy to do? These tartlets will do the trick. You can serve them right away, but they're better after chilling for about an hour in the refrigerator.
—ASHLEY EAGON KETTERING, OHIO

20 Mulled Red Cider

Red wine gives a rosy glow to hot apple cider. The spices are a wonderful complement to both the cider and wine.

—STEVE FOY KIRKWOOD, MISSOURI

PREP/TOTAL TIME: 20 MINUTES
MAKES: 7 SERVINGS (¾ CUP EACH)

    Cinnamon-sugar, optional
 1¾ cups apple cider or juice
  ½ cup sugar
   3 cinnamon sticks (3 inches)
   4 whole cloves
   1 bottle (750 milliliters) dry red wine

1. If desired, moisten the rims of seven mugs with water. Sprinkle cinnamon-sugar on a plate; dip rims in cinnamon-sugar. Set mugs aside.

2. In a large saucepan, combine the cider, sugar, cinnamon sticks and cloves. Cook and stir over medium heat until sugar is dissolved.

3. Add wine and heat through. Remove from the heat. Cover and steep for 10 minutes; strain. Serve in prepared mugs.

Orange-Pecan Pork Roast

Family and friends will "ooh" and "ahh" when you bring in this impressive roast with its orange glaze and pecan topping. It's a real showstopper!

—YVONNE NOVAK SILVER SPRING, MARYLAND

PREP: 20 MINUTES **BAKE:** 1¾ HOURS + STANDING
MAKES: 6-8 SERVINGS

   1 boneless pork loin roast (2½ to 3 pounds)
  ½ cup finely chopped onion
   1 garlic clove, minced
   2 tablespoons canola oil
  ½ cup orange marmalade
  ¼ cup chopped pecans
  ¼ teaspoon ground cinnamon

1. Place roast on a rack in a shallow roasting pan. In a skillet, saute onion and garlic in oil until tender. Add the marmalade, pecans and cinnamon; cook and stir until marmalade is melted. Spoon over roast.

2. Bake, uncovered, at 325° for 1¾ hours or until a thermometer reads 160°. Let stand for 10 minutes before slicing.

10 ⟩ Bacon Blue Cheese Appetizer

PREP/TOTAL TIME: 5 MINUTES
MAKES: 8 SERVINGS

- 1 wedge (8 ounces) blue cheese
- 1 tablespoon honey
- 3 bacon strips, cooked and crumbled
  Assorted crackers

1. Place cheese on a serving dish. Drizzle with honey. Sprinkle with bacon. Serve with crackers.

30 ⟩ Toasted Almond Party Spread

This rich spread goes a long way at holiday parties. Almonds and Swiss cheese are a classic combination that never goes out of style.

—KIM SOBOTA
PLYMOUTH, MINNESOTA

PREP/TOTAL TIME: 25 MINUTES
MAKES: 1½ CUPS

- 1 package (8 ounces) cream cheese, softened
- 1½ cups (6 ounces) shredded Swiss cheese
- ½ cup sliced almonds, toasted, divided
- ⅓ cup mayonnaise
- 2 tablespoons sliced green onions
- ⅛ teaspoon pepper
- ⅛ teaspoon ground nutmeg
  Assorted crackers

1. In a small bowl, beat the cream cheese until smooth. Stir in the Swiss cheese, ⅓ cup almonds, mayonnaise, green onions, pepper and nutmeg.

2. Spoon into a lightly greased pie plate. Bake at 350° for 12-15 minutes or until heated through. Sprinkle with remaining almonds. Serve warm with crackers.

Nothing is easier than this three-ingredient starter. Salty, sweet and rich, it's a surefire people pleaser. **—JAKE HAEN** OCALA, FLORIDA

Pomegranate Ginger Spritzer

A pitcher of this non-alcoholic beverage can conveniently be made hours before guests arrive. Stir in the club soda just before serving.

—TASTE OF HOME TEST KITCHEN

PREP: 10 MINUTES + CHILLING
MAKES: 7 CUPS

- ½ cup sliced fresh gingerroot
- 1 medium lime, sliced
- 3 cups pomegranate juice
- ¾ cup orange juice
- 3 cups chilled club soda

1. Place ginger and lime slices in a pitcher; stir in pomegranate and orange juices. Refrigerate overnight.

2. Just before serving, strain and discard ginger and lime. Stir club soda into juice mixture.

Strawberry Sangria

My friends always request that I serve this pretty and refreshing drink. Perfect summertime sipping!

—TANYA JONES
OKLAHOMA CITY, OKLAHOMA

PREP: 10 MINUTES + CHILLING
MAKES: 6 SERVINGS

- 1 bottle (750 milliliters) white wine
- ½ cup strawberry schnapps
- ¼ cup sugar
- 2 cups sliced fresh strawberries
  Ice cubes

1. In a pitcher, stir the wine, schnapps and sugar until sugar is dissolved; add strawberries. Chill least 2 hours. Serve over ice.

20 ▶ Party Pitas

Whether served as a satisfying lunch or as appealing appetizers, these tasty bites are sure to please!

—JANETTE ROOT ELLENSBURG, WASHINGTON

PREP/TOTAL TIME: 15 MINUTES **MAKES:** 16 PIECES

- 1 package (8 ounces) cream cheese, softened
- ½ cup mayonnaise
- ½ teaspoon dill weed
- ¼ teaspoon garlic salt
- 4 whole pita breads
- 1½ cups fresh baby spinach
- 1 pound shaved fully cooked ham
- ½ pound thinly sliced Monterey Jack cheese

1. Combine the cream cheese, mayonnaise, dill and garlic salt. Cut each pita in half horizontally; spread 2 tablespoons cream cheese mixture on each cut surface.

2. On four pita halves, layer the spinach, ham and cheese. Top with remaining pita halves. Cut each sandwich into four wedges and secure with toothpicks.

10 ▸ Parmesan-Crusted Brie

In no time, this wonderful appetizer cooks to a golden exterior with gooey cheese inside. It's delicious with French bread, crackers or fruit.

—**KAREN GRANT** TULARE, CALIFORNIA

PREP/TOTAL TIME: 10 MINUTES
MAKES: 8 SERVINGS

- 1 **egg**
- 1 **tablespoon water**
- ½ **cup seasoned bread crumbs**
- ¼ **cup grated Parmesan cheese**
- 1 **round (8 ounces) Brie cheese**
- ¼ **cup canola oil**
    Assorted crackers and/or fresh fruit

1. In a shallow bowl, beat egg and water. In another bowl, combine bread crumbs and Parmesan cheese. Dip Brie in egg mixture; coat with crumb mixture. Repeat.

2. In a small skillet, cook Brie in oil over medium heat for 2 minutes on each side or until golden brown. Serve with crackers and/or fruit.

30 ▸ Sausage Cheese Puffs

People are always surprised when I tell them there are only four ingredients in these tasty bite-size puffs. Cheesy and spicy, the golden puffs are a fun novelty at brunch. They also make yummy party appetizers.

—**DELLA MOORE** TROY, NEW YORK

PREP/TOTAL TIME: 25 MINUTES **MAKES:** ABOUT 4 DOZEN

- 1 **pound bulk Italian sausage**
- 3 **cups biscuit/baking mix**
- 4 **cups (16 ounces) shredded cheddar cheese**
- ¾ **cup water**

1. In a large skillet, cook the sausage over medium heat until no longer pink; drain.

2. In a large bowl, combine biscuit mix and cheese; stir in sausage. Add water and toss with a fork until moistened. Shape into 1½-in. balls. Place 2 in. apart on ungreased baking sheets.

3. Bake at 400° for 12-15 minutes or until puffed and golden brown. Cool on wire racks.

Editor's Note: *Baked puffs may be frozen; reheat at 400° for 7-9 minutes or until heated through (they do not need to thawed first).*

10 ▸ Whiskey Sour

Here's a nice, simple drink to make that uses just a few ingredients. No wonder it's a classic.

—**TASTE OF HOME TEST KITCHEN**

PREP/TOTAL TIME: 5 MINUTES
MAKES: 1 SERVING

    Ice cubes
- 2 **ounces whiskey**
- 1½ **ounces sour mix**
GARNISH
    Orange wedge and maraschino cherry

1. Fill a shaker three-fourths full with ice. Add whiskey and sour mix. Cover and shake for 10-15 seconds or until condensation forms on outside of shaker. Strain into a chilled wine glass. Garnish as desired.

10 Martini

PREP/TOTAL TIME: 5 MINUTES
MAKES: 1 SERVING

>   Ice cubes
>   3   ounces gin or vodka
>   ½   ounce dry vermouth
> **GARNISH**
>   Pimiento-stuffed olives

1. Fill a mixing glass or tumbler three-fourths full with ice. Add gin and vermouth; stir until condensation forms on outside of glass. Strain into a chilled cocktail glass. Garnish as desired.

Apple Martini: *Omit vermouth and olives. Reduce vodka to 2 ounces and use 1½ ounces sour apple liqueur and 1½ teaspoons lemon juice. Garnish with a green apple slice.*

Chocolate Martini: *Omit vermouth and olives. Reduce vodka to 2 ounces and use 2 ounces creme de cacao or chocolate liqueur. Garnish with chocolate shavings.*

10 Easy Hummus

Using sun-dried tomato salad dressing instead of tahini adds a new dimension of flavor to hummus.
—JEANNETTE JEREMIAS
KITCHENER, ONTARIO

PREP/TOTAL TIME: 5 MINUTES
MAKES: 1½ CUPS

>   1   can (15 ounces) garbanzo beans or chickpeas, rinsed and drained
>   ½   cup sun-dried tomato salad dressing
>   2   garlic cloves, minced
>   Baked pita chips or assorted fresh vegetables

1. In a food processor, combine the beans, salad dressing and garlic. Cover and process for 30 seconds or until smooth. Serve with chips.

Martinis can be made with either vodka or gin. Our taste panel's preference was for gin, but try them both and decide for yourself. Be warned, this is a strong and serious drink.
—TASTE OF HOME TEST KITCHEN

30 Shrimp & Cucumber Rounds

I always make these appetizers for our get-togethers. They're simple to prepare and a snappy addition to any party buffet.
—**KELLY ALANIZ** EUREKA, CALIFORNIA

PREP/TOTAL TIME: 25 MINUTES **MAKES:** 3 DOZEN

- ½ pound cooked shrimp, peeled, deveined and finely chopped
- ½ cup reduced-fat mayonnaise
- 2 green onions, thinly sliced
- 1 celery rib, finely chopped
- 1 teaspoon dill pickle relish
  Dash cayenne pepper
- 1 medium English cucumber, cut into ¼-inch slices

1. In a small bowl, combine the first six ingredients. Spoon onto cucumber slices. Serve immediately.

Chili Ham Cups

I like to entertain a lot, and have used these tasty cups on several occasions as an appetizer. I like how easy it is to switch up the ingredients for a different flavor. You can really have fun with these!
—**LAURA METZGER** YORK, PENNSYLVANIA

PREP: 15 MINUTES **BAKE:** 20 MINUTES
MAKES: 10 SERVINGS

- 1 package (3 ounces) cream cheese, softened
- 1 cup finely chopped fully cooked ham
- 1 cup (4 ounces) shredded cheddar cheese
- 1 can (4 ounces) chopped green chilies, drained
- ¼ cup sliced ripe olives, drained
- 1 tube (10.2 ounces) refrigerated biscuits
  Salsa and sour cream, optional

1. In a small bowl, combine the cream cheese, ham, cheddar cheese, chilies and olives. Separate the dough into 10 biscuits; press each biscuit onto the bottom and up the sides of a greased muffin cup. Fill with ham mixture.

2. Bake at 375° for 20-25 minutes or until cheese is melted and crust is golden brown. Let stand for 2 minutes before removing from pan. Serve warm. Garnish with salsa and sour cream if desired.

Antipasto Appetizer Salad

Serve this as an appetizer or over torn Romaine lettuce as a salad. I like it with toasted baguette slices on the side.

—TAMRA DUNCAN
LINCOLN, ARKANSAS

PREP: 10 MINUTES + MARINATING
MAKES: 6 CUPS

- 1 jar (16 ounces) roasted sweet red pepper strips, drained
- ½ pound part-skim mozzarella cheese, cubed
- 1 cup grape tomatoes
- 1 jar (7½ ounces) marinated quartered artichoke hearts, undrained
- 1 jar (7 ounces) pimiento-stuffed olives, drained
- 1 can (6 ounces) pitted ripe olives, drained
- 1 teaspoon dried basil
- 1 teaspoon dried parsley flakes
  Pepper to taste
  Toasted baguette slices or Romaine lettuce, torn

1. In a large bowl, combine the first nine ingredients; toss to coat. Cover and refrigerate for at least 4 hours before serving.

2. Serve with baguette slices or over lettuce.

Editor's Note: *This recipe was tested with Vlasic roasted red pepper strips.*

20 Ranch Snack Mix

This is a wonderful fast-to-fix recipe that makes a generous 24 cups and doesn't involve any cooking. It's a cinch to make and really keeps its crunch.

—LINDA MURPHY PULASKI, WISCONSIN

PREP/TOTAL TIME: 15 MINUTES **MAKES:** 6 QUARTS

- 1 package (12 ounces) miniature pretzels
- 2 packages (6 ounces each) Bugles
- 1 can (10 ounces) salted cashews
- 1 package (6 ounces) bite-size cheddar cheese fish crackers
- 1 envelope ranch salad dressing mix
- ¾ cup canola oil

1. In two large bowls, combine the pretzels, Bugles, cashews and crackers. Sprinkle with dressing mix; toss gently to combine. Drizzle with oil; toss until well coated. Store in airtight containers.

20 Sweet Berry Bruschetta

I've made this recipe by toasting the bread on a grill at cookouts, but any way I serve it, I never have any leftovers. The bruschetta is sweet instead of savory, and guests enjoy the change.

—PATRICIA NIEH PORTOLA VALLY, CALIFORNIA

PREP/TOTAL TIME: 20 MINUTES **MAKES:** 10 PIECES

- 10 slices French bread (½ inch thick)
  Cooking spray
- 5 teaspoons sugar, divided
- 6 ounces fat-free cream cheese
- ½ teaspoon almond extract
- ¾ cup fresh blackberries
- ¾ cup fresh raspberries
- ¼ cup slivered almonds, toasted
- 2 teaspoons confectioners' sugar

1. Place bread on an ungreased baking sheet; lightly coat with cooking spray. Sprinkle with 2 teaspoons sugar. Broil 3-4 in. from the heat for 1-2 minutes or until lightly browned.

2. In a small bowl, combine the cream cheese, extract and remaining sugar. Spread over toasted bread. Top with berries and almonds; dust with confectioners' sugar. Serve immediately.

30 Italian Party Appetizers

Quick, easy, delicious, colorful and impressive! This is one great snack to serve with a refreshing white wine to unexpected guests. Easily doubled for a crowd.

—HEATHER NYGREN CUMMING, GEORGIA

PREP/TOTAL TIME: 30 MINUTES **MAKES:** 4 DOZEN

- 4 ounces cream cheese, softened
- 48 Triscuits or other crackers
- ¼ cup prepared pesto
- ¼ cup oil-packed sun-dried tomatoes, patted dry and thinly sliced

1. Spread cream cheese on each cracker. Top with pesto and a tomato slice. Serve immediately.

10 Screwdriver

If you're looking for a mixed drink that is easy on your budget, look no further. With just two simple ingredients, vodka and orange juice, you'll have a classic drink that's a real crowd-pleaser.

—TASTE OF HOME TEST KITCHEN

PREP/TOTAL TIME: 5 MINUTES **MAKES:** 1 SERVING

- ½ to ¾ cup ice cubes
- 2 ounces vodka
- 3 ounces orange juice

GARNISH
   Orange slice

1. Place ice in a rocks glass. Pour the vodka and orange juice into the glass. Garnish as desired.

192

196

185

Desserts

"A quick meal does not have to go without dessert. If you don't think so, just try my creamy 15-minute pie."

JEANETTE FUEHRING CONCORDIA, MISSOURI
about her recipe, No-Cook Coconut Pie, on page 196

Chocolate Cherry Cupcakes

Inside each of these cupcakes is a fruity surprise! Kids and adults will love them.

—BERTILLE COOPER
CALIFORNIA, MARYLAND

PREP: 15 MINUTES
BAKE: 20 MINUTES
MAKES: 2 DOZEN

- 1 package (18¼ ounces) chocolate cake mix
- 1⅓ cups water
- ½ cup canola oil
- 3 eggs
- 1 can (21 ounces) cherry pie filling
- 1 can (16 ounces) vanilla frosting
  Chocolate curls, optional

1. In a large bowl, combine the cake mix, water, oil and eggs; beat on low speed for 30 seconds. Beat on medium for 2 minutes.

2. Spoon batter by ¼ cupfuls into paper-lined muffin cups. Place a rounded teaspoonful of pie filling in the center of each cupcake. Set remaining pie filling aside.

3. Bake at 350° for 20-25 minutes or until a toothpick inserted near the center comes out clean. Remove from pans to wire racks to cool completely.

4. Frost cupcakes; top each with one cherry from pie filling. Refrigerate remaining pie filling for another use. Garnish with chocolate curls if desired.

30 Grilled Peaches 'n' Berries

Highlight the natural sweetness of peak summertime fruit with brown sugar, butter and a squeeze of lemon juice. Foil packets make this a go-anywhere grilled dessert.

—SHARON BICKETT CHESTER, SOUTH CAROLINA

PREP/TOTAL TIME: 30 MINUTES **MAKES:** 3 SERVINGS

- 3 medium ripe peaches, halved and pitted
- 1 cup fresh blueberries
- 2 tablespoons brown sugar
- 2 tablespoons butter
- 1 tablespoon lemon juice

1. Place two peach halves, cut side up, on each of three double thicknesses of heavy-duty foil (12 in. square). Top with blueberries, brown sugar, butter and lemon juice. Fold foil around fruit mixture and seal tightly.

2. Grill, covered, over medium-low heat for 18-20 minutes or until tender. Open foil carefully to allow steam to escape.

Watermelon Ice

Here is pure summer refreshment for a hot and humid day. It's fun to serve in snow-cone cups. Try it with a little lemon or lime juice if you like a brighter fruit flavor.

—DARLENE BRENDEN SALEM, OREGON

PREP: 15 MINUTES + FREEZING **MAKES:** 4-6 SERVINGS

- ½ cup sugar
- ¼ cup watermelon or mixed fruit gelatin powder
- ¾ cup boiling water
- 5 cups seeded cubed watermelon

1. In a large bowl, dissolve sugar and gelatin in boiling water; set aside. Place watermelon in a food processor; cover and puree. Stir into gelatin mixture.

2. Pour into an ungreased pan. Cover and freeze overnight. Remove from the freezer 15 minutes before serving; scrape ice with a fork. Serve in paper cones or serving dishes.

10 ▷ Banana Split Shortcake

PREP/TOTAL TIME: 10 MINUTES **MAKES:** 2 SERVINGS

- 4 slices pound cake (½ inch thick) or 2 individual round sponge cakes
- 1 medium firm banana, sliced
- 2 scoops vanilla ice cream
- 2 tablespoons chocolate syrup

1. Place cake slices on two dessert plates. Top each with banana and ice cream. Drizzle chocolate syrup over the tops.

❝ Two delicious desserts combine to create an out-of-this-world treat. I serve my banana split on a layer of tender pound cake. Yum! ❞

—CHRISTI GILLENTINE TULSA, OKLAHOMA

Easy Grasshopper Ice Cream Pie

This quick pie is such an ego booster! My family compliments me the entire time they're eating it. A big hit at work potlucks, too, it's good to the last crumb.

—KIM MURPHY ALBIA, IOWA

PREP: 15 MINUTES + FREEZING **MAKES:** 8 SERVINGS

- 4 **cups mint chocolate chip ice cream, softened**
- 1 **chocolate crumb crust (8 inches)**
- 5 **Oreo cookies, chopped**
- ⅓ **cup chocolate-covered peppermint candies**
  Chocolate hard-shell ice cream topping

1. Spread ice cream into crust. Sprinkle with cookies and candies; drizzle with ice cream topping. Freeze until firm. Remove from the freezer 15 minutes before serving.

Editor's Note: *This recipe was tested with Junior Mints chocolate-covered peppermint candies.*

10 ▸ Candy Bar Parfaits

My kids just love making their own candy and ice cream treats. These parfaits are such a favorite, we've featured them at build-your-own-parfait birthday parties. To add to the fun, try different nuts and candy bar toppings and offer a variety of ice cream flavors.

—ANGIE CASSADA MONROE, NORTH CAROLINA

PREP/TOTAL TIME: 10 MINUTES **MAKES:** 4 SERVINGS

- ½ **cup coarsely chopped unsalted peanuts**
- ½ **cup coarsely crushed pretzels**
- 1 **milk chocolate candy bar (1.55 ounces), chopped**
- 1 **pint vanilla ice cream, softened**
- ⅓ **cup chocolate syrup**
- 2 **tablespoons peanut butter**

1. In a small bowl, combine the peanuts, pretzels and chopped candy bar; place 2 tablespoons in each of four parfait glasses. Top each with ¼ cup ice cream, 2 tablespoons peanut mixture and another ¼ cup of ice cream.

2. Combine chocolate syrup and peanut butter; drizzle over ice cream. Sprinkle with remaining peanut mixture.

Peanut Butter Brownie Cupcakes

PREP: 15 MINUTES
BAKE: 15 MINUTES + COOLING
MAKES: 1 DOZEN

- 1 package fudge brownie mix (8-inch square pan size)
- ½ cup miniature semisweet chocolate chips
- ⅓ cup creamy peanut butter
- 3 tablespoons cream cheese, softened
- 1 egg
- ¼ cup sugar
  Confectioners' sugar

1. Prepare brownie batter according to package directions; stir in chocolate chips. For filling, in a small bowl, beat peanut butter, cream cheese, egg and sugar until smooth.

2. Fill paper-lined muffin cups one-third full with batter. Drop filling by teaspoonfuls into the center of each cupcake. Cover with remaining batter.

3. Bake at 350° for 15-20 minutes or until a toothpick inserted in brownie portion comes out clean. Cool for 10 minutes before removing from pan to a wire rack to cool completely. Dust tops with confectioners' sugar. Store in the refrigerator.

top tip

I like to dress up brownie mix by stirring almond extract and chocolate chips into the batter. I can never eat just one brownie; they're so good!
—**BETTE B.** LADYSMITH, WISCONSIN

I have made this outstandingly delicious recipe for years. These rich cupcakes are so decadent.
—**CAROL GILLESPIE** CHAMBERSBURG, PENNSYLVANIA

30 Praline Grahams

Someone brought these crunchy, nutty treats to a meeting I attended, and I wouldn't leave without the recipe. They're super easy to fix, inexpensive and delicious. The recipe makes a lot, so it's a great snack for a large gathering.

—MARIAN PLATT SEQUIM, WASHINGTON

PREP/TOTAL TIME: 25 MINUTES **MAKES:** 4 DOZEN

  12 **whole graham crackers**
  ½ **cup butter, cubed**
  ½ **cup packed brown sugar**
  ½ **cup finely chopped walnuts**

1. Line a 15-in. x 10-in. x 1-in. baking pan with heavy-duty foil. Break the graham crackers at indentations; place in a single layer in pan.

2. In a small saucepan, combine butter and brown sugar. Bring to a rolling boil over medium heat; boil for 2 minutes. Remove from the heat; add nuts. Pour over crackers.

3. Bake at 350° for 10 minutes or until lightly browned. Let stand for 2-3 minutes. Remove to a wire rack to cool.

10 Frosty Almond Dessert

You can treat your family to a homemade dessert without a lot of fuss when you whip up this confection. Everyone will love its yummy flavor.

—PHYLLIS SCHMALZ KANSAS CITY, KANSAS

PREP/TOTAL TIME: 10 MINUTES **MAKES:** 4 SERVINGS

  4 **cups low-fat vanilla frozen yogurt**
  1 **cup ice cubes**
  ½ **cup hot fudge ice cream topping**
  ¼ **teaspoon almond extract**
    Whipped topping and baking cocoa, optional

4. In a blender, place half of the yogurt, ice cubes, fudge topping and extract; cover and process for 1-2 minutes or until smooth. Stir if necessary. Pour into two chilled dessert glasses.

5. Repeat with remaining yogurt, ice, fudge topping and extract. Garnish with whipped topping and cocoa if desired.

10 Cool Chocolate Mousse

Four ingredients are all you need for this cool and creamy chocolate treat. It's so easy the kids will love helping you make it.

—**SHIRLEY LITTLE** ALVORD, TEXAS

PREP/TOTAL TIME: 10 MINUTES **MAKES:** 6 SERVINGS

- 2 **cups cold 2% milk**
- 1 **package (5.9 ounces) instant chocolate pudding mix**
- 1 **carton (8 ounces) frozen whipped topping, thawed**
- ½ **cup sour cream**
  Additional whipped topping, optional

1. In a large bowl, whisk milk and pudding mix for 2 minutes. Let stand for 2 minutes or until soft-set. Fold in whipped topping and sour cream. Pour into individual dessert dishes. Dollop with whipped topping if desired.

10 Caramel Apple Dessert

PREP/TOTAL TIME: 10 MINUTES **MAKES:** 6 SERVINGS

- 4 **to 6 medium apples, cut into wedges**
- 1 **jar (12 ounces) caramel ice cream topping**
- 1 **cup roasted chopped peanuts**

1. Just before serving, cut apples and arrange on a platter or individual plates. Heat ice cream topping according to package directions. Place peanuts in a small bowl. To serve, dip apples in warm caramel sauce and then in chopped peanuts.

❝ The whole family has fun dipping apple wedges into the caramel sauce and peanuts. Even our toddler gets in on the act! ❞

—**KATHIE LANDMANN** LEXINGTON PARK, MARYLAND

30 ▶ Honey-Peanut Crispy Bars

My daughters have loved these nutritious snacks since they were in grade school. Now, both are adults and still make these bars when they want a quick treat.
—**URSULA MAURER** WAUWATOSA, WISCONSIN

PREP/TOTAL TIME: 30 MINUTES **MAKES:** 1 DOZEN

> ½ **cup honey**
> ½ **cup reduced-fat chunky peanut butter**
> ½ **cup nonfat dry milk powder**
> 4 **cups Rice Krispies**

1. In a large saucepan, combine the honey, peanut butter and milk powder. Cook and stir over low heat until blended.

2. Remove from the heat; stir in cereal. Press into an 8-in. square dish coated with cooking spray. Let stand until set. Cut into bars.

20 ▶ Cheerio Treats

Peanut butter, Cheerios and M&M's put a sweet spin on crispy bars. Whether I take them to picnics or bake sales, I'm always asked for the recipe. Great for on-the-go snacks or tailgating, too.
—**PENNY REIFENRATH** WYNOT, NEBRASKA

PREP/TOTAL TIME: 20 MINUTES **MAKES:** 15 SERVINGS

> 3 **tablespoons butter**
> 1 **package (10½ ounces) miniature marshmallows**
> ½ **cup peanut butter**
> 5 **cups Cheerios**
> 1 **cup milk chocolate M&M's**

1. Place butter and marshmallows in a large microwave-safe bowl. Microwave, uncovered, on high for 1-2 minutes or until melted. Stir in peanut butter until blended. Add the cereal and M&M's. Spoon into a greased 13-in. x 9-in. pan; press down gently. Cool slightly before cutting.

Editor's Note: *This recipe was tested in a 1,100-watt microwave.*

Marshmallow Pops

These cute and easy pops are great fun for any age. They'd be perfect for your child's next birthday party.

—MARCIA PORCH
WINTER PARK, FLORIDA

PREP: 30 MINUTES + CHILLING
MAKES: 20 SERVINGS

- 2 **cups (12 ounces) semisweet chocolate chips**
- 4½ **teaspoons canola oil**
- 40 **large marshmallows**
- 20 **Popsicle sticks**
  Toppings: assorted sprinkles, flaked coconut and ground walnuts

1. In a microwave, melt chocolate chips and oil. Stir until smooth.

2. Thread two marshmallows onto each wooden stick. Roll marshmallows in melted chocolate, turning to coat. Allow excess to drip off. Roll in toppings of your choice. Place on waxed paper-lined baking sheets. Chill until firm.

Chocolate Chip Butter Cookies

At the downtown Chicago law firm where I work, we often bring in goodies for special occasions. When co-workers hear I've baked these melt-in-your-mouth cookies, they make a special trip to my floor to sample them. Best of all, these crisp, buttery treats can be made in no time.

—JANIS GRUCA MOKENA, ILLINOIS

PREP: 20 MINUTES **BAKE:** 15 MINUTES/BATCH + COOLING
MAKES: ABOUT 4 DOZEN

- 1 **cup butter, cubed**
- ½ **teaspoon vanilla extract**
- 2 **cups all-purpose flour**
- 1 **cup confectioners' sugar**
- 1 **cup (6 ounces) miniature semisweet chocolate chips**
  Melted semisweet and/or white chocolate, optional

1. Melt butter in a microwave; stir in vanilla. Cool completely. In a large bowl, combine flour and confectioners' sugar; stir in butter mixture and chocolate chips (mixture will be crumbly).

2. Shape into 1-in. balls. Place 2 in. apart on ungreased baking sheets; flatten slightly. Bake at 375° for 12 minutes or until edges begin to brown. Cool on wire racks. Dip or drizzle with chocolate if desired.

10 Ambrosia Tarts

I created this dessert for my niece, who loves the tangy-sweet combo of fruit and marshmallows.

—MARILOU ROBINSON
PORTLAND, OREGON

PREP/TOTAL TIME: 10 MINUTES
MAKES: 4 SERVINGS

- 1 **can (11 ounces) mandarin oranges, drained**
- 1 **can (8 ounces) crushed pineapple, drained**
- ½ **cup miniature marshmallows**
- ¼ **cup flaked coconut**
- 1 **cup whipped topping**
- 4 **individual graham cracker shells**

1. In a small bowl, combine the oranges, pineapple, marshmallows and coconut. Fold in whipped topping. Spoon into shells. Chill until serving.

20 Strawberry Mousse

To cut calories from a strawberry pie recipe, I lightened up the filling and served it in dessert dishes instead of a pie crust. This mousse is elegant and refreshing without much fuss.

—WAYDELLA HART PARSONS, KANSAS

PREP/TOTAL TIME: 20 MINUTES **MAKES:** 8 SERVINGS

- 4 cups fresh or frozen unsweetened strawberries
- ½ cup sugar
- 1 package (1 ounce) sugar-free instant vanilla pudding mix
- 1 carton (8 ounces) frozen reduced-fat whipped topping, thawed

1. In a food processor, combine strawberries and sugar; cover and process until smooth. Strain and discard seeds. Return strawberry mixture to the food processor. Add the pudding mix; cover and process until smooth.

2. Transfer to a large bowl; fold in whipped topping. Spoon into dessert dishes. Refrigerate until serving.

Frozen Orange Cream Pie

PREP: 5 MINUTES + FREEZING **MAKES:** 6-8 SERVINGS

- 2½ cups vanilla ice cream, softened
- 1 cup thawed orange juice concentrate
- 3 drops red food coloring, optional
- 1 drop yellow food coloring, optional
- 1 graham cracker crust (9 inches)

1. In a bowl, combine the ice cream and orange juice concentrate. Stir in food coloring if desired. Spoon into crust. Cover and freeze for 8 hours or overnight. Remove from the freezer 10 minutes before serving.

66 Dessert doesn't get much easier than this fun, frosty little pie. Children like it because it tastes like a popular ice cream treat. 99

—NANCY HORSBURGH EVERETT, ONTARIO

10 ⟩ Peanut Butter S'mores

I turn to this recipe when I need something fun and easy for dessert. It's a decadent, extra-sweet take on classic campfire s'mores.

—LILY JULOW GAINESVILLE, FLORIDA

PREP/TOTAL TIME: 10 MINUTES **MAKES:** 4 SERVINGS

- 8 **large chocolate chip cookies**
- 4 **teaspoons hot fudge ice cream topping**
- 4 **large marshmallows**
- 4 **peanut butter cups**

1. Spread bottoms of four cookies with fudge topping. Using a long-handled fork, grill marshmallows 6 in. from medium-hot heat until golden brown, turning occasionally.

2. Carefully place a marshmallow and a peanut butter cup on each fudge-topped cookie; top with remaining cookies. Serve immediately.

10 ⟩ Oreo Cheesecake Pie

This pie is so quick, you'll have it ready in less than 10 minutes. And it's so good, it may disappear just as fast!

—CATHY SHORTALL EASTON, MARYLAND

PREP/TOTAL TIME: 5 MINUTES **MAKES:** 8 SERVINGS

- 1 **carton (24.3 ounces) Philadelphia ready-to-serve cheesecake filling**
- 1½ **cups coarsely crushed Oreos (about 12 cookies), divided**
- 1 **chocolate crumb crust (9 inches)**

1. In a large bowl, combine cheesecake filling and 1¼ cups crushed cookies. Spoon into crust; sprinkle with remaining cookies. Chill until serving.

20 No-Cook Coconut Pie

A quick meal does not have to go without dessert. If you don't think so, just try my creamy 15-minute pie.

—JEANETTE FUEHRING CONCORDIA, MISSOURI

PREP/TOTAL TIME: 15 MINUTES **MAKES:** 6-8 SERVINGS

    2 packages (3.4 ounces each) instant vanilla
       pudding mix
  2¾   cups cold 2% milk
    1 teaspoon coconut extract
    1 carton (8 ounces) frozen whipped topping,
       thawed
  ½   cup flaked coconut
    1 graham cracker crust (9 inches)
       Toasted coconut

1. In a large bowl, whisk the pudding mixes, milk and extract for 2 minutes. Fold in whipped topping and coconut.

2. Pour into the crust. Sprinkle with toasted coconut. Chill until serving.

Lemon Snowflakes

You'll need just four items to whip up these delightful cookies. Confectioners' sugar highlights the cracked tops to give them their snowflake appearance.

—LINDA BARRY DIANNA, TEXAS

PREP: 30 MINUTES **BAKE:** 10 MINUTES/BATCH
MAKES: 5-6 DOZEN

    1 package (18¼ ounces) lemon cake mix
  2¼   cups whipped topping
    1 egg
       Confectioners' sugar

1. In a large bowl, combine the cake mix, whipped topping and egg until well blended. Batter will be very sticky.

2. Drop by teaspoonfuls into confectioners' sugar; roll lightly to coat. Place on ungreased baking sheets. Bake at 350° for 10-12 minutes or until lightly browned and tops are cracked. Remove to wire racks to cool.

30 Caramel Marshmallow Treats

PREP/TOTAL TIME: 30 MINUTES
MAKES: 5 DOZEN

- 1 can (14 ounces) sweetened condensed milk
- 1 package (14 ounces) caramels
- 1 cup butter, cubed
- 1 teaspoon ground cinnamon
- ½ teaspoon vanilla extract
  Rice Krispies, coarsely crushed
- 1 package (16 ounces) large marshmallows

1. Line two baking sheets with waxed paper; set aside.

2. In a large saucepan, cook and stir the milk, caramels and butter over low heat until melted and smooth. Remove from the heat; stir in the cinnamon and vanilla.

3. Place Rice Krispies in a shallow bowl. With a toothpick, dip each marshmallow into warm caramel mixture; turn to coat. Press bottoms into Rice Krispies; place treats on prepared pans. Let stand until set.

I created this candy by combining my husband's favorite cookie recipe and my mom's caramel dip. These sweets really appeal to kids. Plus, they can help make them. —**TAMARA HOLSCHEN** ANCHOR POINT, ALASKA

20 ▶ Easy Tiramisu

PREP/TOTAL TIME: 20 MINUTES **MAKES:** 8 SERVINGS

- 1 **package (10¾ ounces) frozen pound cake, thawed**
- ¾ **cup strong brewed coffee**
- 1 **package (8 ounces) cream cheese, softened**
- 1 **cup sugar**
- ½ **cup chocolate syrup**
- 1 **cup heavy whipping cream, whipped**
- 2 **Heath candy bars (1.4 ounces each), crushed**

1. Cut cake into nine slices. Arrange in an ungreased 11-in. x 7-in. dish, cutting to fit if needed. Drizzle with the coffee.

2. In a small bowl, beat cream cheese and sugar until smooth. Add chocolate syrup. Fold in whipped cream. Spread over cake. Sprinkle with crushed candy bars. Refrigerate until serving.

❝ This treat comes together quickly and can be made the night before. Sometimes I drizzle additional chocolate syrup over the coffee and pound cake. Other times, I add sliced almonds to the topping. ❞

—NANCY BROWN DAHINDA, ILLINOIS

10 ▶ Raspberry Parfaits

Looking for a carefree way to impress someone special? This rich and creamy raspberry parfait is guaranteed to dazzle them!

—JOELYN HANHAM CHESTER, NEW YORK

PREP/TOTAL TIME: 10 MINUTES **MAKES:** 2 SERVINGS

- 2 **ounces cream cheese, softened**
- 2 **tablespoons seedless raspberry jam**
- ½ **cup whipped topping, divided**
- ½ **cup fresh or frozen raspberries**

1. In a small bowl, beat cream cheese and jam until smooth. Fold in ¼ cup whipped topping.

2. Place 2 tablespoons raspberries in each of two small parfait glasses or dessert dishes; layer with cream cheese mixture and remaining berries. Top with remaining whipped topping. Refrigerate parfaits until serving.

239

211

216

Cook Once, Eat Twice

Planned Overs.....204
Freezer Pleasers......218

❝We were happy growing up when there was pork roast on the menu because we were sure that, within the next few days, we'd be feasting on the leftover pork in these tasty sandwiches.❞

GEORGE HASCHER PHOENICIA, NEW YORK
about his recipe, Homemade Barbecues, on page 211

Leftover turkey breast is great for more than just sandwiches.

Butter & Herb Turkey

PREP: 10 MINUTES **COOK:** 5 HOURS
MAKES: 12 SERVINGS (3 CUPS GRAVY)

- 1 bone-in turkey breast (6 to 7 pounds)
- 2 tablespoons butter, softened
- ½ teaspoon dried rosemary, crushed
- ½ teaspoon dried thyme
- ¼ teaspoon garlic powder
- ¼ teaspoon pepper
- 1 can (14½ ounces) chicken broth
- 3 tablespoons cornstarch
- 1 tablespoon cold water

1. Rub turkey with butter. Combine the rosemary, thyme, garlic powder and pepper; sprinkle over turkey. Place in a 6-qt. slow cooker. Pour broth over top. Cover and cook on low for 5-6 hours or until tender.

2. Remove turkey to a serving platter; keep warm. Skim fat from cooking juices; transfer to a small saucepan. Bring to a boil. Combine cornstarch and water until smooth. Gradually stir into the pan. Bring to a boil; cook and stir for 2 minutes or until thickened. Serve with turkey.

30 Turkey Bean Chili

Here's a quick recipe that tastes great. It won a ribbon at the Nebraska State Fair. Once you try it, you'll want to make it again and again. It's that easy.

—LARITA LANG LINCOLN, NEBRASKA

PREP/TOTAL TIME: 30 MINUTES
MAKES: 6 SERVINGS

- 2 cups cubed cooked turkey breast
- 2 cans (14½ ounces each) diced tomatoes, undrained
- 1 can (15 ounces) black beans, rinsed and drained
- 1 can (15 ounces) great northern beans, rinsed and drained
- 1 cup barbecue sauce
- 1 medium onion, chopped
- 1 teaspoon chili powder
- 1 teaspoon ground cumin

1. In a large saucepan, combine all ingredients. Bring to a boil. Reduce heat; simmer, uncovered, for 15-20 minutes to allow flavors to blend.

30 Crescent Turkey Casserole

How do you make a dinner of turkey and vegetables really appealing to kids? You turn it into a pie, of course! My version tastes classic, but won't take any time at all.
—**DANIELA ESSMAN** PERHAM, MINNESOTA

PREP/TOTAL TIME: 30 MINUTES **MAKES:** 4 SERVINGS

- ½ cup mayonnaise
- 2 tablespoons all-purpose flour
- 1 teaspoon chicken bouillon granules
- ⅛ teaspoon pepper
- ¾ cup 2% milk
- 1½ cups cubed cooked turkey breast
- 1 package (10 ounces) frozen mixed vegetables
- 1 tube (4 ounces) refrigerated crescent rolls

1. In a large saucepan, combine the mayonnaise, flour, bouillon and pepper. Gradually add milk; stir until smooth. Bring to a boil over medium heat; cook and stir for 2 minutes or until thickened.

2. Add turkey and vegetables; heat through. Spoon into a greased 8-in. square baking dish.

3. Unroll crescent dough and separate into two rectangles. Seal perforations. Place over turkey mixture. Bake at 375° for 15-20 minutes or until golden brown.

20 Thai Turkey Salad Pitas

Here's a quick and easy way to use up leftover turkey. My son likes to try foods from different cultures, and he really enjoys these pitas. They're great in lunch boxes.
—**RENEE DENT** CONRAD, MONTANA

PREP/TOTAL TIME: 20 MINUTES **MAKES:** 4 SERVINGS

- 2 cups cubed cooked turkey breast
- 2 cups coleslaw mix
- ½ cup golden raisins
- ⅓ cup chopped unsalted peanuts
- 1 green onion, chopped
- ¼ cup lime juice
- ¼ cup honey
- 3 tablespoons soy sauce
- 1 tablespoon sesame oil
- 2 teaspoons chili sauce
- ½ teaspoon garlic powder
- 8 pita pocket halves

1. In a large bowl, combine the first five ingredients. In another bowl, combine the lime juice, honey, soy sauce, oil, chili sauce and garlic powder; pour over turkey mixture and toss to coat. Fill each pita half with ½ cup turkey mixture.

When Mother wanted to serve ham, she went to the smokehouse, took one down from the rafters and sliced off as much as was needed. The rest was hung up again. This recipe is especially sweet and buttery if you use real smoked ham with no water added.

—**MARJORIE SCHMIDT** ST. MARYS, OHIO

Give ham steak a makeover for easy dinners that serve two.

Baked Apple Ham Steaks

PREP: 10 MINUTES **BAKE:** 1¼ HOURS
MAKES: 6-8 SERVINGS

- 2 fully cooked bone-in ham steaks (1 pound each)
- 2 teaspoons ground mustard
- ½ cup packed brown sugar
- 3 medium tart apples
- 2 tablespoons butter
  Pepper to taste

1. Place ham in an ungreased 13-in. x 9-in. baking dish. Rub with mustard and sprinkle with brown sugar. Core apples and cut into ¾-in. slices; arrange in a single layer over ham. Dot with butter and sprinkle with pepper.

2. Cover and bake at 400° for 15 minutes. Reduce heat to 325°; bake for 45 minutes. Uncover and bake 15 minutes longer or until apples are tender.

20 Ham Salad Pockets

Looking for a great way to use up leftover ham? Try these simple low-fat sandwiches. Pineapple and mustard are traditional flavors with baked ham, and they work well in these pita pockets.

—**MITZI SENTIFF** ANNAPOLIS, MARYLAND

PREP/TOTAL TIME: 15 MINUTES
MAKES: 4 SERVINGS

- 1¼ cups cubed fully cooked ham
- ¾ cup unsweetened pineapple tidbits
- 1 large carrot, chopped
- ¼ cup fat-free mayonnaise
- 1 tablespoon honey mustard
- 4 pita pocket halves
- 4 lettuce leaves

1. In a small bowl, combine the ham, pineapple and carrot. Stir in the mayonnaise and mustard until blended. Line each pita half with a lettuce leaf; fill with ham salad.

30 Ham Stew for 2

This dish is one my husband and I enjoy any time of the year. If I don't have leftover ham, I buy a thick slice from the deli and use that. Served with a salad and rolls, it's a quick meal for two.

—JUDY HALL LOCKPORT, ILLINOIS

PREP/TOTAL TIME: 30 MINUTES **MAKES:** 2 SERVINGS

- 2 medium potatoes, peeled and cut into ¾-inch cubes
- 2 medium carrots, sliced
- 1½ cups cubed fully cooked ham
- 1 cup water
- 1 small onion, chopped
- 1 bay leaf
- ½ teaspoon salt
- ¼ teaspoon dried savory
- ⅛ teaspoon pepper
- 3 tablespoons all-purpose flour
- 1 cup milk

1. In a large saucepan, combine the first nine ingredients. Bring to a boil. Reduce heat; cover and simmer until vegetables are tender. In a small bowl, combine flour and milk until smooth. Stir into stew. Bring to a boil; cook and stir for 2 minutes or until thickened. Discard bay leaf before serving.

30 Stuffed-Crust Hawaiian Pizza

I use tortillas as the crust for my simple five-ingredient pizza. It's such a quick and tasty dish. It only takes about half an hour from start to stomach!

—MARY ROBERTS-RATHJE SWISHER, IOWA

PREP/TOTAL TIME: 25 MINUTES **MAKES:** 2 SERVINGS

- 2 flour tortillas (10 inches)
- 1½ cups (6 ounces) shredded part-skim mozzarella cheese, divided
- ¼ cup pizza sauce
- ½ cup pineapple tidbits, drained
- ¾ cup diced fully cooked ham

1. Place one tortilla on a baking sheet coated with cooking spray. Sprinkle with 1 cup cheese. Top with second tortilla; spread with pizza sauce. Sprinkle with pineapple, ham and remaining cheese.

2. Bake at 375° for 15 minutes or until tortillas are crisp and cheese is melted.

You'll find this meal is a nice one to prepare for company or to serve your family for Sunday dinner. All you need with it is a tossed salad and some crusty French bread. —**PELLA VISNICK** DALLAS, TEXAS

Sunday dinner's roasted chicken makes quick weeknight favorites.

Greek Roasted Chicken and Potatoes

PREP: 10 MINUTES **BAKE:** 2 HOURS + STANDING
MAKES: 8-10 SERVINGS

- 1   roasting chicken (6 to 7 pounds)
     Salt and pepper to taste
- 2   to 3 teaspoons dried oregano, divided
- 4   to 6 baking potatoes, peeled and quartered
- ¼   cup butter, melted
- 3   tablespoons lemon juice
- ¾   cup chicken broth

1. Place chicken breast side up on a rack in a roasting pan. Sprinkle with salt and pepper and half of the oregano. Arrange potatoes around the chicken; sprinkle with salt, pepper and remaining oregano. Pour butter and lemon juice over chicken and potatoes. Add chicken broth to pan.

2. Bake, uncovered, at 350° for 2 to 2½ hours or until a thermometer reads 180°, basting frequently with pan drippings. Cover and let stand for 10 minutes before carving. If desired, thicken pan drippings for gravy.

Chicken Biscuit Potpie

This hearty and delicious meal takes just 10 minutes to assemble before popping it in the oven.

—**DOROTHY SMITH** EL DORADO, ARKANSAS

PREP: 10 MINUTES **BAKE:** 25 MINUTES
MAKES: 4 SERVINGS

- 1⅔   cups frozen mixed vegetables, thawed
- 1½   cups cubed cooked chicken
- 1   can (10¾ ounces) condensed cream of chicken soup, undiluted
- ¼   teaspoon dried thyme
- 1   cup biscuit/baking mix
- ½   cup milk
- 1   egg

1. In a large bowl, combine the vegetables, chicken, soup and thyme. Pour into an ungreased deep-dish 9-in. pie plate. Combine the biscuit mix, milk and egg; spoon over chicken mixture.

2. Bake at 400° for 25-30 minutes or until golden brown.

Fruited Chicken Pasta Salad

Here's a fresh five-ingredient salad that's perfect for summer. It makes a great lunch box entree, too. You'll love the combo of sweet and savory flavors.

—BRIDGET FRANCOEUR ADRIAN, MICHIGAN

PREP: 25 MINUTES + CHILLING **MAKES:** 6 SERVINGS

- 2 **cups uncooked bow tie pasta**
- 2 **cups cubed cooked chicken**
- 1 **can (11 ounces) mandarin oranges, drained**
- 1 **cup halved green grapes**
- ½ **cup ranch salad dressing**

1. Cook pasta according to package directions. Meanwhile, in a large bowl, combine the chicken, oranges and grapes.

2. Drain and rinse pasta with cold water; add to chicken mixture. Drizzle with dressing; toss to coat. Refrigerate for at least 1 hour before serving.

30 Cheesy Chicken Vegetable Soup

Kids won't think twice about eating vegetables if they're tucked into this rich and cheesy soup!

—LAVONNE LUNDGREN SIOUX CITY, IOWA

PREP/TOTAL TIME: 30 MINUTES **MAKES:** 7 SERVINGS

- 4 **cups cubed cooked chicken breast**
- 3½ **cups water**
- 2 **cans (10¾ ounces each) condensed cream of chicken soup, undiluted**
- 1 **package (16 ounces) frozen mixed vegetables, thawed**
- 1 **can (14½ ounces) diced potatoes, drained**
- 1 **package (16 ounces) process cheese (Velveeta), cubed**

1. In a Dutch oven, combine the first five ingredients. Bring to a boil. Reduce heat; cover and simmer for 8-10 minutes or until vegetables are tender. Stir in cheese just until melted (do not boil).

This is the meal I have become famous for, and it is so simple to prepare in the slow cooker. The garlic and apple flavors really complement the pork. It's great with steamed fresh asparagus and roasted red potatoes.

—**JENNIFER LOOS** WASHINGTON BORO, PENNSYLVANIA

Use leftover pork roast to create your choice of cuisine. Smart!

Slow-Cooked Pork Roast

PREP: 10 MINUTES **COOK:** 8 HOURS + STANDING
MAKES: 12 SERVINGS

- 1 boneless pork loin roast (3½ to 4 pounds)
- 1 jar (12 ounces) apple jelly
- ½ cup water
- 2½ teaspoons minced garlic
- 1 tablespoon dried parsley flakes
- 1 to 1½ teaspoons seasoned salt
- 1 to 1½ teaspoons pepper

1. Cut the roast in half; place in a 5-qt. slow cooker. In a small bowl, combine the jelly, water and garlic; pour over roast. Sprinkle with parsley, salt and pepper.

2. Cover and cook on low for 8-10 hours or until meat is tender. Let stand for 15 minutes before slicing. Serve with cooking juices if desired.

Pork Spanish Rice

My family wasn't fond of pork roast until I used it in this yummy casserole.

—**BETTY UNRAU** MACGREGOR, MANITOBA

PREP: 20 MINUTES **BAKE:** 20 MINUTES
MAKES: 4 SERVINGS

- 1 medium green pepper, chopped
- 1 small onion, chopped
- 2 tablespoons butter
- 1 can (14½ ounces) diced tomatoes, drained
- 1 cup chicken broth
- ½ teaspoon salt
- ¼ teaspoon pepper
- 1¾ cups cubed cooked pork
- 1 cup uncooked instant rice

1. In a large skillet, saute green pepper and onion in butter until tender. Stir in the tomatoes, broth, salt and pepper. Bring to a boil; stir in pork and rice.

2. Transfer to a greased 2-qt. baking dish. Cover and bake at 350° for 20-25 minutes or until rice is tender and liquid is absorbed. Stir before serving.

30 ▶ Homemade Barbecues

We were happy growing up when there was pork roast on the menu because we were sure that, within the next few days, we'd be feasting on the leftover pork in these tasty sandwiches.

—GEORGE HASCHER PHOENICIA, NEW YORK

PREP/TOTAL TIME: 30 MINUTES **MAKES:** 2-3 SERVINGS

- 2 celery ribs, finely chopped
- 1 medium onion, finely chopped
- 1 teaspoon canola oil
- 1 cup ketchup
- 1 to 1½ teaspoons salt
- 1 teaspoon ground mustard
- 2 cups shredded cooked pork
- 2 to 3 kaiser rolls or hamburger buns, split

1. In a large saucepan, saute celery and onion in oil until tender. Stir in the ketchup, salt and mustard. Add pork. Bring to a boil. Reduce heat; cover and simmer for 20-30 minutes to allow flavors to blend. Serve on rolls.

10 ▶ Chinese Spinach-Almond Salad

This recipe combines power-packed spinach and other veggies with lean meat and heart-healthy almonds. Reduced-fat dressing adds a light Asian touch to each delicious serving. For added crunch, I sometimes toss in some crispy chow mein noodles.

—MARY ANN KIEFFER LAWRENCE, KANSAS

PREP/TOTAL TIME: 10 MINUTES **MAKES:** 4 SERVINGS

- 1 package (6 ounces) fresh baby spinach
- 2 cups cubed cooked pork
- 1 cup bean sprouts
- 2 medium carrots, thinly sliced
- ½ cup sliced fresh mushrooms
- ¼ cup sliced almonds, toasted
- ½ cup reduced-fat sesame ginger salad dressing

1. In a large bowl, combine the first six ingredients. Divide among four salad plates; drizzle with dressing. Serve immediately.

Entertaining doesn't get much easier than serving this tasty five-ingredient ham from the slow cooker. Leftovers are delicious in casseroles.

—HEATHER SPRING SHEPPARD AIR FORCE BASE, TEXAS

Flavorful slow-cooked ham makes these delicious comfort foods.

Zesty Ham

PREP: 5 MINUTES **COOK:** 6 HOURS
MAKES: 15-20 SERVINGS

- ½ cup packed brown sugar
- 1 teaspoon ground mustard
- 1 teaspoon prepared horseradish
- 2 tablespoons plus ¼ cup cola, divided
- 1 fully cooked boneless ham (5 to 6 pounds), cut in half

1. In a small bowl, combine the brown sugar, mustard, horseradish and 2 tablespoons cola. Rub over ham. Transfer to a 5-qt. slow cooker; add remaining cola to slow cooker.

2. Cover and cook on low for 6-8 hours or until a thermometer reads 140°.

30 Quick Antipasto Salad

I used to work in a pizza shop where this salad was the most popular item on the menu. It's great for nights when it's just too hot to cook.

—WEBBIE CARVAJAL ALPINE, TEXAS

PREP/TOTAL TIME: 25 MINUTES
MAKES: 8 SERVINGS

- 1½ cups cubed fully cooked ham
- 1 jar (10 ounces) pimiento-stuffed olives, drained and sliced
- 1 can (3.8 ounces) sliced ripe olives, drained
- 1 package (3½ ounces) sliced pepperoni, quartered
- 8 cups shredded lettuce
- 10 to 12 cherry tomatoes, quartered
- 1 cup Italian salad dressing
- 1½ cups (6 ounces) shredded part-skim mozzarella cheese

1. In a large bowl, combine the ham, olives and pepperoni. On a platter or individual salad plates, arrange the lettuce, olive mixture and tomatoes.

2. Drizzle the salad with dressing and sprinkle with cheese. Serve immediately.

Spinach-Ham Casserole

This is down-home cooking at its best! Ham and veggies join forces with a creamy sauce and pretty lattice topping to create a hearty meal idea.

—TASTE OF HOME TEST KITCHEN

PREP: 25 MINUTES **BAKE:** 20 MINUTES
MAKES: 4 SERVINGS

- 3 **cups cubed fully cooked ham**
- 1 **package (16 ounces) frozen sliced carrots, thawed**
- 1 **can (10¾ ounces) condensed cream of potato soup, undiluted**
- 1 **package (10 ounces) frozen creamed spinach, thawed**
- ¼ **cup water**
- ¼ **teaspoon pepper**
- ⅛ **teaspoon salt**
- 1 **tube (4 ounces) refrigerated crescent rolls**

1. In a large nonstick skillet coated with cooking spray, cook ham over medium heat until lightly browned. Stir in the carrots, soup, spinach, water, pepper and salt; heat through. Pour into a greased 8-in. square baking dish.

2. Unroll crescent dough; separate into two rectangles. Seal perforations. Cut each rectangle lengthwise into four strips; make a lattice crust. Bake at 375° for 18-22 minutes or until bubbly and crust is golden brown.

30 Broccoli-Ham Noodles

My husband, Ronald, works long hours and frequently won't arrive home until after 7 p.m. But these creamy noodles are still tasty after warming in the microwave.

—BARB MARSHALL PICKERINGTON, OHIO

PREP/TOTAL TIME: 25 MINUTES **MAKES:** 8 SERVINGS

- 1 **package (12 ounces) egg noodles**
- 1 **package (16 ounces) frozen broccoli cuts**
- 3 **cups cubed fully cooked ham**
- 1 **cup (4 ounces) shredded part-skim mozzarella cheese**
- 1 **cup (4 ounces) shredded Parmesan cheese**
- ⅓ **cup butter, cubed**
- ½ **cup half-and-half cream**
- ¼ **teaspoon each garlic powder, salt and pepper**

1. In a Dutch oven, cook noodles in boiling water for 5 minutes. Add broccoli and ham; cook 5-10 minutes longer or until noodles are tender.

2. Drain; return to pan. Stir in the remaining ingredients. Cook and stir over low heat until butter is melted and mixture is heated through.

Tender beef makes tasty stew, old-fashioned hash or pasta.

German-Style Beef Roast

PREP: 10 MINUTES **COOK:** 8 HOURS
MAKES: 10 SERVINGS

- 1 boneless beef chuck roast (4 pounds), trimmed
- 1 teaspoon pepper
- 1 large onion, thinly sliced
- 1 bottle (12 ounces) beer or nonalcoholic beer
- 1 cup ketchup
- ¼ cup packed brown sugar
- ¼ cup all-purpose flour
- ¼ cup cold water

1. Cut roast in half; sprinkle with pepper. Place onion and roast in a 5-qt. slow cooker. In a small bowl, combine the beer, ketchup and brown sugar; pour over top. Cover and cook on low for 8-10 hours or until meat is tender.

2. Remove meat to a serving platter; keep warm. Skim fat from cooking juices; transfer to a small saucepan. Bring liquid to a boil.

3. Combine flour and water until smooth; gradually stir into the pan. Bring to a boil; cook and stir for 2 minutes or until thickened. Serve with roast.

20 Easy Beef Stew

This recipe transforms leftover cooked roast beef into a homey stew.

—**VALERIE COOK** HUBBARD, IOWA

PREP/TOTAL TIME: 15 MINUTES
MAKES: 4 SERVINGS

- 2 cups cubed cooked roast beef
- 1 can (15 ounces) mixed vegetables, liquid drained and reserved
- 1 can (10¾ ounces) condensed cream of celery soup, undiluted
- 1 can (10¾ ounces) condensed cream of mushroom soup, undiluted
- ½ teaspoon dried thyme, optional
- ¼ teaspoon dried rosemary, crushed, optional
  Pepper to taste

1. In a large saucepan, combine the beef, vegetables, soups and seasonings. Heat through. If desired, add reserved vegetable liquid to thin the stew.

20 Crispy Hash Cake

This family favorite provides a quick and nourishing meal. I remember Mother made this often when I was growing up. It's a good way to use leftover beef roast, but other types of meat work well, too.

—FLO BURTNETT GAGE, OKLAHOMA

PREP/TOTAL TIME: 15 MINUTES **MAKES:** 2 SERVINGS

- 2 **tablespoons butter**
- 1 **cup cubed cooked roast beef**
- 1 **cup diced cooked potato**
- 1 **medium onion, diced**
- 1 **tablespoon minced parsley**
- ½ **cup milk**
  Salt and pepper to taste

1. In a small heavy skillet, melt butter over medium-high heat. In a small bowl, combine the remaining ingredients; add to the skillet.

2. Cover and cook until hash cake is crisp on the bottom. Turn and brown other side.

20 Roast Beef Pasta Skillet

Leftover beef is the star in a skillet dinner that's perfect for two. Chopped tomato adds a burst of fresh flavor.

—BILL HILBRICH ST. CLOUD, MINNESOTA

PREP/TOTAL TIME: 20 MINUTES **MAKES:** 2 SERVINGS

- 1 **cup uncooked spiral pasta**
- ½ **cup chopped onion**
- 1 **teaspoon olive oil**
- 1 **teaspoon butter**
- 1 **cup cubed cooked roast beef**
- ½ **teaspoon pepper**
- ½ **cup chopped tomato**
- ½ **cup grated Parmesan cheese**

1. Cook pasta according to package directions. Meanwhile, in a large skillet, saute onion in oil and butter until tender. Add roast beef and pepper; heat through. Drain pasta; add to beef mixture. Stir in tomato and cheese.

This simple recipe has become my family's favorite way to eat chicken. The blend of sweet and spicy is perfect!

—**MELISSA BALL** PEARISBURG, VIRGINIA

Grill extra chicken breasts for easy meals in the future.

20 Sweet and Spicy Grilled Chicken

PREP/TOTAL TIME: 20 MINUTES
MAKES: 6 SERVINGS

- 2 tablespoons brown sugar
- 1 tablespoon paprika
- 2 teaspoons onion powder
- 1½ teaspoons salt
- 1 teaspoon chili powder
- 6 boneless skinless chicken breast halves (6 ounces each)

1. Combine the first five ingredients; rub over chicken. Moisten a paper towel with cooking oil; using long-handled tongs, lightly coat the grill rack.

2. Grill chicken, covered, over medium heat or broil 4 in. from the heat for 4-5 minutes on each side or until a thermometer reads 170°.

20 Asparagus Chicken Sandwiches

No one will be able to resist these lovely open-faced sandwiches that definitely say "spring." Enjoy them for lunch or a light dinner. What a great way to use leftover chicken!

—**ANCA CRETAN** HAGERSTOWN, MARYLAND

PREP/TOTAL TIME: 15 MINUTES
MAKES: 4 SERVINGS

- 1 pound fresh asparagus, cut into 3-inch lengths
- 1½ cups reduced-fat sour cream
- 2 teaspoons lemon juice
- 1½ teaspoons prepared mustard
- ½ teaspoon salt
- ½ pound sliced cooked chicken breast
- 4 English muffins, split and toasted
- 2 medium tomatoes, sliced
  Paprika, optional

1. In a large saucepan, bring ½ in. of water to a boil. Add asparagus; cover and boil for 3 minutes. Drain and immediately place asparagus in ice water. Drain and pat dry.

2. In the same pan, combine the sour cream, lemon juice, mustard and salt; heat through (do not boil). Meanwhile, in a microwave, heat the chicken breast.

3. Place two English muffin halves on each plate. Top with chicken, tomatoes, asparagus and sauce. Sprinkle with paprika if desired.

20 Quick Chicken and Corn Wraps

My girls like these tortilla roll-ups very much—they'll ask for them practically every week!

—**SUE SEYMOUR** VALATIE, NEW YORK

PREP/TOTAL TIME: 15 MINUTES **MAKES:** 4 SERVINGS

- 2 **cups cubed cooked chicken breast**
- 1 **can (11 ounces) whole kernel corn, drained**
- 1 **cup salsa**
- 1 **cup (4 ounces) shredded cheddar cheese**
- 8 **flour tortillas (6 inches), warmed**

1. In a large saucepan, combine chicken, corn and salsa. Cook over medium heat until heated through.

2. Sprinkle cheese over tortillas. Place about ½ cup chicken mixture down the center of each tortilla; roll up. Secure with toothpicks.

30 Provolone Chicken Pizza

Enjoy a fresh, cheesy pizza in less time than it takes to order one not even half as good!

—**SHELLY BEVINGTON-FISHER** HERMISTON, OREGON

PREP/TOTAL TIME: 25 MINUTES **MAKES:** 6 SERVINGS

- 1 **prebaked 12-inch thin whole wheat pizza crust**
- ½ **cup reduced-fat ranch salad dressing**
- 6 **slices reduced-fat provolone cheese**
- 2 **cups shredded cooked chicken breast**
- 1 **medium tomato, thinly sliced**
- 2 **green onions, thinly sliced**
- 1 **tablespoon grated Parmesan cheese**

1. Place crust on an ungreased 12-in. pizza pan or baking sheet; spread with salad dressing. Top with provolone cheese, chicken, tomato and onions. Sprinkle with Parmesan cheese.

2. Bake at 450° for 10-12 minutes or until cheese is melted and edges are lightly browned.

Bow Ties & Ham

Here's a dish from our family cookbook, which is filled with recipes from generations of women. We love casseroles! Just pop one in the oven to warm your home and fill your stomach.

—SUZETTE JURY KEENE, CALIFORNIA

PREP: 20 MINUTES
BAKE: 25 MINUTES
MAKES: 2 CASSEROLES
(6 SERVINGS EACH)

- 4 **cups uncooked bow tie pasta**
- 6 **cups frozen broccoli florets**
- 4 **cups cubed fully cooked ham**
- 2 **cartons (10 ounces each) refrigerated Alfredo sauce**
- 2 **cups (8 ounces) shredded Swiss cheese**
- 1 **can (8 ounces) mushroom stems and pieces, drained**

1. Cook the pasta according to package directions, adding the broccoli during the last 5 minutes of cooking. Meanwhile, in a large bowl, combine the ham, Alfredo sauce, cheese and mushrooms. Drain pasta mixture; add to ham mixture and toss to coat.

2. Transfer to two greased 11-in. x 7-in. baking dishes. Cover and freeze one casserole for up to 3 months. Cover and bake remaining casserole at 375° for 20 minutes. Uncover; bake 5-10 minutes longer or until bubbly.

To use frozen casserole: *Thaw in the refrigerator overnight. Remove from refrigerator 30 minutes before heating. Cover and microwave on high for 8-10 minutes or until heated through, stirring once.*

Editor's Note: *This recipe was tested in a 1,100-watt microwave.*

Chicken Tater Bake

You'll please everyone in the family with this inviting and filling dish. It tastes like a chicken potpie with a Tater Tot crust.

—FRAN ALLEN ST. LOUIS, MISSOURI

PREP: 20 MINUTES **BAKE:** 40 MINUTES
MAKES: 2 CASSEROLES (6 SERVINGS EACH)

- 2 **cans (10¾ ounces each) condensed cream of chicken soup, undiluted**
- ½ **cup 2% milk**
- ¼ **cup butter, cubed**
- 3 **cups cubed cooked chicken**
- 1 **package (16 ounces) frozen peas and carrots, thawed**
- 1½ **cups (6 ounces) shredded cheddar cheese, divided**
- 1 **package (32 ounces) frozen Tater Tots**

1. In a large saucepan, combine the soup, milk and butter. Cook and stir over medium heat until heated through. Remove from the heat; stir in the chicken, peas and carrots, and 1 cup cheese.

2. Transfer to two greased 8-in. square baking dishes. Top with Tater Tots; sprinkle with remaining cheese.

3. Cover and freeze one casserole for up to 3 months. Cover and bake the remaining casserole at 350° for 35 minutes. Uncover; bake 5-10 minutes longer or until heated through.

To use frozen casserole: *Remove from the freezer 30 minutes before baking (do not thaw). Cover and bake at 350° for 1½ to 1¾ hours or until casserole is heated through.*

Chicken Potpies

My aunt created this wonderful recipe, and I adjusted it for my own family's tastes. I think they like it so much because of the sage—it brings a totally different flavor to the dish.

—LYSA DAVIS PINE BLUFF, ARKANSAS

PREP: 25 MINUTES **BAKE:** 35 MINUTES + STANDING
MAKES: 2 PIES (6 SERVINGS EACH)

- 2 **cans (9¾ ounces each) chunk white chicken, drained**
- 1 **can (15¼ ounces) lima beans, drained**
- 1 **can (15 ounces) sliced carrots, drained**
- 1 **can (14½ ounces) sliced potatoes, drained**
- 1 **can (10¾ ounces) condensed cream of chicken soup, undiluted**
- 1 **can (10¾ ounces) condensed cream of mushroom soup, undiluted**
- 1 **jar (4½ ounces) sliced mushrooms, drained**
- 1½ **teaspoons rubbed sage**
- ¼ **teaspoon salt**
- ¼ **teaspoon pepper**
- 2 **packages (15 ounces each) refrigerated pie pastry**
- 1 **tablespoon butter, melted**

1. In a large bowl, combine the first 10 ingredients. Line two 9-in. pie plates with bottom crusts. Add filling. Roll out remaining pastry to fit tops of pies; place over filling. Trim, seal and flute edges. Cut slits in pastry; brush with butter.

2. Cover and freeze one potpie for up to 3 months. Bake the remaining potpie at 375° for 35-40 minutes or until golden brown. Let stand for 10 minutes before cutting.

To use frozen potpie: *Remove from freezer 30 minutes before baking. Cover edges of crust loosely with foil; place on a baking sheet. Bake at 425° for 30 minutes. Reduce heat to 375°; remove foil. Bake 55-60 minutes longer or until golden brown. Let stand for 10 minutes before cutting.*

Broccoli-Chicken Spaghetti

It's so nice being able to work ahead! I serve one of these casseroles for supper the night I make it and freeze the other for a no-fuss dinner later.

—JEANETTE FUEHRING CONCORDIA, MISSOURI

PREP: 25 MINUTES **BAKE:** 30 MINUTES
MAKES: 2 CASSEROLES (6 SERVINGS EACH)

- 1½ **pounds boneless skinless chicken breasts**
- 1 **package (1 pound) spaghetti**
- 2 **cups fresh broccoli florets**
- 1 **can (10¾ ounces) condensed cream of chicken soup, undiluted**
- 1 **can (10¾ ounces) condensed cream of mushroom soup, undiluted**
- 1¼ **cups water**
- 1 **package (16 ounces) process cheese (Velveeta), cubed**
- ¼ **teaspoon pepper**

1. Place chicken in a large saucepan and cover with water. Bring to a boil. Reduce heat; cover and simmer for 12-14 minutes or until no longer pink. Meanwhile, cook the spaghetti according to package directions; drain. Drain chicken and cut into cubes; set aside.

2. In a Dutch oven, bring 1 in. of water to a boil. Add the broccoli; cover and cook for 3-5 minutes or until crisp-tender. Drain and set aside. In the same pan, combine soups and water. Stir in cheese; cook and stir until cheese is melted. Stir in the chicken, broccoli, pepper and spaghetti.

3. Transfer to two greased 11-in. x 7-in. baking dishes. Cover and freeze one casserole for up to 3 months. Bake remaining casserole, uncovered, at 350° for 30-40 minutes or until lightly browned and edges are bubbly.

To bake frozen casserole: *Completely thaw in the refrigerator. Cover and bake at 350° for 45-50 minutes or until heated through.*

This soup is great for those very cold winter days or just when you feel like eating good, hot comfort food. I usually serve it with crusty garlic bread or French bread. **—KELLY MILAN** LAKE JACKSON, TEXAS

30 Zesty Hamburger Soup

PREP/TOTAL TIME: 30 MINUTES
MAKES: 10 SERVINGS (3¾ QUARTS)

- 1 pound ground beef
- 2 cups sliced celery
- 1 cup chopped onion
- 2 teaspoons minced garlic
- 4 cups water
- 2 medium red potatoes, peeled and cubed
- 2 cups frozen corn
- 1½ cups uncooked small shell pasta
- 4 pickled jalapeno slices
- 4 cups V8 juice
- 2 cans (10 ounces each) diced tomatoes with green chilies
- 1 to 2 tablespoons sugar

1. In a Dutch oven, cook the beef, celery and onion over medium heat until meat is no longer pink. Add garlic; cook 1 minute longer. Drain. Stir in the water, potatoes, corn, pasta and jalapeno.

2. Bring to a boil. Reduce heat; cover and simmer for 10-15 minutes or until pasta is tender. Add the remaining ingredients. Cook and stir until heated through. Serve immediately or cool and freeze in a freezer container. May be frozen for up to 3 months.

To use frozen soup: *Thaw in the refrigerator overnight. Transfer to a saucepan. Cover and cook over medium heat until heated through.*

Mexican Chicken Alfredo

One family member likes Italian; another prefers Mexican. They'll never have to compromise when this rich and creamy sensation is on the menu!

—TIA WOODLEY
STOCKBRIDGE, GEORGIA

PREP: 25 MINUTES
BAKE: 30 MINUTES
MAKES: 2 CASSEROLES
(4 SERVINGS EACH)

- 1 package (16 ounces) gemelli or spiral pasta
- 2 pounds boneless skinless chicken breasts, cubed
- 1 medium onion, chopped
- ¼ teaspoon salt
- ¼ teaspoon pepper
- 1 tablespoon canola oil
- 2 jars (15 ounces each) Alfredo sauce
- 1 cup grated Parmesan cheese
- 1 cup medium salsa
- ¼ cup 2% milk
- 2 teaspoons taco seasoning

1. Cook the pasta according to package directions.

2. Meanwhile, in a large skillet over medium heat, cook chicken, onion, salt and pepper in oil until chicken is no longer pink. Stir in the Alfredo sauce; bring to a boil. Stir in the cheese, salsa, milk and taco seasoning.

3. Drain the pasta; toss with the chicken mixture. Divide mixture between two greased 8-in. square baking dishes.

4. Cover and freeze one casserole for up to 3 months. Cover and bake the remaining casserole at 350° for 30-35 minutes or until bubbly.

To use frozen casserole: *Thaw in refrigerator overnight. Remove from the refrigerator 30 minutes before baking. Cover and bake at 350° for 50-60 minutes or until bubbly.*

30 Open-Faced Pizza Burgers

I'm not sure where I first saw this recipe, but I'm glad I did! My family requests these burgers often. A dash of oregano livens up the canned pizza sauce.

—SHARON SCHWARTZ BURLINGTON, WISCONSIN

PREP/TOTAL TIME: 30 MINUTES **MAKES:** 12 SERVINGS

- 1½ pounds ground beef
- ¼ cup chopped onion
- 1 can (15 ounces) pizza sauce
- 1 can (4 ounces) mushroom stems and pieces, drained
- 1 tablespoon sugar
- ½ teaspoon dried oregano
- 6 hamburger buns, split and toasted
- 1½ cups (6 ounces) shredded part-skim mozzarella cheese

1. In a large skillet, cook beef and onion over medium heat until meat is no longer pink; drain. Stir in pizza sauce, mushrooms, sugar and oregano. Spoon onto buns; sprinkle with mozzarella cheese.

2. Place on ungreased baking sheets. Broil 4 in. from the heat for 2 minutes or until cheese is melted.

3. To freeze for quick lunches later, place the split and toasted buns on a baking sheet. Spoon the meat mixture onto buns; freeze for 1 hour. Transfer to heavy-duty resealable plastic bags or airtight containers.

To use frozen burgers: *Thaw completely in the refrigerator. Sprinkle with cheese. Broil 4 in. from the heat for 2 minutes or until heated through and cheese is melted.*

Ham 'n' Cheese Pasta

Top a rich casserole with a little crunch, and you've got a dish the whole family will love!

—MARION LITTLE HUMBOLDT, TENNESSEE

PREP: 20 MINUTES **BAKE:** 25 MINUTES
MAKES: 2 CASSEROLES (9 SERVINGS EACH)

- 10 **cups uncooked tricolor spiral pasta**
- 4 **celery ribs, chopped**
- 1 **medium green pepper, chopped**
- ½ **cup chopped onion**
- ¼ **cup butter**
- 3 **cans (10¾ ounces each) condensed cheddar cheese soup, undiluted**
- 3 **cups 2% milk**
- 1 **teaspoon salt**
- 4 **cups cubed fully cooked ham**
- 2 **cans (8 ounces each) mushroom stems and pieces, drained**
- 1 **cup crushed butter-flavored crackers**

1. Cook the pasta according to package directions. Meanwhile, in a Dutch oven, saute the celery, pepper and onion in butter until tender. Stir in the soup, milk and salt.

2. In a very large bowl, combine the soup mixture, ham and mushrooms. Drain pasta; add to soup mixture and toss to coat.

3. Transfer to two greased 13-in. x 9-in. baking dishes. Top with cracker crumbs. Cover and freeze one casserole for up to 3 months. Bake the remaining casserole, uncovered, at 350° for 20-25 minutes or until golden brown.

To use frozen casserole: *Thaw in the refrigerator overnight. Remove from the refrigerator 30 minutes before baking. Bake, uncovered, at 350° for 50-55 minutes or until heated through.*

Baked Beef & Potatoes

I love recipes where you only have to do the prep work once, but you get two meals from it! You can substitute cream of chicken soup for celery, or use peas or green beans instead of mushrooms.

—CATHY CASEMENT-MCDOWELL TULSA, OKLAHOMA

PREP: 10 MINUTES **BAKE:** 50 MINUTES
MAKES: 2 CASSEROLES (4 SERVINGS EACH)

- 2 **pounds ground beef**
- 1 **can (10¾ ounces) condensed cream of mushroom soup, undiluted**
- 1 **can (10¾ ounces) condensed cream of celery soup, undiluted**
- 1¼ **teaspoons dried parsley flakes**
- 1 **teaspoon dried minced onion**
- ¼ **teaspoon pepper**
- 1 **package (32 ounces) frozen cubed hash brown potatoes, thawed**
- 4 **cups (16 ounces) shredded cheddar cheese, divided**
- 1 **can (8 ounces) mushroom stems and pieces, drained**

1. In skillet, cook the beef over medium heat until no longer pink; drain. Meanwhile, in a large bowl, combine the soups, parsley, onion and pepper. Add the potatoes, 2 cups cheese and mushrooms. Stir in beef.

2. Transfer to two greased 8-in. square baking dishes. Sprinkle each with 1 cup cheese. Cover and freeze one casserole for up to 3 months. Cover and bake the remaining casserole at 375° for 45-50 minutes or until potatoes are tender. Uncover and bake for 5-10 minutes or until cheese is melted.

To use frozen casserole: *Thaw in the refrigerator overnight. Remove from the refrigerator 30 minutes before baking. Bake as directed.*

Creamy Chicken Casserole

PREP: 20 MINUTES
BAKE: 40 MINUTES
MAKES: 2 CASSEROLES
(5 SERVINGS EACH)

- 4 **cups uncooked egg noodles**
- 4 **cups cubed cooked chicken**
- 1 **package (16 ounces) frozen peas and carrots**
- 2 **cups milk**
- 2 **cans (10¾ ounces each) condensed cream of celery soup, undiluted**
- 2 **cans (10¾ ounces each) condensed cream of chicken soup, undiluted**
- 1 **cup chopped onion**
- 2 **tablespoons butter, melted**
- ½ **teaspoon salt**
- ½ **teaspoon pepper**

1. Cook the noodles according to package directions. Meanwhile, in a large bowl, combine the remaining ingredients. Drain noodles; add to chicken mixture.

2. Transfer the mixture to two greased 8-in. square baking dishes. Cover and freeze one casserole for up to 3 months.

3. Cover and bake remaining casserole at 350° for 30 minutes. Uncover and bake 10-15 minutes longer or until heated through.

To use frozen casserole: *Thaw in the refrigerator overnight. Remove from refrigerator 30 minutes before cooking. Cover and microwave on high for 10-12 minutes or until heated through, stirring twice.*

Creamy Lasagna Casserole

PREP: 30 MINUTES
BAKE: 25 MINUTES + STANDING
MAKES: 2 CASSEROLES
(4-6 SERVINGS EACH)

- 2 **pounds ground beef**
- 1 **can (29 ounces) tomato sauce**
- 1 **teaspoon salt**
- ½ **teaspoon pepper**
- ½ **teaspoon garlic powder**
- 2 **packages (3 ounces each) cream cheese, softened**
- 2 **cups (16 ounces) sour cream**
- 2 **cups (8 ounces) shredded cheddar cheese, divided**
- 4 **green onions, chopped**
- 12 **to 14 lasagna noodles, cooked and drained**

1. In a Dutch oven, cook beef over medium heat until no longer pink; drain. Add the tomato sauce, salt, pepper and garlic powder. Bring to a boil. Reduce heat; simmer, uncovered, for 15 minutes.

2. In a large bowl, beat cream cheese until smooth. Add the sour cream, 1 cup cheddar cheese and onions; mix well.

3. Spread about ½ cup meat sauce into each of two greased 8-in. square baking dishes. Place two to three noodles in each dish, trimming to fit as necessary. Top each with about ½ cup cream cheese mixture and ⅔ cup meat sauce. Repeat layers twice. Sprinkle ½ cup cheddar cheese over each.

4. Cover and freeze one casserole for up to 1 month. Bake remaining casserole, uncovered, at 350° for 25-30 minutes or until bubbly and heated through. Let stand for 15 minutes before cutting.

To use frozen casserole: *Thaw in the refrigerator for 18 hours. Remove from the refrigerator 30 minutes before baking. Bake, uncovered, at 350° for 40-50 minutes or until heated through.*

I can whip up two rich, amazing mini lasagnas in almost no time. The best part is being able to enjoy the second casserole with virtually no work at all! —**SHELLY KORELL** EATON, COLORADO

30 Cabbage Beef Soup

I didn't have time to make my favorite cabbage rolls one day, so I just threw together this soup and I loved it!

—RENEE LEARY CITRUS SPRINGS, FLORIDA

PREP/TOTAL TIME: 30 MINUTES **MAKES:** 6 SERVINGS

- 1 **pound ground beef**
- 1 **medium onion, chopped**
- 3½ **cups shredded cabbage**
- 1 **medium zucchini, halved and thinly sliced**
- 1 **cup sliced fresh mushrooms**
- 1 **carton (18.3 ounces) ready-to-serve sweet red pepper soup**
- 1 **can (10 ounces) diced tomatoes and green chilies, undrained**
- ¼ **teaspoon hot pepper sauce**
- ¼ **teaspoon salt**
- ¼ **teaspoon pepper**
- ¼ **cup grated Parmesan cheese**

1. In a large saucepan, cook the beef and onion over medium heat until meat is no longer pink; drain. Add the cabbage, zucchini and mushrooms; cook and stir 8 minutes longer.

2. Stir in soup, tomatoes, pepper sauce, salt and pepper. Bring to a boil. Reduce heat; cover and simmer for 5 minutes. Sprinkle each serving with 2 teaspoons cheese.

3. Serve immediately or cool and freeze in a freezer container. May be frozen for up to 3 months.

To use frozen soup: *Thaw in the refrigerator overnight. Transfer to a saucepan. Cover and cook over medium heat until heated through. Sprinkle each serving with 2 teaspoons cheese.*

30 Creamed Turkey with Puff Pastry

Warm and hearty with lots of veggies in every creamy bite, this is classic comfort food. Tastes a lot like potpie, but it's so much quicker!

—NILA GRAHL GURNEE, ILLINOIS

PREP/TOTAL TIME: 25 MINUTES **MAKES:** 12 SERVINGS

- 1 **package (17.3 ounces) frozen puff pastry**
- 4 **cans (18.8 ounces each) chunky chicken corn chowder soup**
- 4 **cups cubed cooked turkey**
- 2 **packages (16 ounces each) frozen peas and carrots, thawed**
- 1 **package (8 ounces) cream cheese, cubed**
- ¼ **teaspoon pepper**

1. Thaw one sheet of puff pastry. Cut pastry into six squares. Cut each square in half diagonally; transfer to two greased baking sheets. Bake at 400° for 10-15 minutes or until golden brown.

2. Meanwhile, in a Dutch oven, combine the soup, turkey, peas and carrots, cream cheese and pepper. Bring to a boil, stirring frequently. Reduce heat; simmer, uncovered, for 5 minutes or until cream cheese is melted. Serve half of the turkey mixture with puff pastry triangles. Cool the remaining turkey mixture; transfer to freezer containers. May be frozen for up to 3 months.

To use frozen turkey mixture: *Thaw mixture in the refrigerator overnight. Thaw remaining puff pastry; prepare and bake pastry triangles as directed. Place turkey mixture in a large saucepan and heat through. Serve with puff pastry triangles.*

Spaghetti Beef Casserole

As the mother of three boys, I have found this casserole to be a lifesaver! It's fast and is always a hit at pregame meals and sports banquets.

—JANE RADTKE GRIFFITH, INDIANA

PREP: 25 MINUTES **BAKE:** 20 MINUTES
MAKES: 2 CASSEROLES
(8 SERVINGS EACH)

- 1½ **pounds uncooked spaghetti**
- 3 **pounds ground beef**
- 1 **cup chopped onion**
- ⅔ **cup chopped green pepper**
- 1 **teaspoon minced garlic**
- 2 **cans (10¾ ounces each) condensed cream of mushroom soup, undiluted**
- 2 **cans (10¾ ounces each) condensed tomato soup, undiluted**
- 1⅓ **cups water**
- 1 **can (8 ounces) mushroom stems and pieces, drained**
- 3 **cups (12 ounces) shredded cheddar cheese, divided**

1. Cook spaghetti according to package directions. Meanwhile, in two large skillets, cook the beef, onion and green pepper over medium heat until meat is no longer pink. Add garlic; cook 1 minute longer. Drain. Stir in the soups, water and mushrooms.

2. Drain spaghetti. Add spaghetti and 1 cup cheese to beef mixture. Transfer to two greased 13-in. x 9-in. baking dishes. Sprinkle with the remaining cheese. Cover and freeze one casserole for up to 3 months. Bake the remaining casserole, uncovered, at 350° for 20-25 minutes or until the cheese is melted.

To use frozen casserole: *Thaw in refrigerator overnight. Remove from refrigerator 30 minutes before baking. Cover and bake at 350° for 1 to 1¼ hours or until heated through and cheese is melted.*

Italian Quiches

This hearty and versatile dish tastes like pizza and can be enjoyed for breakfast as well as supper.

—BERNICE HANCOCK GREENVILLE, PENNSYLVANIA

PREP: 25 MINUTES **BAKE:** 35 MINUTES + STANDING
MAKES: 2 QUICHES (6 SERVINGS EACH)

- 2 **unbaked pastry shells (9 inches)**
- 1 **pound bulk Italian sausage**
- 4 **cups (16 ounces) finely shredded part-skim mozzarella cheese**
- 1 **medium onion, thinly sliced**
- 1 **medium green pepper, thinly sliced**
- 1 **medium sweet red pepper, thinly sliced**
- 6 **eggs**
- 2 **cups milk**
- 1 **teaspoon minced garlic**
- ¼ **cup grated Parmesan cheese**

1. Line unpricked pastry shells with a double thickness of heavy-duty foil. Bake at 400° for 4 minutes. Remove foil; bake 4 minutes longer.

2. In a large skillet, cook sausage over medium heat until no longer pink; drain. Spoon sausage into pastry shells; sprinkle with mozzarella cheese. Top with onion and peppers. In a large bowl, whisk the eggs, milk and garlic. Pour over peppers; sprinkle with Parmesan cheese.

3. Cover and freeze one quiche for up to 3 months. Cover edges of the remaining quiche loosely with foil; place on a baking sheet. Bake at 400° for 35-40 minutes or until a knife inserted near the center comes out clean. Let stand for 10 minutes before cutting.

To use frozen quiche: *Remove from the freezer 30 minutes before baking (do not thaw). Cover edges of crust loosely with foil; place on a baking sheet. Bake at 400° for 50-60 minutes or until a knife inserted near the center comes out clean. Let stand for 10 minutes before cutting.*

Enchilada Casserole

PREP: 20 MINUTES
BAKE: 40 MINUTES
MAKES: 2 CASSEROLES
(4-6 SERVINGS EACH)

- 1½ pounds ground beef
- 1 large onion, chopped
- 1 cup water
- 2 to 3 tablespoons chili powder
- 1½ teaspoons salt
- ½ teaspoon pepper
- ¼ teaspoon garlic powder
- 2 cups salsa, divided
- 10 flour tortillas (8 inches), cut into ¾-inch strips, divided
- 1 cup (8 ounces) sour cream
- 2 cans (15¼ ounces each) whole kernel corn, drained
- 4 cups (16 ounces) shredded part-skim mozzarella cheese

1. In a large skillet, cook the beef and onion over medium heat until meat is no longer pink; drain. Stir in water, chili powder, salt, pepper and garlic powder. Bring to a boil. Reduce heat; simmer, uncovered, for 10 minutes.

2. Place ¼ cup salsa in each of two greased 8-in. square baking dishes. Top each with a fourth of the tortillas and ¼ cup salsa.

3. Divide the meat mixture, sour cream and corn between the two casseroles. Top with remaining tortillas, salsa and cheese.

4. Cover and freeze one casserole for up to 1 month. Cover and bake remaining casserole at 350° for 35 minutes. Uncover; bake 5-10 minutes longer or until casserole is heated through.

To use frozen casserole: *Thaw in the refrigerator for 24 hours. Remove from the refrigerator 30 minutes before baking. Bake as directed above.*

This zippy Mexican casserole is a real winner at our house. If your family has spicier tastes, increase the chili powder and choose a medium or hot salsa. —JULIE JUFFMAN NEW LEBANON, OHIO

Hamburger Baked Beans

I serve this satisfying ground beef-and-bean bake when I need to feed a crowd. And I keep an extra pan of it in my freezer for when I know I'll need a large dish.

—**LOUANN SHERBACH** WANTAGH, NEW YORK

PREP: 15 MINUTES **BAKE:** 45 MINUTES
MAKES: 2 CASSEROLES (10-12 SERVINGS EACH)

- 3 **pounds ground beef**
- 4 **cans (15¾ ounces each) pork and beans**
- 2 **cups ketchup**
- 1 **cup water**
- 2 **envelopes onion soup mix**
- ¼ **cup packed brown sugar**
- ¼ **cup ground mustard**
- ¼ **cup molasses**
- 1 **tablespoon white vinegar**
- 1 **teaspoon garlic powder**
- ½ **teaspoon ground cloves**

1. In a Dutch oven, cook the beef over medium heat until no longer pink; drain. Stir in the remaining ingredients; heat through. Transfer to two greased 2-qt. baking dishes. Cover and freeze one dish for up to 3 months.

2. Cover and bake the second dish at 400° for 30 minutes. Uncover; bake 10-15 minutes longer or until bubbly.

To use frozen casserole: *Thaw in the refrigerator. Cover and bake at 400° for 40 minutes. Uncover; bake 15-20 minutes longer or until bubbly.*

Chili Tots

Cook once and eat twice with my hearty Southwestern casserole. With help from a few convenience products, it quickly goes together before you freeze it or pop it into the oven to bake.

—**LINDA BALDWIN** LONG BEACH, CALIFORNIA

PREP: 15 MINUTES **BAKE:** 35 MINUTES
MAKES: 2 CASSEROLES (6 SERVINGS EACH)

- 1 **pound ground beef**
- 2 **cans (15 ounces each) chili without beans**
- 1 **can (8 ounces) tomato sauce**
- 1 **can (2¼ ounces) sliced ripe olives, drained**
- 1 **can (4 ounces) chopped green chilies**
- 2 **cups (8 ounces) shredded cheddar cheese**
- 1 **package (32 ounces) frozen Tater Tots**

1. In a large skillet, cook the beef over medium heat until no longer pink; drain. Stir in the chili, tomato sauce, olives and chilies. Transfer to two greased 8-in. square baking dishes. Sprinkle with cheese; top with Tater Tots. Cover and freeze one casserole for up to 3 months.

2. Cover and bake the remaining casserole at 350° for 35-40 minutes or until heated through.

To use frozen casserole: *Remove from the freezer 30 minutes before baking (do not thaw). Cover and bake at 350° for 1¼ to 1½ hours or until heated through.*

Sweet-Sour Ham Balls

Pineapple, brown sugar and mustard combine to create a delightful sauce for these sweet-savory meatballs. I like to keep a batch on hand for when I'm planning to host card parties and other occasions.

—DOROTHY PRITCHETT WILLS POINT, TEXAS

PREP: 20 MINUTES **BAKE:** 45 MINUTES
MAKES: 2 BATCHES (ABOUT 30 HAM BALLS EACH)

- 4 **eggs, lightly beaten**
- ¼ **cup chopped onion**
- 1½ **cups soft bread crumbs**
- 2 **pounds ground ham**
- 1 **pound ground pork**
- 2 **cans (8 ounces each) crushed pineapple, undrained**
- 1 **cup packed brown sugar**
- ¼ **cup prepared mustard**
- 2 **tablespoons cider vinegar**

1. In a large bowl, combine the eggs, onion and bread crumbs. Crumble meat over mixture and mix well. Shape into 1½-in. balls. Place in two greased 13-in. x 9-in. baking dishes.

2. In a blender, combine pineapple, brown sugar, mustard and vinegar; cover and process until smooth. Pour over ham balls. Transfer to freezer bags; seal and freeze. Or, bake, uncovered, at 350° for 45-50 minutes or until a thermometer reads 160°; basting occasionally with sauce.

To use frozen ham balls: *Completely thaw uncooked ham balls with sauce in the refrigerator. Bake as directed in recipe.*

Roasted Tomato Soup

Just before the first frost, we gather up all of the tomatoes from my mom's garden to create this flavor-packed soup. Although it sounds like a lot of garlic, the flavor becomes mellow and sweet when it's roasted.

—KAITLYN LERDAHL
MADISON, WISCONSIN

PREP: 25 MINUTES
COOK: 40 MINUTES
MAKES: 6 SERVINGS

- 15 **large tomatoes (5 pounds), seeded and quartered**
- ¼ **cup plus 2 tablespoons canola oil, divided**
- 8 **garlic cloves, minced**
- 1 **large onion, chopped**
- 2 **cups water**
- 1 **teaspoon salt**
- ½ **teaspoon crushed red pepper flakes, optional**
- ½ **cup heavy whipping cream**
  Fresh basil leaves, optional

1. Place tomatoes in a greased 15-in. x 10-in. x 1-in. baking pan. Combine ¼ cup oil and garlic; drizzle over tomatoes. Toss to coat. Bake at 400° for 15-20 minutes or until softened, stirring occasionally. Remove and discard skins.

2. Meanwhile, in a Dutch oven, saute onion in remaining oil until tender. Add the tomatoes, water, salt and pepper flakes, if desired. Bring to a boil. Reduce heat; cover and simmer for 30 minutes or until flavors are blended. Cool slightly.

3. In a blender, process the soup in batches until smooth. Stir in the cream; heat through. Serve immediately or cool soup; transfer to freezer containers. Cover and freeze for up to 3 months.

To use frozen soup: *Thaw in the refrigerator overnight. Place in a large saucepan; heat through. Garnish with basil if desired.*

2 tablespoons honey
⅛ teaspoon cayenne pepper

1. Cut ribs into serving-size pieces; place in a 3-qt. microwave-safe dish with water, liquid smoke if desired and onion powder. Cover and microwave on high for 15-20 minutes or until meat is tender.

2. Meanwhile, in a small saucepan, combine the remaining ingredients. Bring to a boil. Reduce heat; simmer, uncovered, for 5-8 minutes or until slightly thickened, stirring occasionally.

3. Drain ribs. Moisten a paper towel with cooking oil; using long-handled tongs, lightly coat the grill rack. Grill ribs, covered, over medium heat for 8-10 minutes or until browned, turning occasionally and basting with sauce.

4. Serve immediately or cool the ribs. Cover tightly with foil; place in a freezer container and freeze for up to 3 months.

To use frozen ribs: *Thaw in the refrigerator overnight. Place in a baking pan; cover and bake at 325° for 35-40 minutes or until heated through.*

Editor's Note: *This recipe was tested in a 1,100-watt microwave.*

Chicken & Sausage Manicotti

Here's a scrumptious meal idea the whole gang will love. For a tasty change, try it with ground turkey or beef instead of the sausage.

—FRAN SCOTT BIRMINGHAM, MICHIGAN

PREP: 30 MINUTES **BAKE:** 55 MINUTES + STANDING
MAKES: 2 CASSEROLES (7 SERVINGS EACH)

 1 pound sliced fresh mushrooms
 2 medium green peppers, chopped
 2 medium onions, chopped
 1 tablespoon olive oil
 4 garlic cloves, minced
 3 jars (26 ounces each) spaghetti sauce
1¼ cups water
1½ pounds chicken tenderloins, halved lengthwise
 4 teaspoons dried basil
 2 teaspoons chicken seasoning
 2 packages (8 ounces each) uncooked manicotti shells
 1 pound fully cooked andouille or Italian sausage links, halved lengthwise and sliced
½ pound each shredded mozzarella and cheddar cheeses

> ❝ These ribs are tangy and tender. The Chinese-style glaze gives them a different and unique taste. ❞

—JAMIE WETTER BOSCOBEL, WISCONSIN

Chinese Country-Style Pork Ribs

PREP: 25 MINUTES **GRILL:** 10 MINUTES
MAKES: 8 SERVINGS

 4 pounds bone-in country-style pork ribs
½ cup water
 1 tablespoon Liquid Smoke, optional
½ teaspoon onion powder
½ cup chili sauce
¼ cup hoisin sauce

1. In a Dutch oven, saute the mushrooms, peppers and onions in oil until tender. Add the garlic; cook 1 minute longer. Stir in spaghetti sauce and water.

2. Sprinkle the chicken with basil and chicken seasoning. Stuff chicken into uncooked manicotti shells. Spread 1 cup sauce mixture in each of two greased 13-in. x 9-in. baking dishes. Arrange the manicotti over sauce; sprinkle with sausage. Pour remaining sauce over top; sprinkle with cheeses.

3. Cover and freeze one casserole for up to 3 months. Cover and bake the remaining casserole at 375° for 55-65 minutes or until bubbly and pasta is tender. Let stand for 10 minutes before serving.

To use frozen manicotti: *Thaw in the refrigerator overnight. Remove from refrigerator 30 minutes before baking. Bake, covered, at 375° for 55-65 minutes or until pasta is tender. Let stand 10 minutes.*

Editor's Note: *This recipe was tested with McCormick's Montreal Chicken Seasoning. Look for it in the spice aisle.*

“ Loaded with beans, peppers, tomatoes and corn, this hearty chili is sure to be a family hit. I often take it to potlucks and always come home with an empty pot! ”

—**NANCY FOREMAN** EAST WENATCHEE, WASHINGTON

Ranch Bean Chili

PREP: 25 MINUTES **COOK:** 20 MINUTES
MAKES: 8 SERVINGS (3 QUARTS)

- 1 **pound lean ground beef (90% lean)**
- ¾ **cup chopped onion**
- 1 **medium green pepper, chopped**
- 1 **each small sweet orange, red and yellow peppers, chopped**
- 1 **teaspoon minced garlic**
- 2 **cans (16 ounces each) kidney beans, rinsed and drained**
- 1 **can (16 ounces) chili beans, undrained**
- 1 **can (14½ ounces) diced tomatoes, undrained**
- 1 **can (11½ ounces) tomato juice**
- 1⅓ **cups fresh or frozen corn**
- 1 **cup water**
- 1 **envelope ranch salad dressing mix**

1. In a Dutch oven, cook the beef, onion and peppers over medium heat until the meat is no longer pink; drain. Add garlic; cook 1 minute longer. Stir in the remaining ingredients. Bring to a boil. Reduce heat; cover and simmer for 15 minutes.

2. Serve desired amount of chili. Cool the remaining chili; transfer to freezer containers. Cover and freeze for up to 3 months.

To use frozen chili: *Thaw in the refrigerator. Place in a saucepan; heat through.*

Cordon Bleu Casserole

I got this recipe from a friend years ago. I freeze several disposable pans to share with neighbors or for nights when I know I'll be short on time but still want a good meal.

—REA NEWELL DECATUR, ILLINOIS

PREP: 20 MINUTES
BAKE: 40 MINUTES
MAKES: 2 CASSEROLES
(6 SERVINGS EACH)

- 2 packages (6 ounces each) reduced-sodium stuffing mix
- 1 can (10¾ ounces) condensed cream of chicken soup, undiluted
- 1 cup milk
- 8 cups cubed cooked chicken
- ½ teaspoon pepper
- ¾ pound sliced deli ham, cut into 1-inch strips
- 1 cup (4 ounces) shredded Swiss cheese
- 3 cups (12 ounces) shredded cheddar cheese

1. Prepare the stuffing mixes according to package directions. Meanwhile, in a large bowl, combine soup and milk; set aside.

2. Divide the chicken between two greased 13-in. x 9-in. baking dishes. Sprinkle with the pepper. Layer with the ham, Swiss cheese, 1 cup cheddar cheese, soup mixture and stuffing. Sprinkle with the remaining cheddar cheese.

3. Cover and freeze one casserole for up to 3 months. Cover and bake the remaining casserole at 350° for 30 minutes. Uncover and bake 10-15 minutes longer or until heated through.

To use frozen casserole: *Thaw in the refrigerator overnight. Remove from refrigerator 30 minutes before baking. Bake, covered, at 350° for 45 minutes. Uncover; bake 10-15 minutes or until heated through.*

Hearty Chicken Enchiladas

My husband and I really like Mexican food, and this is our favorite dish. You can switch it up to suit your taste by adding corn, rice or refried beans.

—JENNY MILLER RALEIGH, NORTH CAROLINA

PREP: 30 MINUTES + SIMMERING **BAKE:** 25 MINUTES
MAKES: 2 CASSEROLES (2 SERVINGS EACH)

- 1 pound boneless skinless chicken breasts
- 2 cans (15 ounces each) enchilada sauce
- 1 can (4 ounces) chopped green chilies
- 1 can (15 ounces) black beans, rinsed and drained
- 8 flour tortillas (6 inches)
- 1 cup (4 ounces) shredded Mexican cheese blend
  Sour cream, optional

1. In a 3-qt. slow cooker, combine the chicken, enchilada sauce and chilies. Cover and cook on low for 6-8 hours or until meat is tender.

2. Remove chicken and shred with two forks. Reserve 1⅔ cups cooking juices. Pour the remaining cooking juices into a large bowl; add the beans and shredded chicken. Coat two freezer-safe 8-in. square baking dishes with cooking spray; add ½ cup reserved juices to each.

3. Place about ⅓ cup chicken mixture down the center of each tortilla. Roll up and place seam side down in prepared dishes. Pour remaining reserved juices over top; sprinkle with cheese.

4. Cover and freeze one dish for up to 3 months. Cover and bake the second dish at 350° for 20 minutes. Uncover; bake 5 minutes longer or until cheese is lightly browned. Serve with sour cream if desired.

To use frozen enchiladas: *Thaw in the refrigerator overnight. Remove from the refrigerator 30 minutes before baking. Bake as directed.*

Chicken Club Casseroles

Here's a warm and welcoming main dish that tastes as fresh and delicious after it's frozen as it does right out of the oven!

—**JANINE SMITH** COLUMBIA, SOUTH CAROLINA

PREP: 20 MINUTES **BAKE:** 35 MINUTES
MAKES: 2 CASSEROLES (5 SERVINGS EACH)

- 4 **cups uncooked spiral pasta**
- 4 **cups cubed cooked chicken**
- 2 **cans (10¾ ounces each) condensed cheddar cheese soup, undiluted**
- 1 **cup crumbled cooked bacon**
- 1 **cup 2% milk**
- 1 **cup mayonnaise**
- 4 **medium tomatoes, seeded and chopped**
- 3 **cups fresh baby spinach, chopped**
- 2 **cups (8 ounces) shredded Colby-Monterey Jack cheese**

1. Cook the pasta according to package directions. Meanwhile, in a large bowl, combine the chicken, soup, bacon, milk and mayonnaise. Stir in tomatoes and spinach.

2. Drain pasta; stir into chicken mixture. Transfer to two greased 8-in. square baking dishes. Sprinkle with cheese.

3. Cover and freeze one casserole for up to 3 months. Cover and bake the remaining casserole at 375° for 35-40 minutes or until bubbly and cheese is melted.

To use frozen casserole: *Thaw in the refrigerator overnight. Remove from the refrigerator 30 minutes before baking. Cover and bake at 375° for 60-70 minutes or until bubbly.*

Hearty Macaroni Casserole

Give Jack Frost the cold shoulder by setting a warming casserole on the table. This hearty meal satisfies the biggest of appetites. Enjoy one dish and freeze the other, or serve them both when entertaining.

—**JOY SAUERS** SIOUX FALLS, SOUTH DAKOTA

PREP: 20 MINUTES **BAKE:** 30 MINUTES
MAKES: 2 CASSEROLES (4 SERVINGS EACH)

- 1 **package (7¼ ounces) macaroni and cheese dinner mix**
- 1 **pound ground beef**
- 1 **cup chopped green pepper**
- ½ **cup chopped onion**
- 1 **can (14½ ounces) Italian diced tomatoes, drained**
- 2 **cups (8 ounces) shredded cheddar cheese, divided**
- 1 **cup French-fried onions**

1. Prepare the macaroni and cheese according to package directions. Meanwhile, in a large skillet, cook the beef, green pepper and onion over medium heat until meat is no longer pink; drain. Add to prepared macaroni. Stir in tomatoes.

2. Divide half of the mixture between two greased 1½-qt. baking dishes; sprinkle each with ½ cup cheese. Top with remaining mixture.

3. Sprinkle remaining cheese over one casserole. Cover and freeze for up to 3 months. Sprinkle second casserole with French-fried onions. Bake, uncovered, at 350° for 30 minutes or until heated through.

To use frozen casserole: *Completely thaw in the refrigerator. Remove from the refrigerator 30 minutes before baking. Bake as directed.*

Ground beef, cheese and, of course, Tater Tots make this homey casserole a crowd-pleaser. Cayenne pepper and hot Italian sausage give it a pleasant kick. —RYAN JONES CHILLICOTHE, ILLINOIS

Tater Tot Casseroles

PREP: 25 MINUTES
BAKE: 45 MINUTES
MAKES: 2 CASSEROLES
(6 SERVINGS EACH)

- ¾ pound bulk hot Italian sausage
- ¾ pound lean ground beef (90% lean)
- 1 small onion, chopped
- 2 cans (10¾ ounces each) condensed cream of celery soup, undiluted
- 2 cups frozen cut green beans, thawed
- 1 can (15¼ ounces) whole kernel corn, drained
- 2 cups (8 ounces) shredded Colby-Monterey Jack cheese, divided
- ½ cup 2% milk
- 1 teaspoon garlic powder
- ¼ teaspoon seasoned salt
- ¼ to ½ teaspoon cayenne pepper
- 1 package (32 ounces) frozen Tater Tots

1. In a Dutch oven, cook the sausage, beef and onion over medium heat until the meat is no longer pink; drain. Add the soup, beans, corn, 1 cup cheese, milk, garlic powder, seasoned salt and cayenne. Transfer to two greased 11-in. x 7-in. baking dishes. Top with Tater Tots; sprinkle with remaining cheese.

2. Cover and freeze one casserole for up to 3 months. Cover and bake remaining casserole at 350° for 40 minutes. Uncover and bake 5-10 minutes longer or until bubbly.

To use frozen casserole: *Thaw in the refrigerator overnight. Remove from refrigerator 30 minutes before baking. Cover and bake at 350° for 50 minutes. Uncover and bake 5-10 minutes longer or until bubbly.*

Spaghetti Casserole

This quick hot dish makes wonderful use of convenience products like canned spaghetti and jarred mushrooms. The kids will love how cheesy it is. It's perfect for when their friends stay over.

—PAT RICHTER LAKE PLACID, FLORIDA

PREP: 15 MINUTES
BAKE: 25 MINUTES
MAKES: 2 CASSEROLES
(4 SERVINGS EACH)

- 1½ **pounds ground beef**
- 1 **cup chopped green pepper**
- ½ **cup chopped onion**
- 1 **teaspoon salt**
- ½ **teaspoon pepper**
- 1 **teaspoon minced garlic**
- 3 **cans (14¾ ounces each) spaghetti in tomato sauce with cheese**
- 1 **jar (6 ounces) sliced mushrooms, drained**
- 1 **can (2¼ ounces) sliced ripe olives, drained**
- 2 **cups (8 ounces) shredded cheddar cheese**
- 1 **cup grated Parmesan cheese**

1. In a large skillet, cook the beef, green pepper, onion, salt and pepper over medium-high heat for 10-12 minutes or until the meat is no longer pink. Add garlic; cook 1 minute longer. Drain. Stir in the spaghetti, mushrooms and olives.

2. Transfer to two greased 8-in. square baking dishes. Sprinkle with cheeses. Cover and freeze one casserole for up to 3 months. Bake remaining casserole, uncovered, at 350° for 25-30 minutes or until bubbly and golden brown.

To use frozen casserole: *Remove from the freezer 30 minutes before baking (do not thaw). Cover and bake at 350° for 1 hour. Uncover; bake 15-20 minutes longer or until heated through.*

Ham & Cheese Potato Casserole

My recipe makes two cheesy and delicious casseroles. Have one tonight and put the other on ice for a weeknight that has a packed schedule. It's like having money in the bank when things get hectic!

—KARI ADAMS FORT COLLINS, COLORADO

PREP: 15 MINUTES **BAKE:** 50 MINUTES + STANDING
MAKES: 2 CASSEROLES (5 SERVINGS EACH)

- 2 **cans (10¾ ounces each) condensed cream of celery soup, undiluted**
- 2 **cups (16 ounces) sour cream**
- ½ **cup water**
- ½ **teaspoon pepper**
- 2 **packages (28 ounces each) frozen O'Brien potatoes**
- 1 **package (16 ounces) process cheese (Velveeta), cubed**
- 2½ **cups cubed fully cooked ham**

1. In a large bowl, combine the soup, sour cream, water and pepper. Stir in the potatoes, cheese and ham.

2. Transfer to two greased 11-in. x 7-in. baking dishes. Cover and freeze one casserole for up to 3 months. Cover and bake the remaining casserole at 375° for 40 minutes. Uncover and bake 10-15 minutes longer or until bubbly. Let stand for 10 minutes before serving.

To use frozen casserole: *Thaw in the refrigerator overnight. Remove from the refrigerator 30 minutes before baking. Bake as directed.*

Mostaccioli

PREP: 25 MINUTES
BAKE: 25 MINUTES
MAKES: 2 CASSEROLES
(6 SERVINGS EACH)

- 1 package (16 ounces) mostaccioli
- 1½ pounds ground beef
- 1¼ cups chopped green pepper
- 1 cup chopped onion
- 1 jar (26 ounces) spaghetti sauce
- 1 can (10¾ ounces) condensed cheddar cheese soup, undiluted
- 1½ teaspoons Italian seasoning
- ¾ teaspoon pepper
- 2 cups (8 ounces) shredded part-skim mozzarella cheese, divided

1. Cook mostaccioli according to package directions. Meanwhile, in a large skillet, cook the beef, green pepper and onion over medium heat until meat is no longer pink; drain. Stir in spaghetti sauce, soup, Italian seasoning and pepper.

2. Drain the mostaccioli. Add the mostaccioli and 1½ cups cheese to the beef mixture. Transfer to two greased 11-in. x 7-in. baking dishes. Sprinkle with remaining cheese.

3. Cover and freeze one casserole for up to 3 months. Cover and bake the remaining casserole at 350° for 20 minutes. Uncover; bake 5-10 minutes longer or until bubbly and cheese is melted.

To use frozen casserole: *Thaw in the refrigerator overnight. Remove from the refrigerator 30 minutes before baking. Cover and bake at 350° for 50-60 minutes or until heated through and cheese is melted.*

A friend shared the recipe for this cheesy baked pasta years ago. I love to serve it with a salad and garlic bread. It's great for entertaining!
—MARGARET MCNEIL GERMANTOWN, TENNESSEE

30 Chili Hot Dog Spaghetti

I've been making this fun spaghetti for over 35 years. It's one of my husband's favorite dishes. Lower-fat franks and reduced-fat cheese can be used and it's just as good.
—**KAREN TAUSEND** BRIDGEPORT, MICHIGAN

PREP/TOTAL TIME: 30 MINUTES **MAKES:** 6 SERVINGS

- 8 ounces uncooked spaghetti
- 1 package (1 pound) hot dogs, sliced
- ½ cup chopped onion
- ½ cup chopped celery
- 2 tablespoons canola oil
- 1 can (15 ounces) tomato sauce
- 1 tablespoon prepared mustard
- 1 teaspoon chili powder
- ½ teaspoon Worcestershire sauce
- ¼ teaspoon salt
- ¼ teaspoon pepper
- 1 cup (4 ounces) shredded cheddar cheese

1. Cook spaghetti according to package directions. Meanwhile, in a large skillet, saute the hot dogs, onion and celery in oil until the vegetables are tender. Add the tomato sauce, mustard, chili powder, Worcestershire sauce, salt and pepper; cook and stir until heated through.

2. Drain spaghetti; toss with hot dog mixture. Serve immediately, sprinkling each serving with cheese. Or cool spaghetti; transfer to freezer containers and freeze for up to 3 months.

To use frozen spaghetti: *Thaw in the refrigerator overnight. Place in a saucepan and heat through. Sprinkle each serving with cheese.*

20 Salsa Sloppy Joes

PREP/TOTAL TIME: 20 MINUTES **MAKES:** 8 SERVINGS

- 1 pound ground beef
- 1⅓ cups salsa
- 1 can (10¾ ounces) condensed tomato soup, undiluted
- 1 tablespoon brown sugar
- 8 hamburger buns, split

1. In a large skillet, cook the beef over medium heat until no longer pink; drain. Stir in the salsa, soup and brown sugar. Cover and simmer for 10 minutes to allow flavors to blend.

2. Serve immediately on buns, or cool mixture before placing in a freezer container. Cover and freeze for up to 3 months.

To use frozen sloppy joes: *Thaw beef mixture in the refrigerator; place in a saucepan and heat through. Serve on buns.*

> ❝ I created these sandwiches when I realized I did not have a can of sloppy joe sauce. The sweet brown sugar in this recipe complements the tangy salsa.❞

—**KRISTA COLLINS** CONCORD, NORTH CAROLINA

30 Presto Sloppy Joes

Five ingredients are all you need for these hearty sandwiches that are great for family gatherings. Onion soup mix and sweet relish add zesty flavor.

—**MARGE NAPALO** BRUNSWICK, OHIO

PREP/TOTAL TIME: 30 MINUTES **MAKES:** 14 SERVINGS

- 3 **pounds ground beef**
- 3 **cups ketchup**
- ⅔ **cup sweet pickle relish**
- 1 **envelope onion soup mix**
- 14 **hamburger buns, split**

1. In a Dutch oven, cook beef over medium heat until no longer pink; drain. Stir in the ketchup, relish and soup mix; heat through. Serve immediately on buns, or cool mixture before placing in a freezer container. Cover and freeze for up to 3 months.

To use frozen sloppy joes: *Thaw beef mixture in the refrigerator; place in a saucepan and heat through. Serve on buns.*

Greek Meat Loaves

Here's a twist on traditional meat loaf that will be a hit, especially when served with a Greek garden salad and good bread.

—**RADELLE KNAPPENBERGER** OVIEDO, FLORIDA

PREP: 20 MINUTES **BAKE:** 50 MINUTES
MAKES: 2 LOAVES (6 SERVINGS EACH)

- 2 **eggs, lightly beaten**
- ½ **cup ketchup**
- ¼ **cup 2% milk**
- 1 **large red onion, finely chopped**
- ¾ **cup quick-cooking oats**
- ⅓ **cup oil-packed sun-dried tomatoes, patted dry and finely chopped**
- ⅓ **cup pitted Greek olives, chopped**
- 2 **garlic cloves, minced**
- 1 **teaspoon salt**
- 1 **teaspoon pepper**
- 2 **pounds lean ground beef (90% lean)**
- ½ **cup crumbled feta cheese**

1. In a large bowl, combine the first 10 ingredients. Crumble beef over mixture and mix well. Pat into two greased 8-in. x 4-in. loaf pans. Cover and freeze one meat loaf for up to 3 months.

2. Bake remaining meat loaf, uncovered, at 350° for 50-60 minutes or until no pink remains and a thermometer reads 160°. Let stand for 5 minutes. Transfer to a serving plate; sprinkle with cheese.

To use frozen meat loaf: *Thaw in the refrigerator overnight. Bake as directed; sprinkle with cheese.*

Ham & Noodle Casseroles

PREP: 20 MINUTES
BAKE: 25 MINUTES
MAKES: 2 CASSEROLES
(8 SERVINGS EACH)

1½ **pounds uncooked egg noodles**
3 **pounds cubed fully cooked ham**
4 **cans (10¾ ounces each) condensed cream of chicken soup, undiluted**
4 **cups frozen cut green beans, thawed**
1 **cup 2% milk**
¼ **cup butter, melted**
2 **cups (8 ounces) shredded Colby-Monterey Jack cheese**

1. Cook the pasta according to package directions. Meanwhile, in a large bowl, combine the ham, soup, beans and milk. Drain pasta; pour over ham mixture and toss to coat. Transfer to two greased 13-in. x 9-in. baking dishes.

2. Drizzle each dish with butter; sprinkle with the cheese. Cover and freeze one casserole for up to 3 months. Bake the remaining casserole, uncovered, at 350° for 25-30 minutes or until the casserole is heated through.

To use frozen casserole: *Thaw in the refrigerator overnight. Remove from the refrigerator 30 minutes before baking. Bake, uncovered, at 350° for 40-45 minutes or until heated through.*

General Index

Alphabetical Index